Praise for *Real Heroes*

"If you love a good biography, you'll love Larry Reed's *Real Heroes*. Instead of a single biography, you get many great stories of liberty's heroes, from Cato the Younger to Adam Smith to Ludwig Erhard. A great book from one of liberty's own heroes."
 —**Senator Rand Paul**

"What a riveting and upbeat book! *Real Heroes* is hard to put down. I'm still taking notes on it to supplement my teaching."
 —**Burton W. Folsom Jr.**, professor of history, Hillsdale College

"A free and flourishing society requires liberty, and liberty requires vigilance and courage. This book will empower the rising generation to stand up and fight for what is right by giving us examples of brave souls who have done so. It's a treasure trove of heroic stories that encourage and inspire."
 —**Anne Rathbone Bradley**, vice president of economic initiatives
  at the Institute for Faith, Work, and Economics

"No matter their time or place, the men and women we meet in this book share a passion for liberty and justice. Reed presents a road map to strong character and a challenge to build a freer society."
 —**Jim DeMint**, Heritage Foundation president and former U.S. senator

"Reed demystifies the concept of what it means to be a hero and brings readers to the edge of their seats with uniquely compelling tales of triumph. This long-overdue book will change the way we see not only heroes but also ourselves."
 —**T. K. Coleman**, education director for Praxis

"Integrating the importance of human liberty with moral responsibility and personal character, Reed has penned a compelling outline of the case for freedom through the lens of forty diverse and intriguing portraits."
 —**Rev. Robert Sirico**, president of the Acton Institute

"Cheers to Larry Reed and ISI Books for this fun and fulfilling book of heroes to remember and rediscover."
 —**Paul Kengor**, professor of political science at Grove City College

"Rarely does a book come along at precisely the right time. In an age when the word *hero* is too often confused with celebrity, Reed gives us a much-needed corrective, told in a lively style so that the stories jump from the pages to inspire us."
 —**Roger Ream**, president of the Fund for American Studies

"In a world in which crassness and hedonism seem to be the norm, it is refreshing to read the tales of noble characters. This is an inspiring book for anyone who aspires to live a life of meaning and purpose. This book will encourage your inner hero to come forth and lead you to your proper role in the world."
    —**Magatte Wade**, award-winning entrepreneur, founder of Tiossan

"*Real Heroes* is a crucial reminder of the key values needed in greater supply if we're to preserve the freedom and prosperity we've so fortunately been given."
    —**Peter Goettler**, president of the Cato Institute

"I love Larry's emphasis on character. It's the biggest issue of our time for all walks of life, from business to media to politics. Nobody explains its importance through historical examples better than he does."
    —**Donald G. Smith**, investor, New York City

"This book could not come at a better time. It is in the most trying of times that heroes can save us. They teach us about good and evil, give us hope, and inspire us to become our best selves. An enjoyable read, *Real Heroes* is packed with fascinating stories, inspirational quotes, and takeaway lessons."
    —**Romina Boccia**, Heritage Foundation

"Reed brings to life dozens of stories where high character animates courage and triumph. I cannot recommend it highly enough."
    —**Kent Lassman**, president and CEO of the Competitive Enterprise Institute

"*Real Heroes* is an exciting and inspiring study of people who dared to challenge the consensus of their time and put their necks on the line for what they believed in. A timely and important book, especially for young people."
    —**Nathan Bond**, cofounder and CEO of Rifle Paper Co.

"Reed's powerful book motivates the reader to go out into the world and stand strong for the ideas of liberty. The stories here are highly educational, fun to read, and inspiring."
    —**Wolf von Laer**, CEO of Students for Liberty

"*Real Heroes* illustrates the true peacemakers of the world. Reed tells the stories of individuals who dedicated their lives to the fight for liberty and prosperity. You'll be motivated with every turn of the page."
    —**Cliff Maloney Jr.**, executive director of Young Americans for Liberty

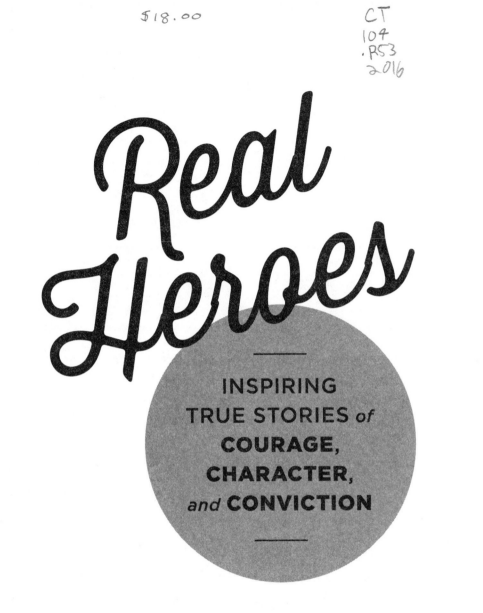

Real Heroes

INSPIRING
TRUE STORIES *of*
COURAGE,
CHARACTER,
and **CONVICTION**

LAWRENCE W. REED

ISI
BOOKS

Lawrence W. Reed
Strategic Objectives Speaker
2016

Library of Congress Cataloging-in-Publication Data

Names: Reed, Lawrence W., author.
Title: Real heroes : inspiring true stories of courage, character, and conviction / Lawrence W. Reed.
Description: Wilmington, Delaware : ISI Books, 2016.
Identifiers: LCCN 2016033560 | ISBN 9781610171427 (pbk.)
Subjects: LCSH: Heroes—Biography.
Classification: LCC CT104 .R53 2016 | DDC 808.8/0352—dc23 LC record available at https://lccn.loc.gov/2016033560

Published in the United States by:

ISI Books
Intercollegiate Studies Institute
3901 Centerville Road
Wilmington, Delaware 19807-1938
www.isibooks.org

Manufactured in the United States of America

To

Ron and Jenny Manners of Perth, Australia

and

Ned and Elfie Gallun of Mayville, Wisconsin

Two very special couples—heroes of impeccable character who work tirelessly to advance all the right causes, especially liberty and entrepreneurship

Contents

Foreword

by Christopher Long
President, Intercollegiate Studies Institute

When Larry Reed came to me with the idea of publishing *Real Heroes*, it took my colleagues and me about five minutes to decide that we wanted to be part of this exciting project.

The Intercollegiate Studies Institute and the Foundation for Economic Education, the organization Larry has headed since 2008, have closely aligned missions: we both focus on teaching young people the principles of a free society. This is no accident. ISI's founder, Frank Chodorov, and its first president, William F. Buckley Jr., were good friends with FEE founder Leonard Read. In the early 1950s Read and other FEE officers helped launch ISI.

ISI and FEE are committed to the principles that sustain a free, prosperous, and virtuous society in which individuals can pursue their dreams and aspirations. We know that it's one thing to be inspired by ideas but quite another to put them into action.

In an 1891 address to the Yale Philosophical Club, William James said that "the higher fidelities, like justice, truth, or freedom," are what motivate people. But he stressed that "the deepest difference...in the moral life of man is the difference between the easy-going and the strenuous mood." He added, "The strenuous type of character will on the battle-field of human history always outwear the easy-going type."

So ideas are crucial, but they aren't enough. To make a positive impact on the world, you also need the courage of your convictions—the courage and integrity to advance your core principles, to persevere even when it's not easy or comfortable to do so.

That's the beauty of *Real Heroes*. In this book Larry Reed takes the essential ideas that ISI and FEE have been teaching for decades—

fundamental concepts like liberty, personal responsibility, entrepreneurship, integrity, and virtue—and brings them to life. This book is not an abstract reflection on principles; here you'll meet real, flesh-and-blood people who have spoken truth to power and put their principles into practice.

Lovers of liberty need a book like *Real Heroes*. We know that our side has the winning ideas. But sometimes we are ineffective at communicating them. Too often we forget that the way you inspire and motivate people is through stories and relatable examples.

Larry Reed doesn't make that mistake. Instead he follows the example of his predecessor Leonard Read, whose short, easy-to-understand essay "I, Pencil" has opened the minds of millions of people to the power of free markets and the folly of central planning.

Larry has also learned from one of the heroes in this book, Frédéric Bastiat, whom he calls "liberty's masterful storyteller." It is exciting to know that *Real Heroes* will introduce a new generation to Bastiat's genius, and to the stories of dozens of other men and women who have led lives of courage and purpose.

Our world desperately needs more heroes—more models of character, courage, and conviction whom we can admire and emulate.

Such models are exactly what Larry Reed offers in *Real Heroes*. I have been inspired by the exceptional men and women Larry profiles, and I am sure you will be too.

ISI is excited to publish this book. I encourage you not only to read these remarkable stories but also to share *Real Heroes* far and wide—whether it's with your classmates, your students, your children or grandchildren, your church group, or your book club. In so doing, you will inspire a new generation of heroes for liberty.

Christopher Long is president of the Intercollegiate Studies Institute and publisher of ISI Books.

Introduction

———•———

Just for a moment, imagine a world without heroes.

Such a world could still have lots of good and decent people. Mixed in with the bad and the rotten, however, they would not stand out. And in the absence of anyone who would speak truth to power no matter the consequences, the antiheroes just might take charge, making life almost unlivable for the rest of us.

I'm reminded of the animated 1998 DreamWorks film *Antz*. The setting is an ant colony in which all ants are expected to behave as an obedient blob. No heroes to challenge conventional wisdom. No exceptional ants that might inspire vision or change in the others. In the short run this is very convenient for the tyrant ants, but their selfish misrule leaves the entire society vulnerable to attack. The debilitating collectivist mind-set is shaken by a single ant, who ultimately saves the colony through his individual initiative. In risking everything to assert his values and uniqueness, he transcends the blob and becomes a hero.

Far more than ants, humans need heroes. It's not enough, though, to need them. We must value them. And we can't just *say* we value them. We must recognize them and impart to others the lessons that their heroic deeds teach.

Relating stories of heroic people, I hope and believe, can encourage the proliferation of the traits we admire in heroes. I would like nothing better than for heroism to become so common as to be the norm, not the exception.

The Character of Heroes

What makes someone a hero?

Is it fame, power, money, creative talent, athletic ability, good looks? Despite what our culture typically celebrates, it's none of those things. Yes, some heroes are famous, or powerful, or wealthy, or artistic, or athletic, or good-looking. But that's not *why* they are heroes.

If I had to pick one term above all others as essential to heroism, it would be this: *character.*

A person's character is nothing more than the sum of his or her choices. Fortunately, character is something every one of us has control over. Yet most of us cut corners all the time, sacrificing character for money, attention, power, or other ephemeral gratifications.

Heroes don't squander their character that way. As someone once said, they don't "borrow from integrity to pay expediency." What unites heroes across time periods and cultures is that they exemplify character through their words and actions. They embody traits like honesty, gratitude, intellectual humility, personal responsibility, self-discipline, inventiveness, entrepreneurship, vision, compassion, and optimism. And they display these traits continually. The heroism of the people I profile arises not from a single, momentary act but rather from a lifetime of choices.

Why care about character? Here's one good reason: it is indispensable to a successful career and a happy life. Sure, we all can think of unethical people who have made a lot of money or gotten ahead in their chosen field. But usually it's just a matter of time before their poor choices catch up with them. As Shakespeare reminds us, "At length truth will out."

Here's another reason: character is essential to liberty.

It's easy to take our freedoms for granted. But the kind of free society we enjoy is hardly the norm in human history, which is marked (and marred) by tyranny, slavery, genocide, and religious persecution.

Often the "road to serfdom," in the famous phrase of Nobel Prize winner F. A. Hayek, begins with small incursions on liberty. But just as you can't borrow from integrity to pay expediency, you can't sacrifice liberty for short-term convenience. Perhaps the most important lesson from the past five thousand years of history is this: no people who lost their character kept their liberties.

That's why so many of the heroes profiled in this book have risked their lives to defend liberty and resist oppression, from Cicero in ancient Rome, to Anne Hutchinson in seventeenth-century America, to Witold Pilecki in Nazi-occupied Poland, to Haing Ngor in Pol Pot's Cambodia.

Courage and Conviction

As those examples suggest, *courage* is another common thread among heroes.

Heroes are rarely, if ever, timid and retiring. If a hero has to stick her neck out to get a job done, she does it. The hero ventures forth in directions the less brave won't dare. In so doing, she provides an inspiring example. "Courage is contagious," evangelist Billy Graham said. "When a brave man takes a stand, the spines of others are stiffened."

I've heard it said that there are only three kinds of people in the world: a very small minority that makes things happen, a somewhat larger minority that watches things happen, and the vast majority of people who never know what happened. Heroes are surely of the first group. As I researched and wrote this book, the courage of these remarkable people awed me again and again.

When I say *courage*, I don't refer simply to physical courage (though that is something many heroes display). I mean *moral* courage as well.

To have moral courage means to do the right thing no matter the risks to yourself. How do you know the right thing to do? You have to have *conviction* as well. Almost all heroes are men or women who stand not for what they think others will fall for but for principles they value because those principles are sound and right.

Many of the people you will read about in this book stood for principles that were unpopular or that put them at odds with the ruling class. Cato the Younger fiercely defended Rome's republican values against Julius Caesar's power grabs; the abolitionist Thomas Clarkson campaigned against slavery even though the institution was widely accepted and a source of wealth for many powerful people; the British politician Katharine Atholl denounced Nazi Germany and Soviet communism even when she incurred the wrath of the prime minister.

Character, courage, and conviction: these heroic traits are inextricably linked. A person of *conviction* has a guiding set of principles; a person of *character* stands by those principles even in difficult times; and a person of *courage* understands that it is not enough to stick to your principles quietly—sometimes you must take action to defend and advance them.

Flesh-and-Blood Heroes

Great movements, countries, moments, and achievements are marked by heroic individuals. We all can name the really famous ones. For the most part, those are not the people you'll encounter in this book. Instead I chose people most readers will know little if anything about. I did so for several reasons.

First, these "real heroes" deserve to be known, and their stories should inspire us all.

Second, heroism comes in many forms; it is not unique to a certain sex, race, or country. Here you will meet many different kinds of heroes. Some lived in the distant past; some live and work among us today. Some come from the United States; others come from the opposite side of the globe. Some are statesmen, others scientists; some are athletes, others inventors; some are entrepreneurs, others theologians; some are writers, others teachers.

Third, by choosing little-known subjects, I want to suggest that in our midst are a great many other heroes we ought to learn about and draw inspiration from. Are you looking for them? By your example, are you encouraging heroism? When you come upon heroes, do you thank them?

Finally, heroes do not (or should not) stand at a far remove from the rest of us. They are not demigods who have little connection to our lives. The whole point of heroes is that they are flesh-and-blood models for all of us. We admire them, yes—but we also should learn from them so we can emulate their heroic character, choices, and actions.

America is a country with a history of heroes, but at times it seems that we've forgotten more than we're producing. Maybe there's a connection there. If we forget our heroes, how can their examples serve as inspirations?

Who in his right mind doesn't yearn for a world where at least *some* people live lives worth admiring—and emulating? A world without heroes is not the one in which we live, fortunately; nor is it one to which we should aspire.

1

Cicero

Enemy of the State, Friend of Liberty

Question: If you could go back in time and spend an hour in conversation with ten people—each one separately and privately—whom would you choose?

My list isn't exactly the same from one day to the next, but at least a couple of the same names are always on it, without fail. One of them is Marcus Tullius Cicero. He was the greatest citizen of the greatest ancient civilization, Rome. He was its most eloquent orator and its most distinguished man of letters. He was elected to its highest office. More than anyone else, Cicero introduced to Rome the best ideas of the Greeks. More of his written and spoken work survives to this day—including hundreds of speeches and letters—than that of any other historical figure before AD 1000. Most important, he gave his life for peace and liberty as the greatest defender of the Roman Republic before it plunged into the darkness of a "welfare-warfare" state.

Cato Institute scholar Jim Powell opened his remarkable book *The Triumph of Liberty: A 2,000-Year History, Told Through the Lives of Freedom's Greatest Champions* with a chapter on this Roman hero— a chapter he closed with this fitting tribute: "Cicero urged people to reason together. He championed decency and peace, and he gave the modern world some of the most fundamental ideas of liberty. At a time when speaking freely was dangerous, he courageously denounced tyranny. He helped keep the torch of liberty burning bright for more than two thousand years."

Who *wouldn't* want to have an hour with this man?

Father of the Country

Cicero was born in 106 BC in the small town of Arpinum, about sixty miles southeast of Rome. He began practicing law in his early twenties. His most celebrated case required him to defend a man accused of murdering his father. He secured an acquittal by convincing the jury that the real murderers were closely aligned to the highest public officials in Rome. It was the first but not the last time that he put himself in grave danger for what he believed to be right.

In 70 BC, ten years after his victory in that murder trial, Cicero assumed a role uncommon for him—that of prosecutor. It was a corruption case involving Gaius Verres, the politically powerful former governor of Sicily. Aggrieved Sicilians accused Verres of abuse of power, extortion, and embezzlement. The evidence Cicero gathered appeared overwhelming, but Verres was confident he could escape conviction. His brilliant defense lawyer, Hortensius, was regarded as Cicero's equal. Both Verres and Hortensius believed they could delay the trial a few months until a close ally became the new judge of the

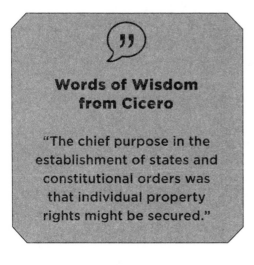

Words of Wisdom from Cicero

"The chief purpose in the establishment of states and constitutional orders was that individual property rights might be secured."

extortion court. But Cicero outmaneuvered them at every turn. Verres, all but admitting his guilt, fled into exile. Cicero's speeches against him, *In Verrem*, are still read in some law schools today.

Roman voters rewarded Cicero with victory in one office after another as he worked his way up the ladder of government. Along the way, the patrician nobility of Rome never quite embraced him because he hailed from a slightly more humble class, the so-called equestrian order. He reached the pinnacle of office in 63 BC, when, at age forty-three, Romans elected him coconsul.

The consulship was the republic's highest office, though authority under the Roman Constitution was shared between two coequal consuls. One could veto the decisions of the other, and both were limited to a single one-year term. Cicero's coconsul, Gaius Antonius Hybrida, was so overshadowed by his colleague's eloquence and magnetism that he's but a footnote today. In contrast, Cicero emerged as the savior of the republic amid a spectacular plot to snuff it out.

The ringleader of the vast conspiracy was a senator named Lucius Sergius Catiline. This disgruntled, power-hungry Roman assembled an extensive network of fellow travelers, including some fellow senators. The plan was to ignite a general insurrection across Italy, march on Rome with the aid of mercenaries, assassinate Cicero and his coconsul, seize power, and crush all opposition. Cicero learned of the plot and quietly conducted his own investigations. Then, in a series of four powerful orations before the Senate, with Catiline himself present for the first, he cut loose. The great orator mesmerized the Senate with these opening lines and the blistering indictment that followed: "How long, O Catiline, will you abuse our patience? And for how long will that madness of yours mock us? To what end will your unbridled audacity hurl itself?"

Before Cicero was finished, Catiline fled the Senate. He rallied his dwindling army but was ultimately killed in battle. Other top conspirators were exposed and executed. Cicero, on whom the Senate had conferred emergency power, walked away from that power and restored the republic. He was given the honorary title of *Pater Patriae* (Father of the Country).

"I Shall Not Tremble"

But Rome at the time of the Catilinarian conspiracy was not the Rome of two or three centuries earlier, when honor, virtue, and character were the watchwords of life. By Cicero's time, the place was rife with corruption and power lust. The outward appearances of a republic were undermined daily by civil strife and a growing welfare-warfare state. Many who publicly praised republican values were privately conniving to secure power or wealth through political connections. Others were corrupted or bribed into silence by government handouts. Cicero's voice was soon to be drowned out amid political intrigue, violence, and popular apathy.

In 60 BC, Julius Caesar, then a senator and military general with boundless ambition, tried to get Cicero to join a powerful partnership that became known as the First Triumvirate, but Cicero's republican sentiments prompted him to reject the offer. Two years later and barely five years after crushing Catiline's conspiracy, Cicero found himself on the wrong side of senatorial intrigue. Political opponents connived to thwart his influence, resulting in a brief exile to northern Greece.

He returned to a hero's welcome but retired to his writing. Over the next decade he gifted the world with impressive literary and philosophical work, one of my favorites being *De Officiis* ("On Duties"). In it he wrote: "The chief purpose in the establishment of states and constitutional orders was that individual property rights might be secured.... It is the peculiar function of state and city to guarantee to every man the free and undisturbed control of his own property."

Politics, however, wouldn't leave Cicero alone. Rivalry between Caesar and another leading political figure and general, Pompey, exploded into civil war. Cicero reluctantly sided with the latter, whom he regarded as less dangerous to the republic. But Caesar triumphed over Pompey, who was killed in Egypt, and then cowed the Senate into naming him dictator for life. A month later, Caesar was assassinated in the Senate by pro-republican forces. When Mark Antony attempted to succeed Caesar as dictator, Cicero spearheaded the republican cause once again, delivering a series of fourteen powerful speeches known as the Philippics.

Cicero's oratory never soared higher. Antony, Cicero declared, was nothing but a bloodthirsty tyrant-in-waiting. "I fought for the republic when I was young," he said. "I shall not abandon her in my old age. I scorned the daggers of Catiline; I shall not tremble before yours. Rather, I would willingly expose my body to them, if by my death the liberty of the nation could be recovered and the agony of the Roman people could at last bring to birth that with which it has been so long in labor."

Antony and his fellow conspirators named Cicero an enemy of the state and sent the assassin Herennius to take him out. On December 7, 43 BC, the killer found his target. The great statesman bared his neck and faced his assailant with these last words: "There is nothing proper about what you are doing, soldier, but do try to kill me properly."

With one sword stroke to the neck, the life of the last major obstacle to dictatorship was extinguished. At that moment, the five-hundred-year-old republic expired, too, to be replaced by an imperial autocracy. Roman liberty was gone. On the orders of Antony, Cicero's hands and head were severed and nailed to the speaker's platform in the Roman Forum. Antony's wife personally pulled out Cicero's tongue and, in a rage against his oratory, stabbed it repeatedly with her hairpin.

Powell reports in *The Triumph of Liberty* that a century after the ghastly deed, the Roman writer Quintilian declared that Cicero was "the name not of a man but of eloquence itself." Thirteen centuries later, when the printing press was invented, the first book it produced was the Gutenberg Bible; the second was Cicero's *De Officiis*. Three more centuries after that, Thomas Jefferson called Cicero "the first master of the world." And John Adams proclaimed, "All the ages of the world have not produced a greater statesman and philosopher" than Marcus Tullius Cicero.

Giving His Life

For nearly five centuries, the Roman Republic bestowed upon the world a previously unseen degree of respect for individual rights and the rule of law. The unwritten Roman constitution boasted features we would recognize today: checks and balances, the separation of powers, guarantee of due process, vetoes, term limits, habeas corpus, quorum requirements, impeachments, regular elections. They were buttressed by the traits of strong character (*virtus*) that were widely taught in Roman homes. When the republic expired, the world would not see such wondrous achievements on a comparable scale for a thousand years.

To the moment of his assassination, Cicero defended the republic against the assaults that he knew would send Rome into tyranny. Some might say Cicero's labors to save the Roman Republic were a waste of time. He gave his life for an ideal that he was able to extend tenuously for maybe a couple of decades.

But if I had an hour with Cicero, I would thank him. I would want him to know of the inspiration he remains to lovers of liberty everywhere, more than two millennia after he lived. I would share with him one of my favorite remarks about heroism, from the screenwriter and film producer Joss Whedon: "The thing about a hero is, even when it doesn't look like there's a light at the end of the tunnel, he's going to keep digging, he's going to keep trying to do right and make up for what's gone before, just because that's who he is."

And that is exactly who Cicero *was*.

Lessons from Cicero

Display moral courage: Cicero stood for his principles even when he knew that he was putting himself in danger. His principled position ultimately cost him his life. His courage in the face of mortal threats remains an inspiration to this day.

Defend liberty: Cicero believed the primary purpose of government was to defend the liberty and property of its citizens. He resisted would-be tyrants at every turn, and through the centuries his writings have influenced countless lovers of liberty, including America's Founders.

2

Cato the Younger

Ambition in the Service of Principle

In the estimations of many historians, two men hold the honor as the most notable defenders of the Roman Republic. Marcus Tullius Cicero was one. Marcus Porcius Cato, or "Cato the Younger," was the other.

Since there was a "younger," there must have been an "elder," too. Cato the Elder was the great-grandfather of the younger. Both men, separated by more than a century, were influential in public office. Think of the elder as the social conservative, concerned in his day with preserving the customs and traditions of Rome. The younger was one of history's early libertarians, interested more in personal and political liberties, because he believed that if they were lost, nothing else mattered. Both were men of admirable features, but it is this second one to whom I refer in the balance of this essay as simply "Cato."

By the time of Cato's birth in 95 BC, the Roman Republic had been in place for four centuries. It had risen from obscurity to political and economic dominance in the Mediterranean. Rome was easily the world's wealthiest and most powerful society. It wasn't a libertarian paradise—slavery was a part of its makeup, as it was (even more brutally so) everywhere else—but Rome had taken liberty to a zenith the world had never seen before and wouldn't see again for a long time after it finally fell.

But all this was hanging by a thread as Cato came of age.

Tyranny's Implacable Foe

Cato was just five years of age when Rome went to war with its former allies in the Italian peninsula—the so-called Social War. Although the conflict lasted just two years, its deleterious effects were huge. The decades to follow would be marked by the rise of factions and conflict. As power concentrated in the hands of military figures, men in service increasingly placed loyalty to their generals ahead of loyalty to the larger society. A welfare-warfare state was putting down deep roots. The limited government, personal responsibility, and extensive civil society so critical to the republic's previous success were in a century-long process of collapse. Even many of those who recognized the decay around them nonetheless succumbed to the temptations of power or subsidies or both.

Cato did not succumb. Before the age of thirty, he had become a supremely disciplined individual, a devotee of Stoicism in every respect. He commanded a legion in Macedon and won immense loyalty and respect from the soldiers for the example he set, living and laboring from day to day just as he required of his men. He first won election to public office—to the post of *quaestor*, supervising financial and budgetary matters for the state—in 65 BC and quickly earned a reputation as meticulous and honest. He held previous quaestors accountable for their dishonesty and misappropriation of funds, which he himself uncovered.

Later he served in the Roman Senate, where he never missed a session and criticized other senators who did. Through his superb oratory in public and deft maneuverings in private, he worked tirelessly to restore fealty to the ideals of the fading Republic.

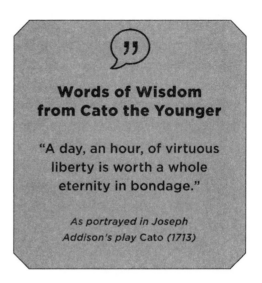

Words of Wisdom from Cato the Younger

"A day, an hour, of virtuous liberty is worth a whole eternity in bondage."

As portrayed in Joseph Addison's play Cato (1713)

Since the days of the Gracchus brothers (Gaius and Tiberius) in the previous century, more and more Roman leaders were rising to power by expensive promises to redistribute land ownership or provide free grain and other subsidies. Cato saw the debilitating effect such cynical demagoguery was exacting from the public's character and opposed it at first. The one time he compromised on this issue was when he supported an expansion of the dole as the only way to prevent a demagogue named Julius Caesar from coming to power. It was a tactic he hoped would be temporary, but it ultimately failed, becoming the only blot on an otherwise virtuous and principled public career.

It was Cato's fierce and relentless opposition to Caesar that made him most remarkable. He saw in the power-hungry general a mortal threat to the republic and tried to block his every move. He filibustered for hours on end to prevent a vote on Caesar's bid to attain Rome's highest office, the consulship. Caesar eventually got the job, but while in office, Cato vexed him more than any other senator did. Caesar even ordered Cato dragged from the Senate in the middle of one of his orations, whereupon another senator declared, according to historian Cassius Dio, that he "would rather be in jail with Cato than in the Senate with Caesar."

In *Rome's Last Citizen: The Life and Legacy of Cato, Caesar's Mortal Enemy*, authors Rob Goodman and Jimmy Soni underscore Cato's implacable resistance:

> It had been an unprecedented year of obstruction and deadlock, all spearheaded by Cato. Never before had a senator brought forth such a range of legislation to the same dead halt in a matter of months. The tax contracts, the postwar plans for the East, the land reform, Caesar's triumph (a costly public spectacle), Caesar's bid for a strong consulship and a provincial command—Cato had not stood against them alone, but he was the common thread between each filibuster and each "no."

Cato stood in the way of Caesar's ambitious agenda but couldn't prevent his post-consulship appointment as a provincial governor. In that post, Caesar mustered his forces for an assault on the very republic he had governed as a consul. In 49 BC he famously crossed the Rubicon River and headed for Rome to seize power.

As a sign of strength and magnanimity, Caesar might have pardoned his old foe. Some contemporaries and present-day historians believe that was, in fact, Caesar's intent and would have been a politically smart thing to do. "But Cato would not give Caesar the gift of his silence; he had scripted his own scene," Goodman and Soni write. "He would not recognize a tyrant's legitimacy by accepting his power to save. As Cato saw it, Caesar broke the law even in offering pardons, because he offered them on no authority but his own. To accept forgiveness would be conceding Caesar's right to forgive, and Cato would not concede that."

So in April 46 BC in Utica, using his own sword, Cato committed suicide rather than be ruled by the man whose power lust was about to extinguish the old republic. While Cato lived, write Goodman and Soni, "every Roman who feared that the traditional virtues were guttering out, who saw the state's crisis as a moral crisis—as the product of terrifyingly modern avarice or ambition—looked, in time, to Cato."

A Hero of Liberty

With Cicero's death three years later under the orders of Caesar's successor, Marc Antony, the republic died and the dictatorship of the empire commenced.

Centuries later, in April 1713, Joseph Addison's play *Cato: A Tragedy* debuted in London. Depicting the ancient Roman as a hero of republican liberty, the play resonated for decades thereafter in both Britain and America. George Washington read it over and over, inspired by this self-sacrificing hero. General Washington ordered it performed for his bedraggled troops at Valley Forge during the awful winter of 1777–78. Congress had forbidden the performance, thinking the play's sad conclusion would dispirit the troops, but Washington knew that Cato's resistance to tyranny would inspire them. And it did.

"Few leaders have ever put ambition so squarely in the service of principle," write Goodman and Soni. "These were the qualities that set Cato apart from his fellows—and that made posterity take notice."

Putting ambition in the service of principle instead of one's own power or wealth: now that's a virtue to which every man and woman in public office—or any other walk of life—should aspire today.

Lessons from Cato the Younger

Stand on principle: Cato's tenure in public office was marked by honesty and fealty to republican values. As his biographers noted, "Few leaders have ever put ambition so squarely in the service of principle." Cato took his own life rather than live under the rule of a tyrant.

Practice self-discipline: A devotee of Stoicism, Cato was supremely disciplined. As a leader, he inspired loyalty and respect by never asking those he commanded to do something he would not himself do.

3

Augustine

Searching for Truth and Wisdom

To write about a man known chiefly as a theologian—a bishop in the early Catholic Church, no less—might suggest at first a discourse on religious issues. Augustine of Hippo (later canonized as Saint Augustine) is unquestionably a giant of Christian thought and teaching. On matters of salvation, grace, free will, original sin, and "just war," his brilliant observations continue to spark lively debate throughout Christendom and beyond. He could be regarded as a hero for those contributions alone, but they are largely matters for readers to explore on their own.

Augustine was also a hero because he took charge of his troubled, wayward life and transformed it. Then, once committed to the highest standards of personal conduct and scholarly inquiry, he offered pioneering insights on liberty critical to the development of Western philosophy. One does not have to be a person of any particular faith to learn a great deal from this man.

The Roman province of Africa produced no more consequential figure than Augustine, born in 354 in Thagaste, now called Souk Ahras, in modern-day Algeria. It was a momentous time to be alive. By the fourth century, the old Roman Republic and its liberties had been snuffed out for four hundred years, succeeded by the increasingly corrupt, tyrannical, and dysfunctional welfare-warfare state that we know as the Roman Empire. Augustine would live to see the Visigoths sack the "Eternal City" of Rome in the year 410. Twenty years later, as the Vandals laid siege to Augustine's own city of Hippo in North Africa, he died at age seventy-five. His life was proof that even as the world you know crumbles into dust, you can still make a difference for the betterment of humanity's future.

"An Unjust Law Is No Law at All"

Augustine's youth was hedonistic and self-centered, in spite of the earnest prayers and intense counseling of his devoutly Christian mother, Monica. His father, a volatile and angry tax collector who converted to Christianity on his deathbed, died when his son was a teenager. Augustine's voracious sexual appetite led him into numerous affairs, which he regretted in later life.

Though a bright student with remarkable rhetorical skills, he found plenty of time to get into trouble. Years later in his magnificent autobiography, *The Confessions*, he recalled with analytic introspection an incident in which he and some young friends stole pears from a man's orchard. He did not steal the fruit because he was hungry, he wrote, but purely because "it was not permitted." Noting this as evidence of his flawed character, he explained, "It was foul, and I loved it. I loved my own error—not that for which I erred, but for the error itself."

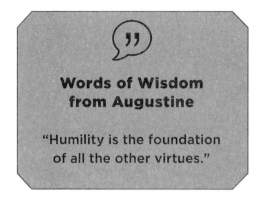

Words of Wisdom from Augustine

"Humility is the foundation of all the other virtues."

In his twenties, Augustine bought into the cult of Manichaeism, a strange concoction of Christian, Buddhist, Gnostic, astrological, and pagan elements. He also flirted with Neoplatonism, a school of philosophy drawing heavily from Plato and from one of Plato's later followers, Plotinus. While Augustine's mother despaired at her son's shifting fancies, two encounters—one with a book and one with a man—ultimately fulfilled her hopes and changed his life.

The book was *Hortensius* by the great Roman republican Cicero. Though the text was eventually lost to history, scholars have reconstructed its core message through citations by contemporaries and by Augustine himself. According to Robin Lane Fox's magisterial biography, *Augustine: Conversions to Confessions*, "Cicero defined philosophy as the 'love of wisdom' (*philo-sophia*), words which struck home to his young reader." It ignited what Augustine termed "an incredible blaze" in his heart for truth and a disdain for pseudo-philosophers, hypocrites, and deceivers. Cicero's emphasis on acquiring knowledge would play a key role even in Augustine's sexual life. He concluded that the passions of the flesh were a distraction from his growing love of wisdom, though this was a transition that took a little time. Before becoming a celibate priest in his early thirties, he famously asked God, "Give me chastity...but not yet."

The other life-altering encounter was with Ambrose, the bishop of Milan, one of the greatest orators in the Roman world. Augustine credited the bishop as the decisive factor in his own conversion to Christianity. That conversion would dominate his every waking moment in the second half of his life.

Before his fortieth birthday, it was apparent to contemporaries that, thanks to Cicero and Ambrose and, secondarily, his mother,

Augustine had developed a remarkable, searching intellect combined with a deeply Christian conscience. His account of his conversion in *The Confessions* is a classic of Christian theology and a seminal text in the history of autobiography. It's been described as "an outpouring of thanksgiving and penitence" and includes observations about the nature of time, causality, free will, and other central topics in philosophy. Augustine's *City of God* is also highly regarded and still widely read today. He wrote the book as an encouragement to his fellow Christians in an increasingly violent world. It was a ringing defense of Christianity in the face of erroneous claims that Rome declined because it had abandoned the old pagan gods.

Of special interest to me is that in his writings and sermons, Augustine says things that resonate with lovers of liberty.

Augustine was more than a little skeptical of earthly political power. "The dominion of bad men is hurtful chiefly to themselves who rule," he said,

> for they destroy their own souls by greater license in wickedness; while those who are put under them in service are not hurt except by their own iniquity. For to the just all the evils imposed on them by unjust rulers are not the punishment of crime, but the test of virtue. The good man, though a slave, is free; the wicked, though he reigns, is a slave, and not the slave of a single man, but—what is worse—the slave of as many masters as he has vices.

Augustine did not subscribe to any sort of "divine right" of rulers. Nor did he believe that legislation or decrees should pass unquestioned. "An unjust law is no law at all," he maintained. To Augustine, government was at best a necessary evil that could only grow more evil the bigger it becomes. In this passage from *The City of God*, he questioned the legitimacy of government itself:

> Justice being taken away, then, what are kingdoms but great robberies? For what are robberies themselves, but little kingdoms?

The band itself is made up of men; it is ruled by the authority of a prince, it is knit together by the pact of the confederacy; the booty is divided by the law agreed on. If, by the admittance of abandoned men, this evil increases to such a degree that it holds places, fixes abodes, takes possession of cities, and subdues peoples, it assumes the more plainly the name of a kingdom, because the reality is now manifestly conferred on it, not by the removal of covetousness, but by the addition of impunity. Indeed, that was an apt and true reply which was given to Alexander the Great by a pirate who had been seized. For when that king had asked the man what he meant by keeping hostile possession of the sea, he answered with bold pride, "What thou meanest by seizing the whole earth; but because I do it with a petty ship, I am called a robber, whilst thou who doest it with a great fleet art styled an emperor."

Writing for the blog *Discourses on Liberty*, Will Harvard notes, "The fact that man has dominion over other men is not a product of God's intended world, but rather the result of sin." Augustine argued that a rational creature made in God's image was meant to have dominion over nature, not over fellow men. At a time when slavery was common and widely viewed as acceptable, declaring it unequivocally sinful was positively bold and refreshing. Augustine even used church funds to purchase the freedom of individual slaves. The scholar from Thagaste also railed against torture and capital punishment. And theft, in his view, was "absolute wickedness" because it violated something sacred: "the law written in our hearts."

Rome had its own immorality to blame for its decline and vulnerability to invasion, Augustine thundered. He argued that the old pagan gods imparted no morality to their followers in either Rome or Greece. Romans had allowed their personal and civic virtues to erode. If legionnaires failed to prevent the assaults they had once repulsed, it was because Rome was rotten at its core. Lust for power and ill-gotten gain had come to plague a people who once rose to greatness because of honesty, self-discipline, mutual respect, and responsibility. The welfare-warfare state of the late empire was a den of iniquity presided over by a nest of vipers. Why should decline come as a surprise?

In *Augustine: A Very Short Introduction*, Henry Chadwick observes:

> With remarkable prescience of what was to come in the West within a generation of his death, Augustine suggested that the world would be a happier place if the great and proud empire were succeeded by a number of smaller states. The kingdom of God had as much room for Goths as for Romans.
>
> Augustine's language angered imperialist patriots. He was aware that empires come and go. He did not think the Roman empire was doomed, as some contemporary pessimists were saying. Rome would collapse only if the Romans did. People cursed the times they lived in; but (in Augustine's words) "whether times are good or bad depends on the moral quality of individual and social life, and is up to us." Each generation, he remarked, thinks its own times uniquely awful, that morality and religion have never been more threatened. He thought it his duty to attack fatalism and to arouse people to a sense of being responsible if things went wrong. They could have a say in what happened next.

Augustine was a man of peace. He urged Christians in particular to engage only in voluntary interactions with themselves and others unless and until a grave wrong required violence to be stopped. His was, in effect, an early defense of *self-defense* and of a concept now known in libertarian circles as the nonaggression principle.

Humility

Of all the virtues of personal character, Augustine reserved the highest praise for one that's often overlooked in our times. "Humility," he asserted, "is the foundation of all the other virtues; hence, in the soul in which this virtue does not exist there cannot be any other virtue except in mere appearance."

Until the twentieth century, most cultures held that having too high an opinion of oneself was the root of most of the world's troubles. Misbehavior—from drug addiction to cruelty to wars—resulted from hubris or pride, a haughtiness of spirit that needed to be deterred or disciplined. The idea that you were bigger or better, or more self-righteous, or somehow immune from the rules that govern others— *the absence of humility*, in other words—gave you license to do unto others what you would never allow them to do unto you.

These days, it's a different story. Being humble rubs against what millions have been taught under the banner of "self-esteem." Even as our schools fail to teach us elemental facts and skills, they teach us to feel good in our ignorance. We explain away bad behavior as the result of the guilty feeling bad about themselves. We manufacture excuses for them, form support groups for them, and resist making moral judgments, lest we hurt their feelings. We don't demand repentance and self-discipline as much as we pump up their egos.

In an extraordinary 2002 article in the *New York Times*, "The Trouble with Self-Esteem," psychologist Lauren Slater concluded that "people with high self-esteem pose a greater threat to those around them than people with low self-esteem, and feeling bad about yourself is not the cause of our country's biggest, most expensive social problems."

Augustine, who was quite familiar with the bloviating demagogues of the late Roman Empire, would surely agree.

In the second half of his life, Augustine was keenly focused on truth and wisdom. He knew that a humble person is a teachable person because he's not so puffed up that his mind is closed. A humble person reforms himself before he attempts to reform the world. A humble person treats others with respect, and that includes other people's lives, rights, and property. A humble person takes criticism or adversity as an opportunity to grow, to build character. A humble person knows that graduation from formal schooling is not the end of learning but only a noteworthy start of what ought to be a lifelong adventure. Augustine regarded the power-seeking know-it-alls of his day the same way that the Austrian economist and Nobel laureate F. A. Hayek saw "central planners" more than fifteen centuries later: as dangerous fools armed with a "pretense of knowledge."

Legacy

Augustine has deeply influenced many leading figures through the centuries: men and women such as Thomas Aquinas, Martin Luther, John Calvin, Soren Kierkegaard, Russell Kirk, Hannah Arendt, and a long list of popes, preachers, philosophers, and politicians.

But even in his day, Augustine inspired appreciation from unlikely quarters. Within weeks of his death in 430, Hippo fell to the Vandals, who burned the city to the ground. They spared only two buildings: Augustine's cathedral and his library.

Lessons from Augustine

Be humble and virtuous: Augustine embodied humility, which he called "the foundation of all the other virtues." He understood that humility encourages an attitude of self-improvement, the key to bettering society. He saw Rome's decline as the inevitable result of its moral degeneration.

Pursue truth and wisdom: Augustine turned away from his useful hedonism partly because he read Cicero and embraced the "love of wisdom." Inspired by truth and wisdom, he became one of the greatest thinkers and theologians of the late Roman Republic.

4

Anne Hutchinson

The Spirit of Religious Liberty

Opinions of Anne Hutchinson have, shall we say, covered the waterfront.

In his masterful tome *Conceived in Liberty*, the twentieth-century economist and libertarian historian Murray Rothbard cast her as a staunch individualist and the greatest threat to the "despotic Puritanical theocracy of Massachusetts Bay."

John Winthrop, the second, sixth, ninth, and twelfth governor of the Massachusetts Bay Colony, thought she was a "hell-spawned agent of destructive anarchy" and "a woman of haughty and fierce carriage, a nimble wit and active spirit, a very voluble tongue, more bold than a man."

The state of Massachusetts apparently agrees with Rothbard. A monument in the State House in Boston today calls her a "courageous exponent of civil liberty and religious toleration." She was, in fact, the preeminent female crusader for a free society in eighteenth-century New England, for which she paid first with banishment and ultimately with her life.

Cast Out

Anne Hutchinson's story is bound intimately to the "antinomian" or "free grace" controversy involving both religion and gender. It raged in Massachusetts for the better part of two years, from 1636 to 1638. Hutchinson was an unconventional, charismatic woman who dared to challenge church doctrine as well as the role of women in even discussing such things in a male-dominated society. In *Saints and Sectaries: Anne Hutchinson and the Antinomian Controversy in the Massachusetts Bay Colony*, historian Emery John Battis wrote, "Gifted with a magnetism which is imparted to few, she had, until the hour of her fall, warm adherents far outnumbering her enemies, and it was only by dint of skillful maneuvering that the authorities were able to loosen her hold on the community."

Antinomianism literally means "against the law" and was a term of derision applied against Hutchinson and her "free grace" followers. While the Puritan establishment in Massachusetts argued, as good "Reformers" of the day did, that Christian understanding derived from scripture alone ("*Sola Scriptura*"), the antinomians placed additional emphasis on an "inner light" by which the Holy Spirit imparted wisdom and guidance to believing individuals, one at a time.

"As I do understand it," Hutchinson explained, "laws, commands, rules and edicts are for those who have not the light which makes plain the pathway. He who has God's grace in his heart cannot go astray."

Barely a century after Martin Luther sparked the great divide known as the Reformation, the Protestant leaders of Massachusetts

**Words of Wisdom
from Anne Hutchinson**

"But now having seen him
which is invisible I fear not
what man can do unto me."

saw antinomianism as dangerously heretical. Their theological forebears broke from Rome in part because they saw the teachings of priests, bishops, and popes as the words of presumptuous intermediaries— diversions by mortals from the divine word of God. When Anne Hutchinson and other antinomians spoke of this supplemental "inner light," it seemed to the Puritan establishment that the Reformation itself was being undone. Worse still, Hutchinson accused church leaders in Massachusetts of reverting to the pre-Reformation notion of "justification by works" instead of the Martin Luther/John Calvin perspective of justification by faith alone through God's "free grace."

In England, where she was born in 1591, Hutchinson had followed the teachings of the dynamic preacher John Cotton, from whom she traced some of her antiestablishment ideas. When Cotton was compelled to leave the country in 1633, Hutchinson and her family followed him to New England. There she would live until her death just ten years later, stirring up one fuss after another while serving as an active midwife and caregiver to the sick. That she found the time to do all this while raising fifteen children of her own is a tribute to her energy and passion.

Hutchinson organized discussion groups ("conventicles") attended by dozens of women and eventually many men, too. This in itself was a bold move. It was empowering especially to the women, who were supposed to remain quiet and subordinate to their husbands, particularly in matters of religion and governance. But Hutchinson's meetings were full of critical talk about the "errors" in recent sermons and the intolerant ways in which the men of Massachusetts ran the colony. Her influence grew rapidly, and by all accounts Boston became a stronghold of antinomianism while the countryside aligned with the establishment. It was only a matter of time before religious and gender differences spilled over into politics.

In 1636 Hutchinson and her "free grace" allies such as Cotton, Reverend John Wheelwright, and Governor Henry Vale came under blistering attack by the orthodox Puritan clergy. In churches and public meetings, they were assailed as heretics and disturbers of the peace who threatened the very existence of the Puritan experiment in New England. Accusations of immoral sexual conduct, thoroughly unfounded, swirled. Cotton was sidelined by the pressure. Wheelwright was found guilty of "contempt & sedition" for having "purposely set himself to kindle and increase" strife within the colony and was banished from Massachusetts. Vale was defeated for reelection, and a Hutchinson enemy, John Winthrop, became governor in 1637. Despite initial wavering under the intense pressure, Hutchinson held firm.

In November 1637, Winthrop arranged for Hutchinson to be put on trial on the charge of slandering the ministers of Massachusetts Bay. He declared that she had "troubled the peace of the commonwealth and churches" by promoting unsanctioned opinions and holding unauthorized meetings in her home. Though she had never voiced her views outside the conventicles she held, or ever signed any statements or petitions about them, Winthrop portrayed her as a coconspirator who had goaded others to challenge authority. Before the court, with Hutchinson present, he charged: "You have spoken divers things as we have been informed [which are] very prejudicial to the honour of the churches and ministers thereof, and you have maintained a meeting and an assembly in your house that hath been condemned by the general assembly as a thing not tolerable nor comely in the sight of God nor fitting for your sex."

Hutchinson mostly stonewalled the prosecution, but occasionally shot back with a fiery rejoinder like this one: "Do you think it not lawful for me to teach women, and why do you call me to teach the court?"

The first day of the trial went reasonably well for her. One biographer, Richard Morris, said she "outfenced the magistrates in a battle of wits." Another biographer, Eve LaPlante, wrote, "Her success before the court may have astonished her judges, but it was no surprise to her. She was confident of herself and her intellectual tools, largely because of the intimacy she felt with God."

But on the second day Hutchinson cut loose with this warning:

> You have no power over my body, neither can you do me any harm—for I am in the hands of the eternal Jehovah, my Saviour. I am at his appointment, the bounds of my habitation are cast in heaven, no further do I esteem of any mortal man than creatures in his hand, I fear none but the great Jehovah, which hath foretold me of these things, and I do verily believe that he will deliver me out of your hands. Therefore take heed how you proceed against me—for I know that, for this you go about to do to me, God will ruin you and your posterity and this whole state.

What Winthrop and his prosecutors hadn't yet proved, Hutchinson handed them in one stroke. This was all the evidence of "sedition" and "contempt of court" that they needed. She was convicted, labeled an instrument of the devil and "a woman not fit for our society," and banished from Massachusetts Bay.

This was the verdict of her *civil* trial. She would be detained for four months under house arrest, rarely able to see her family, until a *church* trial that would determine her fate as a member of the Puritan faith. In that trial, because she would not admit to certain theological mistakes, she was formally excommunicated with this denunciation from Reverend Thomas Shepard: "I do cast you out and deliver you up to Satan...and account you from this time forth to be a Heathen and a Publican.... I command you in the name of Christ Jesus and of this Church as a Leper to withdraw yourself out of the Congregation."

"The Spirit of Liberty"

Hutchinson, husband William, and their children departed Boston in April 1638. They trudged for nearly a week in the snow to get to Providence, Rhode Island, founded by Roger Williams as a haven for persecuted minorities.

In 1642, not long after her husband died, Anne and a number of her children relocated to New Netherland, in what is now the Bronx, New York. On a terrible day in August 1643, Anne and her entire family but for one daughter were massacred by marauding Siwanoy Indians.

The woman who rocked a colony was gone, but as Rothbard writes, "the spirit of liberty that she embodied and kindled was to outlast the despotic theocracy of Massachusetts Bay."

As America's first feminist, and a woman of conscience and principle, Anne Hutchinson planted seeds of religious liberty that would grow and help establish a new nation a little more than a century later.

Lessons from Anne Hutchinson

Have the courage of your convictions: Long before "women's liberation," Anne Hutchinson spoke and acted with every bit as much courage and candor as any man. She showed no fear in challenging what she regarded as errors from the pulpit and assaults from governing authorities against free thought.

Defend religious liberty: Hutchinson's resistance led to her banishment, but she set an example that would, long after her death, help make religious liberty a central element of the American founding.

5

Adam Smith

Ideas Change the World

Adam Smith entered a world that his reason and eloquence would later transform. He was baptized on June 5, 1723, in Kirkcaldy, Scotland. It's presumed that he was born either on that day or a day or two before. He would become the Father of Economics as well as one of history's most eloquent defenders of free markets.

The late British economist Kenneth E. Boulding paid this tribute to his intellectual predecessor: "Adam Smith, who has strong claim to being both the Adam and the Smith of systematic economics, was a professor of moral philosophy and it was at that forge that economics was made."

Economics in the late eighteenth century was not yet a focused subject of its own but rather a poorly organized compartment of what was known as "moral philosophy." Smith's first book, *The Theory of Moral Sentiments*, was published in 1759, when he held the chair of moral philosophy at Glasgow University. He was the first moral philosopher to recognize that the business of enterprise—and all the motives and actions in the marketplace that give rise to it—was deserving of careful, full-time study as a modern discipline of social science.

The culmination of his thoughts in this regard came in 1776. As American colonists were declaring their independence from Britain, Smith was publishing his own shot heard round the world, *An Inquiry into the Nature and Causes of the Wealth of Nations*, better known ever since as simply *The Wealth of Nations*. (One of my most prized possessions is the two-volume 1790 edition of the book, gifted to me by an old friend; it was the last edition to incorporate edits from Smith himself, just before he died in that same year.)

Smith's choice of the longer title is revealing. Note that he didn't set out to explore the nature and causes of the *poverty* of nations. Poverty, in his mind, was what happens when nothing happens, when people are idle by choice or force, or when production is prevented or destroyed. He wanted to know what brings the things we call material wealth into being, and why. It was a searching examination that would make him a withering critic of the existing political and economic order.

A Bigger Pie

For three hundred years before Smith, western Europe was dominated by an economic system known as "mercantilism." Though it provided for modest improvements in life and liberty over the feudalism that preceded it, it was a system rooted in error that stifled enterprise and treated individuals as pawns of the state.

Mercantilist thinkers believed that the world's wealth was a fixed pie, giving rise to endless conflict between nations. After all, if you

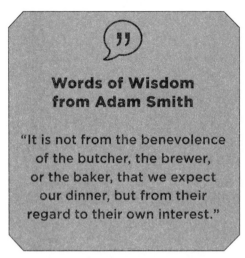

**Words of Wisdom
from Adam Smith**

"It is not from the benevolence
of the butcher, the brewer,
or the baker, that we expect
our dinner, but from their
regard to their own interest."

think there's only so much and
you want more of it, you've got
to take it from someone else.

Mercantilists were eco-
nomic nationalists. Foreign
goods, they thought, were sufficiently harmful to the domestic economy that government
policy should promote exports
and restrict imports. Mercantilists wanted their nations'
exports to be paid for not with
foreign goods but in gold and
silver. To the mercantilist, the precious metals were the very defini-
tion of wealth, especially to the extent that they piled up in the monarch's coffers.

In Smith's contrarian view, wealth was not gold and silver. Precious metals, though reliable as media of exchange and for their own
industrial uses, were no more than claims against the real thing. All
the gold and silver in the world would leave one starving and freezing if it couldn't be exchanged for food and clothing. Wealth to the
world's first economist was plainly this: *goods and services.*

Whatever increased the supply and quality of goods and services,
lowered their price, or enhanced their value made for greater wealth
and higher standards of living. The "pie" of national wealth isn't fixed;
you can bake a bigger one by producing more.

Baking that bigger pie, Smith showed, results from investments in
capital and the division of labor. His famous example of the special-
ized tasks in a pin factory demonstrated how the division of labor produces far more than if each of us acted in isolation to produce everything himself. It was a principle that Smith showed works for nations
precisely because it works for the individuals who make them up.

He was consequently an economic *internationalist*, one who
believed in the widest possible cooperation between peoples irrespec-

tive of political boundaries. He was a consummate free trader at a time when trade was hampered by an endless roster of counterproductive tariffs, quotas, and prohibitions.

Smith wasn't hung up on the old mercantilist fallacy that more goods should be exported than imported. He exploded this "balance of trade" fallacy by arguing that, since goods and services constituted a nation's wealth, it made no sense for government to make sure that more left the country than came in.

Self-interest had been frowned upon for ages as acquisitive, antisocial behavior, but Smith celebrated it as an indispensable spur to economic progress. "It is not from the benevolence of the butcher, the brewer, or the baker, that we expect our dinner," he wrote, "but from their regard to their own interest." He added that self-interest is an unsurpassed incentive: "The natural effort of every individual to better his own condition...is so powerful, that it is alone, and without any assistance, not only capable of carrying on the society to wealth and prosperity, but of surmounting a hundred impertinent obstructions with which the folly of human laws too often encumbers its operations."

Mercantilists wanted governments to bestow monopoly privileges on a favored few. In Britain, the king even granted a protected monopoly over the production of playing cards to a particular highly placed noble. But Smith showed that this view reflected a misunderstanding of self-interest, the profit motive, and the operation of prices. To satisfy his own desires, a person must produce what others want at a price they can afford. Prices send signals to producers so that they will know what to make more of and what to provide less of. It wasn't necessary, Smith said, for the king to assign tasks and bestow monopolies to see that things get done. Prices and profit would act as an "invisible hand" with far more efficiency than any monarch or parliament. And competition would see to it that quality is improved and prices are kept low. Nobel Prize–winning economist F. A. Hayek wrote in his book *The Fatal Conceit*:

Adam Smith was the first to perceive that we have stumbled upon methods of ordering human economic cooperation that exceed the limits of our knowledge and perception. His "invisible hand" had perhaps better have been described as an invisible or unsurveyable pattern. We are led—for example by the pricing system in market exchange—to do things by circumstances of which we are largely unaware and which produce results that we do not intend. In our economic activities we do not know the needs which we satisfy nor the sources of the things which we get.

The Father of Economics placed much more faith in people and markets than in kings and edicts. With characteristic eloquence, he declared, "In the great chess-board of human society, every single piece has a principle of motion of its own, altogether different from that which the legislature might choose to impress upon it." That is why, as Nobel laureate economist Richard Stone explains, "Smith was passionately opposed to all laws and practices that tended to discourage production and increase prices," and why he "devotes chapter after chapter to exposing the harm caused by the combination of two things he particularly disliked: monopoly interests and government intervention in private economic arrangements."

Smith displayed an understanding of government that eclipses that of many citizens today when he wrote:

> It is the highest impertinence and presumption...in kings and ministers, to pretend to watch over the economy of private people, and to restrain their expense.... They are themselves always, and without any exception, the greatest spendthrifts in the society. Let them look well after their own expense, and they may safely trust private people with theirs. If their own extravagance does not ruin the state, that of their subjects never will.

Smith wasn't perfect. He left a little more room for government than many of us are comfortable with, especially in light of what we've learned of the political process in the centuries since. Much of what we now know in economics he left to later scholars to correct or discover (the Austrian school's seminal contributions regarding the source of value and marginal utility being two of the most important). But Smith's books, as Austrian economist Ludwig von Mises noted, represented "the keystone of a marvelous system of ideas."

The last formal job that Smith held in his life was, ironically, commissioner of customs in Scotland. How could such an eminent free trader preside over the collection of the very tariffs he had so eloquently debunked? He certainly evidenced no change of mind on the fundamental virtue of freer trade. E. G. West, in his excellent 1969 biography of Smith, wrote, "To enter the service of the Customs would not be to compromise on his principles. On the contrary, he would be enabled more practically to study further ways of achieving economies." And achieving economies is exactly what Smith did over seven years in the job. Net revenues to the Treasury, we learn in West's book, rose dramatically during Smith's tenure, not from higher rates but from reduction in the costs of collection that Smith had put in place.

Freedom and Prosperity

The ideas of Adam Smith exerted enormous influence before he died in 1790 and especially in the nineteenth century. America's Founders were greatly affected by his insights. *The Wealth of Nations* became required reading among men and women of ideas the world over. No one had more thoroughly blown away the intellectual edifice of big government than the professor from Kirkcaldy.

A tribute as much to him as to any other individual thinker, the world in 1900 was much freer and more prosperous than anyone could have imagined in 1776. The triumphs of trade and globalization in our own time are further testimony to his enduring legacy. A think tank in Britain bears his name and seeks to make his legacy better known.

Ideas really do matter. They can change the world. Adam Smith proved that, and we are all immeasurably better off for the ideas he shattered and the ones he set in motion.

Lessons from Adam Smith

Understand the power of good ideas: Adam Smith demolished the premises of the suffocating system of mercantilism and in so doing planted the seeds for the greatest flowering of the free economy since ancient Rome. His ideas changed the world for the better.

Don't fall for government promises to "fix" the economy: The experience of the past 240 years has borne out the case Smith made so persuasively: that the "invisible hand" of free prices, competitive markets, and self-interest (properly understood) yields far more economic good for society than the "iron fist" of rulers and their bureaucracies.

6

Mercy Otis Warren

Conscience of Great Causes

Two centuries before "women's lib," in the run-up to America's Revolutionary War, Mercy Otis Warren was already a liberated woman by the standards of her day. And she did the liberating herself.

In the latter half of the eighteenth century, Warren was an accomplished poet, playwright, pamphleteer, and historian—though much of what she wrote was anonymous, in part to get a hearing where a woman might not otherwise be listened to. She also risked reprisal from King George III and the British troops with her subversive rhetoric in favor of American liberty and independence.

She was a close friend and confidante to almost all the major figures of the revolution: the Adamses (Samuel as well as John and

Abigail), the Washingtons (both George and Martha), Thomas Jefferson, John Hancock, and Patrick Henry, among others. Many of the plans and activities of the Sons of Liberty and, later, the Committees of Correspondence were hatched in her Massachusetts home.

For decades, she advocated for women's rights at a time when progress on that front must have seemed glacial at best. When the Constitution was debated, she was an outspoken anti-Federalist who insisted on the adoption of a Bill of Rights. She was the first person, man or woman, to pen a history of the conflict with Britain.

It's for eminently good reason that Mercy Otis Warren is regarded in history as the "conscience of the revolution."

"We Will Be Free"

Born in 1728 in West Barnstable, Massachusetts, Warren was home-schooled by parents who encouraged every sign of interest in her studies in general and literature in particular. Her mother was a descendant of a passenger aboard the *Mayflower*, the ship that brought the Pilgrims to New England in 1620. Her father was a vocal opponent of British rule in the colonial legislature. Both her father and her brother led the fight against the king's writs of assistance (searches without warrants), and her brother is credited with the first usage of the phrase "No taxation without representation." Husband James affectionately labeled her "the scribbler."

As tensions rose between the mother country and the colonies, Warren was drawn into the fray. "Every domestic enjoyment depends on the unimpaired possession of civil and religious liberty," she wrote. Encroachments on that liberty, particularly when they came under orders from the unpopular British governor of Massachusetts, Thomas Hutchinson, earned Warren's opprobrium.

Hutchinson was the model for (and intended target of) her famous play *The Adulateur*, which appeared in 1772. It foretold the coming of the revolution through the words of a disagreeable and imperious official named Rapatio. Published anonymously, it enjoyed an enthusiastic reception. "With the publication of *The Adulateur*," writes biographer Nancy Rubin Stuart, "Mercy made her debut as the patriots' secret pen, whose barbed lampoons provoked laughter and longing for liberation from British rule."

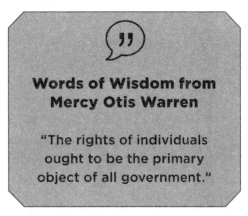

Words of Wisdom from Mercy Otis Warren

"The rights of individuals ought to be the primary object of all government."

With war clouds gathering in 1775, Warren saw the contending sides in stark terms: "America stands armed with resolution and virtue; but she still recoils at the idea of drawing the sword against the nation from whom she derived her origin. Yet Britain, like an unnatural parent, is ready to plunge her dagger into the bosom of her affectionate offspring."

During the war, Warren not only wrote plays and pamphlets that championed the American cause; she also dared to promote women's rights. Her tragedy *The Ladies of Castile*, set in Spain during the reign of Emperor Charles V, is regarded as the most feminist of her patriotic works. The play's heroine warns the audience:

Though weak compassion sinks the female mind
And our frail sex dissolve in pity's tears;
Yet justice' sword can never be resheath'd
'Till Charles is taught to know we will be free;
And learns the duty that a monarch owes,
To heaven—the people—and the rights of man.

After the United States secured independence, Warren turned her attention to ensuring that the government did not stray from the principles of republicanism. In February 1788, during debates over the ratification of the Constitution, she published a nineteen-page pamphlet called "Observations on the New Constitution, and on the

Federal and State Conventions." In it she argued that the Constitution as it stood threatened to violate individuals' and states' rights. "All writers on government agree...that man is born free and possessed of certain unalienable rights—that government is instituted for the protection, safety, and happiness of the people," she wrote. But the Constitution would "betray the people of the United States into an acceptance of a most complicated system of government, marked on the one side with the dark, secret and profound intrigues of the statesman...and on the other, with the ideal project of young ambition...to intoxicate the inexperienced votary."

She concluded that without provisions to ensure explicitly freedoms of speech and press, limits on the judiciary, guarantees of trial by jury, and other protections, the Constitution would undermine what Americans had fought for. She demanded the addition of, in her words, "a bill of rights to guard against the dangerous encroachments of power."

Ultimately, in large measure because the arguments of Warren and her anti-Federalist compatriots finally swayed James Madison, the Bill of Rights became the first ten amendments to the Constitution.

Setting a High Standard

Warren was deeply offended when President John Adams signed into law the infamous Alien and Sedition Acts in 1798. They led to the closure of newspapers critical of the administration, which Warren saw as the grossest violation of American liberty—and she said so without reservation. Her fierce objections strained her relationship with the president but did not injure her long-standing friendship with his wife, Abigail. Warren's warnings against a postwar lapse in revolutionary principles helped bring about the ouster of John Adams and the election of Thomas Jefferson in 1800.

Her last major work was *History of the Rise, Progress, and Termination of the American Revolution.* Appearing it 1805, it was the first important history of the period from 1765 to 1789. President Jefferson ordered copies for himself and for every member of his cabinet and no doubt took note of her concern for the country's future. She wrote:

> The people of the United States are bound together in sacred compact and a union of interests which ought never to be separated. But the confederation is recent, and their experience immatured; they are, however, generally sensible ... [understanding that history demonstrates that] deception as well as violence have operated to the subversion of the freedom of the people.

Warren knew full well that the imperfect Constitution, even improved with a Bill of Rights, was still a scrap of paper. Whether or not it lived to protect Americans' hard-won freedom depended on the wisdom and spirit of the people. She had already witnessed a dismaying retreat from constitutional principles in the Adams administration. She worried that with the passing of the revolutionary generation, future Americans might embrace diminutions of their liberties through moral corruption, false promises, lies, and unprincipled compromise. "The characters of nations," she observed, "have been disgraced by their weak partialities, until their freedom has been irretrievably lost in that vortex of folly which throws a lethargy over the mind, till awakened by the fatal consequences which result from arbitrary power, disguised by specious pretexts amidst a general relaxation of manners [i.e., personal character]."

When Warren died in 1814 at age eighty-six, she was celebrated as a principled defender of the revolution, an eloquent advocate of liberty and limited government, and the epitome of what it meant to be a true "conscience" of great causes. In the two centuries since, how faithfully have Americans lived up to her standards of conscience for those same causes?

Lessons from Mercy Otis Warren

Educate yourself: The homeschooled Mercy Otis Warren drew on her extensive studies to become an accomplished poet, playwright, pamphleteer, and historian—and an influential voice for American independence, the Bill of Rights, and women's rights.

Speak out for your principles: Warren steadfastly supported the cause of American liberty whether that meant defying the British Crown and Parliament, risking her longtime friendship with John Adams, or challenging the common belief of her era that politics and war were subjects only men were to discuss.

7

Edmund Burke

Eloquence and Conviction

Murray Rothbard, the Austrian school economist, regarded the young Edmund Burke as a libertarian and even a philosophical anarchist. Russell Kirk, the renowned man of letters and author of *The Conservative Mind*, viewed Burke as the progenitor of the modern conservative movement.

Rothbard and Kirk differed on many things, but on this they agreed: Edmund Burke was one of the greatest political thinkers of the past three hundred years, a man to whom lovers of liberty owe a considerable intellectual debt.

Resisting "Injustice, Oppression, and Absurdity"

Born in 1729 in Dublin, Ireland, Burke moved to England in 1750 to study law, and he considered himself at least as much English as he was Irish. By his early thirties he had gained a reputation as a promising writer and political commentator, and in 1766 he began a long career as a Whig member of the House of Commons. In *The Triumph of Liberty*, Jim Powell writes: "Burke wasn't a great orator—indeed, his speeches, which were sometimes three hours long, emptied the seats in Parliament. But Burke had acquired deep knowledge of history which gave him valuable perspective, and he developed a passionate pen." And he deployed his considerable skills on behalf of causes that, though not always popular, reflected his commitment to principle.

One such issue was his defense of America and his opposition to conflict with the colonies. On this matter he spoke out against the king, his ministers, and a majority of Parliament. The beginning of George III's reign in 1760 had marked the end of a long period of British "salutary neglect" of colonial America. Most of the British government was intent on letting Americans know who was boss. Burke spoke out nonetheless—passionately and repeatedly.

In 1774 Burke rose in Parliament to deliver an eloquent appeal to leave the colonists alone on the all-important issue of "taxation without representation":

> Again and again, revert to your old principles—seek peace and ensue it; leave America, if she has taxable matter in her, to tax herself. I am not here going into the distinctions of rights, nor attempting to mark their boundaries. I do not enter into these metaphysical distinctions; I hate the very sound of them. Leave the Americans as they anciently stood, and these distinctions, born of our unhappy contest, will die along with it.... Be content to bind America by laws of trade; you have always done it.... Do not burthen them with taxes.... But if intemperately, unwisely, fatally, you sophisticate and poison the very source

of government by urging subtle deductions, and consequences odious to those you govern, from the unlimited and illimitable nature of supreme sovereignty, you will teach them by these means to call that sovereignty itself in question.... If that sovereignty and their freedom cannot be reconciled, which will they take? They will cast your sovereignty in your face. No body of men will be argued into slavery.... Tell me, what one character of liberty the Americans have, and what one brand of slavery they are free from, if they are bound in their property and industry by all the restraints you can imagine on commerce, and at the same time are made pack-horses of every tax you choose to impose, without the least share in granting them. When they bear the burthens of unlimited monopoly, will you bring them to bear the burthens of unlimited revenue too? The Englishman in America will feel that this is slavery; that it is legal slavery, will be no compensation either to his feelings or to his understandings.

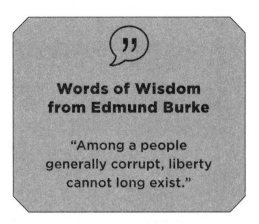

Words of Wisdom from Edmund Burke

"Among a people generally corrupt, liberty cannot long exist."

A year later, as the bonds between Britain and America were breaking, he once again urged peace and reconciliation. He poignantly reminded his colleagues in the House of Commons that Americans were fellow Englishmen:

They are therefore not only devoted to liberty, but to liberty according to English ideas and on English principles. The people are Protestants...a persuasion not only favourable to liberty, but built upon it.... My hold of the colonies is in the close affection which grows from common names, from kindred blood, from similar privileges, and equal protection. These are ties which, though light as air, are as strong as links of iron. Let the colonies always keep the idea of their civil rights associated with your government—they will cling and grapple to you, and no force under heaven will be of power to tear them from their allegiance. But let it be once understood that your government may be one thing and their privileges another, that these two things may exist without any mutual relation—the cement is gone, the cohesion is loosened, and everything hastens to decay and dissolution. As long as you have the wisdom to keep the sovereign authority of this country as the sanctuary of liberty, the sacred temple consecrated to our common faith, wherever the chosen race and sons of England worship freedom, they will turn their faces towards you.... Slavery they can have anywhere. It is a weed that grows in every soil. They may have it from Spain, they may have it from Prussia. But, until you become lost to all feeling of your true interest and your natural dignity, freedom they can have from none but you.

War with America, in Burke's view, could lead only to disaster. Even if Britain were successful, it would come at a great cost in lives, treasure, and goodwill. "The use of force alone is but *temporary*," he warned. "It may subdue for a moment; but it does not remove the necessity of subduing again: and a nation is not governed, which is perpetually to be conquered." He openly declared that to support the war was to "wish success to injustice, oppression and absurdity."

Limiting Government Power

Burke criticized the overreach of government in all spheres, arguing that treating people as pawns of power bred only violence and disorder. "People crushed by law," he reasoned, "have no hopes but from power. If laws are their enemies, they will be enemies to laws; and those who have much to hope and nothing to lose, will always be dangerous." In his famous letter to the sheriffs of Bristol in 1777, he noted that liberty is usually lost not in one fell swoop but one slice at a time: "The true danger is when liberty is nibbled away, for expedients, and by parts." He was a leader in Parliament's debates—perhaps the most important one in his day—in favor of enacting constitutional limitations on government power, whether it emanated from the king or from Parliament itself.

The Anglican Burke championed the unpopular cause of Catholic emancipation, supporting the right of Catholics to hold positions in government and opposing the appropriation of public funds for the support of the Anglican Church in Ireland.

He was an ardent free trader at a time when Adam Smith's ideas against protectionism were only beginning to take root: "Free trade is not based on utility but on justice." He spoke of "the advantage of free intercourse between all parts of the same kingdom" as well as "the evils attending restriction and monopoly." Echoing Smith, he asserted that "the gain of others is not necessarily our loss, but on the contrary, an advantage by causing a greater demand for such wares as we have for sale."

Enjoying special privileges bestowed by the British government, the East India Tea Company by the 1780s dominated the political and economic life of India. Abuses of Indians were rampant, leading Burke to champion the impeachment of Warren Hastings, the British governor-general of Bengal. Piers Brendon, in his *The Decline and Fall of the British Empire: 1781–1997*, recalls that Burke's piercing, well-documented indictment labeled Hastings a "captain-general of iniquity," a man "who never dined without creating a famine," a blackguard whose heart was "gangrened to the core," and a despoiler who resembled both a "spider of Hell" and a "ravenous vulture devouring the carcasses of the dead." Though the House of Commons did impeach Hastings, his friends in the House of Lords refused to convict.

"Architects of Ruin"

The French Revolution that began in 1789 provided Burke with an issue that has surely defined him and his political philosophy more than any other. His powerful treatise in 1790, *Reflections on the Revolution in France*, is perhaps the best-known contemporaneous critique of the revolution and the primary source for Russell Kirk's claim that Burke is the father of modern conservative political theory. Though he applauded the spirit of liberty that provoked the upheaval, he quickly saw where the French were tragically headed. They were becoming, in his words,

> the ablest architects of ruin that had hitherto existed in the world. In that very short space of time they had completely pulled down to the ground, their monarchy; their church; their nobility; their law; their revenue; their army; their navy; their commerce; their arts; and their manufactures.... [There was a danger of] an imitation of the excesses of an irrational, unprincipled, proscribing, confiscating, plundering, ferocious, bloody and tyrannical democracy.

When the French added hyperinflation and price controls to their panoply of tyranny in the mid-1790s, Burke showed himself to be a staunch defender of sound money. He upbraided the French for the destruction of private property and commercial order that their depreciating paper money engendered:

> Your legislators, in everything new, are the very first who have founded a commonwealth on gaming, and infused this spirit into it as its vital breath. The great object of these politics is to metamorphose France from a great kingdom into one great play table; to turn its inhabitants into a nation of gamesters.... With you, a man can neither earn nor buy his dinner without a speculation. What he receives in the morning will not have

the same value at night.... Industry must wither away. Economy must be driven from your country. Careful provision will have no existence.

Burke understood a cardinal rule of society—namely, that there's a vital connection between liberty and personal character. "All who have ever written on government are unanimous," he wrote, "that among a people generally corrupt, liberty cannot long exist." His most eloquent statement of this principle appeared in a letter to a member of the National Assembly in 1791:

> Men are qualified for civil liberty in exact proportion to their disposition to put moral chains upon their own appetites—in proportion as their love to justice is above their rapacity—in proportion as their soundness and sobriety of understanding is above their vanity and presumption,—in proportion as they are more disposed to listen to the counsels of the wise and good, in preference to the flattery of knaves. Society cannot exist, unless a controlling power upon will and appetite be placed some-where; and the less of it there is within, the more there must be without. It is ordained in the eternal constitution of things, that men of intemperate minds cannot be free. Their passions forge their fetters.

Liberty and Authority

Edmund Burke died in 1797 at age sixty-eight, leaving behind a legacy of eloquence in the defense of liberty and of those oppressed by authority, from Catholics to Americans to Indians. Winston Churchill summed him up well when he wrote:

> On the one hand he is revealed as a foremost apostle of Liberty, on the other as the redoubtable champion of Authority. But a

charge of political inconsistency applied to this life appears a mean and petty thing. History easily discerns the reasons and forces which actuated him, and the immense changes in the problems he was facing which evoked from the same profound mind and sincere spirit these entirely contrary manifestations. His soul revolted against tyranny, whether it appeared in the aspect of a domineering Monarch and a corrupt Court and Parliamentary system, or whether, mouthing the watch-words of a non-existent liberty, it towered up against him in the dictation of a brutal mob and wicked sect. No one can read the Burke of Liberty and the Burke of Authority without feeling that here was the same man pursuing the same ends, seeking the same ideals of society and Government, and defending them from assaults, now from one extreme, now from the other.

Lessons from Edmund Burke

Resist assaults on liberty wherever they occur: Often taking unpopular positions, Edmund Burke rose in Parliament to defend the rights of Americans, Catholics, and Indians. He also warned that the anti-liberty excesses of the French Revolution would generate great bloodshed.

Cherish liberty, order, and tradition: Burke saw liberty as impossible without order and respect for honorable traditions; he also championed liberty as a natural source of order itself.

8

Thomas Clarkson

A Moral Steam Engine That Never Quit

At sea in late November 1781, the captain of the British slave ship *Zong* did the unspeakable. He ordered his crew to throw 133 chained black Africans overboard to their deaths. He reckoned that by falsely claiming the ship had run out of fresh water, he could collect more for the "cargo" from the ship's insurer than he could fetch at a slave auction in Jamaica.

The captain and crew were found out, but no one in the *Zong* affair was prosecuted for murder. A London court ruled the matter a civil dispute between an insurance firm and a client. As for the Africans, the judge declared that their drowning was "just as if horses were killed," which was not far removed from the conventional wisdom of the time.

Slavery, after all, was an ancient institution. The number of people who have walked the earth in bondage far exceeds the number who have enjoyed even a modest measure of liberty. As horrifying as the *Zong* captain's actions were, the standard treatment aboard slave ships was little better. Mortality rates aboard such vessels reached appalling levels, sometimes running as high as 50 percent. Even if an African captive survived the Middle Passage across the Atlantic, that was only the start of a hellish experience: life at the end of a lash, filled with endless and often excruciating toil, with death coming at an early age.

Moved by the fate of the *Zong*'s victims and the indifference of the court, a vice chancellor at the University of Cambridge chose this question for the university's Latin essay contest for 1785:

"Anne liceat invitos in servitutem dare?"—Is it lawful to make slaves of others against their will?

The contest was known throughout Britain, and the honor of winning it was highly prized.

A twenty-five-year-old Cambridge student named Thomas Clarkson decided to try his luck in the essay contest. That contest started Clarkson on a quest that would define his life and change world history: the quest to consign slavery to the ash heap of history.

Mobilizer

Before he entered the essay contest, Thomas Clarkson hoped to become a minister. He had not previously displayed an interest in the topic of slavery. Still, he plunged into his research with the vigor, meticulous care, and mounting passion that would characterize nearly every day of his next sixty-one years. Clarkson won first prize for his essay, which drew on the vivid testimony of those who had seen the unspeakable cruelty of the slave trade firsthand.

What Clarkson had learned in writing his essay distressed him to his core. Shortly after claiming the prize, he was riding on horseback along a country road when his conscience gripped him. Slavery, he later wrote, "wholly engrossed" his thoughts. He could not complete the ride without frequent stops to dismount and walk, tortured by the awful visions of the traffic in human lives. At one point, falling to the ground in anguish, he determined that if what he had written in his essay were indeed true, it led to only one conclusion: "It was time some person should see these calamities to their end."

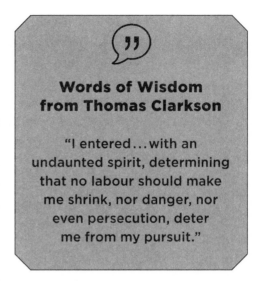

Words of Wisdom from Thomas Clarkson

"I entered...with an undaunted spirit, determining that no labour should make me shrink, nor danger, nor even persecution, deter me from my pursuit."

The significance of those few minutes in time is summed up in a splendid book by Adam Hochschild, *Bury the Chains: Prophets and Rebels in the Fight to Free an Empire's Slaves*:

> If there is a single moment at which the antislavery movement became inevitable, it was the day in 1785 when Thomas Clarkson sat down by the side of the road at Wades Mill.... For his Bible-conscious colleagues, it held echoes of Saul's conversion on the road to Damascus. For us today, it is a landmark on the long, tortuous path to the modern conception of universal human rights.

Thus began Clarkson's all-consuming focus on a moral ideal: no man can rightfully lay claim, moral or otherwise, to owning another. Casting aside his plans for a career as a man of the cloth, he risked everything for the single cause of ending the evil of slavery.

He sought out and befriended the one group that had already embraced the issue: the Quakers. But the Quakers were few in number, and British society wrote them off as an odd fringe element. Quaker men even refused to remove their hats for any man, including the king, because they believed it offended a higher authority. Clarkson knew that antislavery would have to become a mainstream, fashionable educational effort to have any hope of success.

On May 22, 1787, Clarkson brought together twelve men, including a few leading Quakers, at a London print shop to plot the course. Alexis de Tocqueville later described the results of that meeting as "extraordinary" and "absolutely without precedent" in the history of the world. This tiny group, which named itself the Society for the Abolition of the African Slave Trade, was about to take on a firmly established institution in which a great deal of money was made and on which considerable political power depended.

Powered by an evangelical zeal, Clarkson's committee became what might be described as the world's first think tank. Noble ideas and unassailable facts were its weapons.

"Looking back today," writes Hochschild, "what is more astonishing than the pervasiveness of slavery in the late 1700s is how swiftly it died. By the end of the following century, slavery was, at least on paper, outlawed almost everywhere." Thomas Clarkson was the prime architect of "the first, pioneering wave of that campaign"—the antislavery movement in Britain, which Hochschild properly describes as "one of the most ambitious and brilliantly organized citizens' movements of all time."

The credit for ending slavery in the British Empire is most often given to William Wilberforce. He was the longtime parliamentarian who never gave in to overwhelming odds, introducing bill after bill to abolish the slave trade, and later slavery itself. His boyhood pastor was John Newton, the former slave trader who converted to Christianity, renounced slavery, and wrote the enduring, autobiographical hymn "Amazing Grace."

Wilberforce was a hero in his own right, but Thomas Clarkson was prominent among those who proposed to Wilberforce that he be the movement's man in Parliament. Moreover, it was the information Clarkson gathered while crisscrossing the British countryside—logging thirty-five thousand miles on horseback—that Wilberforce often used in parliamentary debate. Clarkson was the mobilizer, the energizer, the fact finder, and the very conscience of the movement.

Indomitable

In *Thomas Clarkson: Friend of Slaves*, biographer Earl Leslie Griggs writes that this man on fire was "second to no one in indefatigable energy and unremitting devotion to an ideal" and that "he inspired in his friends confidence in his ability to lead them."

In a diary entry for Wednesday, June 27, 1787, Clarkson tells of the moment he arrived in the slave ship port of Bristol. Genuine misgivings about his work gave way to a steely determination that served him well in the battles ahead:

I began now to tremble, for the first time, at the arduous task I had undertaken, of attempting to subvert one of the branches of the commerce of the great place which was then before me. I began to think of the host of people I should have to encounter in it. I anticipated much persecution in it also; and I questioned whether I should even get out of it alive. But in journeying on, I became more calm and composed. My spirits began to return. In these latter moments I considered my first feelings as useful, inasmuch as they impressed upon me the necessity of extraordinary courage, and activity, and perseverance, and of watchfulness, also, over my own conduct, that I might not throw any stain upon the cause I had undertaken. When, therefore, I entered the city, I entered it with an undaunted spirit, determining that no labour should make me shrink, nor danger, nor even persecution, deter me from my pursuit.

Clarkson translated his prizewinning essay from Latin into English and supervised its distribution by the tens of thousands. He helped organize boycotts of the West Indian rum and sugar produced with slave labor. He gave lectures and sermons. He wrote many articles and at least two books. He helped British seamen escape from the slave-carrying ships they were pressed into against their will. He filed murder charges in courts to draw attention to the actions of fiendish slave ship captains. He convinced witnesses to speak. He gathered testimony, rustled up petition signatures by the thousands, and smuggled evidence from under the noses of his adversaries. His life was threatened many times, and once, surrounded by an angry mob, he very nearly lost it.

The long hours, the often thankless and seemingly fruitless forays to uncover evidence, the risks and the costs that came in every form, the many low points when it looked like the world was against him— all of that went on and on, year after year. None of it ever made the smallest dent in Thomas Clarkson's iron will.

When Britain went to war with France in 1793, Clarkson and his committee saw their early progress in winning converts evaporate. The opposition in Parliament argued that abandoning the slave trade would hand a lucrative business to a formidable enemy. And the public saw winning the war as more important than freeing people of another color and another continent.

The indomitable Clarkson did not relent. He, Wilberforce, and the committee kept spreading the message.

At Clarkson's instigation, a diagram of a slave ship became a tool in the debate. Depicting hundreds of slaves crammed like sardines in horrible conditions, the diagram proved pivotal in winning over the public.

Clarkson's committee also enlisted the help of famed pottery maker Josiah Wedgwood in producing a famous medallion with the image of a kneeling, chained black man, uttering the words, "Am I not a man and a brother?"

Clarkson's imprint was on almost everything the committee did. It even produced one of the first newsletters and, as Hochschild suggests, one of the first direct-mail campaigns for the purpose of raising money.

The effort finally paid off. The tide of public opinion swung to the abolitionists' side. Parliament outlawed the slave trade when it approved one of Wilberforce's bills in 1807, some twenty years after Clarkson formed his committee. After twenty-six more years of laborious effort by Clarkson, Wilberforce, and others, Britain passed legislation in 1833 to free all slaves within its realm. The law took effect in 1834, forty-nine years after Clarkson's epiphany on a country road. It became a model for peaceful emancipation everywhere. Wilberforce died shortly afterward, but his friend devoted much of the next thirteen years to the movement to end slavery and improve the lot of former slaves worldwide.

"Courageous, Visionary, Disciplined, Self-Sacrificing"

Clarkson died at the age of eighty-six, in 1846. He had been the last living member of the committee that gathered at that London print shop back in 1787. Hochschild tells us that the throngs of mourners "included many Quakers, and the men among them made an almost unprecedented departure from sacred custom" by removing their hats.

In *Thomas Clarkson: A Biography*, Ellen Gibson Wilson summed up her subject well when she wrote, "Thomas Clarkson (1760–1846) was almost too good to be true—courageous, visionary, disciplined, self-sacrificing—a man who gave a long life almost entirely to the service of people he never met in lands he never saw." With good reason the poet Samuel Taylor Coleridge called Clarkson a "moral steam engine" and "the Giant with one idea."

As a former university professor, I've read thousands of students' essays. Occasionally, the process of researching and writing influenced a student's future pursuits. But of all the student essays ever written, I doubt that any had as profound an effect on its author and on the world as the one that Clarkson penned 230 years ago. It struck a spark, which lit a beacon, which saved millions of lives and changed the world.

Lessons from Thomas Clarkson

Fight for what is right, even against long odds: In the 1780s it would have seemed fanciful to believe that the greatest slave-trading power of the day, Britain, could be brought to its moral senses and abolish an institution that was widely accepted around the world. But to Thomas Clarkson, the obstacles to abolition didn't matter. He set himself to accomplish what was right.

Never doubt the power of perseverance: Clarkson's story illustrates how much just a few people can accomplish when they are armed with passion, a righteous cause, and a willingness to persevere no matter the threats and setbacks. As Clarkson wrote, "extraordinary courage, and activity, and perseverance" are necessary to see through a just cause.

9

Frédéric Bastiat

Liberty's Masterful Storyteller

"Sometimes standing against evil is more important than defeating it," wrote novelist N. D. Wilson. "The greatest heroes stand because it is right to do so, not because they believe they will walk away with their lives. Such selfless courage is a victory in itself."

In the last six of his forty-nine years of life, brought to an untimely end by tuberculosis, the classical liberal Frenchman Frédéric Bastiat produced an astonishing volume of books and essays in defense of free markets and free people. He towered over the smug intellectuals and politicians of his native France, most of whom were mired in the country's ancient traditions of statist central planning of the economy.

"Life, liberty, and property do not exist because men have made laws," Bastiat reasoned. "On the contrary, it was the fact that life, liberty, and property existed beforehand that caused men to make laws in the first place."

Bastiat also gave us perhaps the world's most succinct description of the redistributive apparatus of government: "The State is the great fiction through which everyone lives at the expense of everyone else."

If a posthumous Nobel Prize were to be awarded to just one person for crystal-clear writing and masterful storytelling in economics, no one would be more deserving of it than Bastiat. His selfless courage in expressing timeless, irrefutable truths while almost all around him wallowed in fallacy constitutes a great moral victory indeed.

Spying the Statist Threat

Bastiat was born in 1801 in the port village of Bayonne in southern France. He was just fourteen when the French defeat at Waterloo dispatched the dictatorship of Napoleon Bonaparte and put the old monarchy back in place.

As a teenager, Bastiat worked for his family's export business, where he experienced firsthand the absurdity of protectionism and other wealth-stifling trade restrictions. In *The Triumph of Liberty*, Jim Powell writes: "He observed, for instance, how the 1816 French tariff throttled trade, resulting in empty warehouses and idle docks around Bayonne. In 1819, the government put steep tariffs on corn, meat, and sugar, making poor people suffer from needlessly high food prices. High tariffs on English and Swiss cotton led to widespread smuggling."

Inheriting the estate of his grandfather upon the elder's death in 1825, Bastiat could afford to devote considerable time to thought, reading, and debate. In the early 1830s he was elected to two minor public positions: justice of the peace and county assemblyman.

Bastiat published his first article in 1844. He was forty-three years old, but he understood the economic world better than almost anyone twice his age, and he knew better than anybody how to explain it with an economy of words. He employed everyday language and a conversational tone, and he was devastatingly to the point. To this day, nobody can read Bastiat and wonder, "Now what was that all about?"

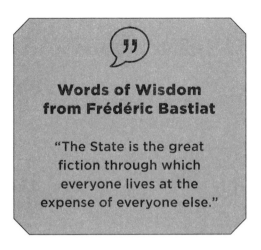

Words of Wisdom from Frédéric Bastiat

"The State is the great fiction through which everyone lives at the expense of everyone else."

He was unequivocal in his opposition to limitless government. "It is not true," he wrote, "that the function of law is to regulate our consciences, our ideas, our wills, our education, our opinions, our work, our trade, our talents, or our pleasures. The function of law is to protect the free exercise of these rights, and to prevent any person from interfering with the free exercise of these same rights by any other person."

David Hart is the editor of Liberty Fund's English translation of *The Collected Works of Frédéric Bastiat*. He writes:

Bastiat thought the modern bureaucratic and regulatory State of his day was based on a mixture of outright violence and coercion on the one hand, and trickery and fallacies (sophisms) on the other. The violence and coercion came from the taxes, tariffs, and regulations, which were imposed on taxpayers, traders, and producers; the ideological dimension that maintained the current class of plunderers came from a new set of "political" and "economic sophisms" that confused, misled, and tricked a new generation of "dupes" into supporting the system. The science of political economy, according to Bastiat, was to be the means by which the economic sophisms of the present would be exposed, rebutted, and finally overturned, thus depriving the current plundering class of its livelihood and power.

Blocked Suns and Broken Windows

Economics these days can be dull and lifeless. Bastiat proved that economics doesn't have to be that way. He could make core economic truths lively and unforgettable, and could tell a story that pierced you with its brilliance.

One of his most memorable analogies comes from "The Candlemakers' Petition," in which candlemakers protest to the government "the unfair competition of a foreign rival." The candlemakers declare: "This foreign manufacturer of light has such an advantage over us that he floods our domestic markets with his product. And he offers it at a fantastically low price."

That competitor turns out to be the sun.

Bastiat wittily demolished the proposed "remedy" of the protectionist candlemakers—forbidding windows or requiring that they be painted black—and explained that it is to society's advantage to accept all the free sunlight it can get and use the resources that might otherwise go to candles to meet other needs.

Bastiat relentlessly assaulted protectionist arguments such as those of the candlemakers. Why should two countries that dig a tunnel through their mountainous border to facilitate travel and trade then undo the advantages by imposing burdensome taxes at both ends? If an exporter sells his goods abroad for more than they were worth at home, then buys valuable goods with the proceeds to bring back to his homeland, why would anyone condemn the transactions as yielding a balance-of-trade "deficit"? If you're a protectionist before reading Bastiat, after reading his work you'll either repent or remain forever in darkness with no excuse that you weren't instructed otherwise.

Bastiat's 1850 essay "That Which Is Seen and That Which Is Not Seen" introduced his famous parable of the broken window. It's a brilliant exposition of what would later become known as "opportunity cost," a core concept in economics. If a hoodlum breaks a baker's window, the economy in general is not "stimulated" because the baker must now do business with a glazier. Less visible but just as real is the fact that to replace the broken glass, the baker must cancel his plans to buy other things, such as a suit of clothes. The act of destruction means a gain for the glazier, but that gain is more than offset by the losses of the baker and the tailor.

Bastiat served the last two years of his life in France's Constituent and Legislative Assemblies, where he worked tirelessly to convince fellow members of the merits of freedom and free markets. These colleagues proved to be his toughest audience. Most were more interested in selfish and ephemeral satisfactions (such as power, money, reelection, and the dispensing of favors to friends) than in eternal truths.

He could be devilishly brilliant in denouncing those colleagues who presumed to plan the lives of others, as in this admonition: "Ah, you miserable creatures! You who think that you are so great! You who judge humanity to be so small! You who wish to reform everything! Why don't you reform yourselves? That task would be sufficient enough." Or in this one, my personal favorite: "If the natural tendencies of mankind are so bad that it is not safe to permit people to be free, how is it that the tendencies of these organizers are always good? Do not the legislators and their appointed agents also belong to the human race? Or do they believe that they themselves are made of a finer clay than the rest of mankind?"

Bastiat's most famous work is *The Law*, which appeared the year he died. In only about fifty pages, Bastiat reveals the dangers of statism and presents a brilliant defense of the free society. Were this timeless essay required reading in schools today, it would transform the world, as it has opened minds and changed lives for many decades.

Permanent Principles

Our world is beset with economic fallacies that are, for the most part, modern versions of those that Bastiat demolished in the mid-nineteenth century. The answers to the vexing problems those fallacies produce are rarely to be found in proposals that empower bureaucracy while imposing tortuous regulations on private behavior. The answers are far more likely to lie in the profound and permanent principles that Frédéric Bastiat did so much to illuminate.

Jim Powell offers this tribute to a great champion of liberty:

And so that frail Frenchman whose public career spanned just six years, belittled as a mere popularizer, dismissed as a dreamer and an ideologue, turns out to have been right. Even before Karl Marx began scribbling *The Communist Manifesto* in December 1847, Frédéric Bastiat knew that socialism is doomed. Marx called for a vast expansion of government power to seize privately owned land, banks, railroads, and schools, but Bastiat warned that government power is a mortal enemy, and he was right. He declared that prosperity is everywhere the work of free people, and he was right again. He maintained that the only meaningful way to secure peace is to secure human liberty by limiting government power, and he was right yet again. Bastiat took the lead, he stood alone when he had to, he displayed a generous spirit, he shared epic insights, he gave wings to ideas, and he committed his life for liberty. He earned his place among the immortals.

Lessons from Frédéric Bastiat

Tell stories: In a field full of dull presentations, Frédéric Bastiat told lively stories that made his arguments accessible. His stories—the parable of the broken window, "The Candlemakers' Petition," etc.—allowed him to make a powerful case for freedom and free markets.

Explode statist myths: Proponents of more government power are still very much with us. Bastiat shows us how to destroy their arguments using wit and logic.

10

Prudence Crandall

In Defiance of Racism

On April Fools' Day in 1833, the little hamlet of Canterbury, Connecticut, was in an uproar. A new private school had opened that day, and it was no joke. A few blocks away, with local politicians leading the charge, angry townspeople gathered at the Congregational Church to demand that the state legislature put the school out of business. The air was thick with denunciations of the owner and operator, a twenty-nine-year-old teacher and entrepreneur named Prudence Crandall.

What was so reprehensible about this school? Just two years earlier, Crandall had opened her first one, in the same building, to universal acclaim. She and her sister Almira had bought and paid for the spacious, Georgian-style 1805 mansion with a $500 down payment and a $1,500 mortgage. They called it the Canterbury Female Boarding School. The reviews from the families of its more than two dozen white female students were stellar.

But the new school that Prudence opened on April 1, 1833, carried a name that sent shock waves throughout Connecticut: Miss Crandall's School for Young Ladies and Little Misses of Color.

Prudence Crandall had done the unthinkable. She was determined to run a school exclusively for—hold on to your hat—*young black girls*. Crandall would be vilified and threatened in the most vicious and disgusting terms. She would be arrested. She would endure three court cases against her. She would see her school vandalized.

"I Will Be Heard"

You might ask: Racism in Connecticut? Weren't such ugly sentiments confined to the Deep South? Not at all. In America's early days, racism was common in all parts of the country, as it was in most of the world. Slavery itself was not foreign to New England. Although slavery by then had largely died out in Connecticut, its effects were still visible. Crandall biographer Donald E. Williams Jr. notes that "many of the free blacks Prudence Crandall saw in northeastern Connecticut were former slaves," since farmers in Canterbury had owned slaves through the end of the eighteenth century. The slave trade had still been legal in America when Crandall was born in 1803.

Growing up in a Quaker home, Crandall was steeped in the values of peace, tolerance, and goodwill. They were reinforced when she attended a Quaker boarding school in Providence, Rhode Island, founded by noted abolitionist Moses Brown. Friends and family claimed she was a born teacher, devoted to cultivating young minds through excellence in the classroom. Her dream was to teach in a school of her own.

The year that Crandall opened her first school, 1831, saw two momentous events in the history of slavery. First, the century's biggest slave uprising, the Nat Turner rebellion, claimed the lives of dozens of whites and blacks and sparked a new level of race-based fear and bigotry. Second, the fiery abolitionist William Lloyd Garrison began publishing his famous newspaper, *The Liberator*. Garrison stirred passions on both sides of the slavery question with this declaration in his first issue:

Words of Wisdom from Prudence Crandall

"What shall I do? Shall I be inactive and permit prejudice, the mother of abominations, to remain undisturbed? Or shall I venture to enlist in the ranks of those who with the Sword of Truth dare hold combat with prevailing iniquity?"

I am aware that many object to the severity of my language; but is there not cause for severity? I will be as harsh as truth, and as uncompromising as justice. On this subject, I do not wish to think, or speak, or write, with moderation. No! No! Tell a man whose house is on fire to give a moderate alarm; tell him to moderately rescue his wife from the hands of the ravisher; tell the mother to gradually extricate her babe from the fire into which it has fallen—but urge me not to use moderation in a cause like the present. I am in earnest—I will not equivocate—I will not excuse—I will not retreat a single inch—*and I will be heard*. The apathy of the people is enough to make every statue leap from its pedestal, and to hasten the resurrection of the dead.

America's First Integrated School

Only white girls enrolled at Crandall's Canterbury Female Boarding School in its first year. But in the second, a very bright black girl named Sarah Harris approached Crandall and expressed interest in attending. Harris, the daughter of free black parents in Canterbury, was a young lady of solid reputation in the community. She wanted to be a teacher herself someday and was, in Crandall's words, "correct in her deportment...pleasing in her personal appearance and manners."

Concerned that a white backlash might ensue and endanger the school's financial survival, Crandall hesitated at first before deciding that rejecting Sarah (whose parents offered to pay full tuition) would be an unconscionable insult to her own values. "I told her if I was injured on her account I would bear it," Crandall later said. Sarah Harris became the first black student in the first integrated school of any kind—public or private—in the United States. Crandall explained the decision this way:

> I said in my heart, here are my convictions. What shall I do? Shall I be inactive and permit prejudice, the mother of abominations, to remain undisturbed? Or shall I venture to enlist in the ranks of those who with the Sword of Truth dare hold combat with prevailing iniquity? I contemplated for a while the manner in which I might best serve the people of color. As wealth was not mine, I saw no other means of benefiting them than by imparting to those of my own sex that were anxious to learn all the instruction I might be able to give, however small the amount.

Local reaction to the news of Sarah's enrollment in the fall of 1832 was swift and fierce. Overnight, Prudence Crandall was transformed from hero to villain. Ugly rumors spread that her real goal was to stoke conflict and even foster—*heaven forbid*—interracial marriage. Local business and political leaders visited Crandall to insist that Sarah be expelled. Parents of the white students began withdrawing their daughters or threatening to do so if Sarah didn't disappear.

Less determined or more timid people in Crandall's shoes might have folded. After all, she had put all her hopes as well as her savings into the school. Why risk failure and opprobrium over a single student when, with a simple dismissal, all would be well again?

The fools of Canterbury underestimated Prudence Crandall. Not only did she refuse to cave in; she came up with a revolutionary idea. "Under the circumstances," she declared, "I made up my mind that, if it were possible, I would teach colored girls exclusively."

Over at *The Liberator* in Boston, Garrison offered his full support and promised to help recruit free black students from every New England state if that's what it would take to make the Crandall school a success. For the sum of twenty-five dollars per quarter, half paid in advance, black female students would have a school of their own where they could get a first-class education.

Prudence Crandall would soon be a household name from Maine to Georgia.

Backlash

Six weeks after that fateful April 1, the Connecticut General Assembly passed the infamous "Black Law," which made it illegal for out-of-state black students to attend any Connecticut school without the permission of local town authorities. At least twenty were already enrolled at the Crandall school, most of them from other New England states.

All but a handful of her friends deserted Crandall. Local vendors wouldn't do business with her. The threats mounted, but her resolve to press on only strengthened. No mere law would shut her school, she defiantly declared.

The students themselves were subjected to abuse by hostile townspeople. Stagecoach drivers refused to provide them with transportation. None of the doctors in town would provide necessary medical attention. After somebody poisoned the school's well, others prevented Crandall from obtaining water elsewhere. She hauled it in herself from her father's farm. When the girls went outside, they were often met with angry epithets from egg- and stone-throwing hooligans of all ages. One seventeen-year-old student, Anna Eliza Hammond, was even arrested, but with the help of donations from abolitionists, she was released upon posting $10,000 bond.

On August 23, 1833, Crandall was arrested for violating the Black Law. After a night in jail, she appeared in court, where she benefited greatly from good lawyers financed by the Boston businessman, philanthropist, and abolitionist Arthur Tappan.

Crandall's legal defense rested on the argument that free blacks from other states were U.S. citizens and, as such, were entitled to the same rights as all citizens. If they chose to attend a private school, with their own money, there was nothing the state of Connecticut could constitutionally do to deny them that right.

The first of three trials ended with a hung jury. The second found Crandall guilty when the judge upheld the Black Law, arguing that blacks were not citizens and, by virtue of their skin color, were not guaranteed any constitutional rights. On appeal, Connecticut's highest court overturned the decision on a minor procedural issue.

Although the decision in the third case would have allowed the school to operate, the behavior of many Canterbury residents was too much for Crandall and her students to take. A mob broke into the school and damaged windows and furniture. Constant threats to assault the students and to burn the school to the ground (it was set on fire at least once) forced a painful decision. The one thing that Crandall could not countenance was the thought of harm to her students. On September 10, 1834, she closed the school and left the state with her new husband, Baptist preacher Calvin Philleo.

Belated Recognition

In the years that followed, Prudence Crandall lived in Massachusetts, Rhode Island, New York, and Illinois before finally settling in Kansas, where she died in 1890 at the age of eighty-six.

In 1885, interviewed in her tiny eight-by-twelve-foot cabin, Crandall told a Topeka newspaper reporter:

> The aspirations of my soul to benefit the colored race were never greater than at the present time. I hope to live long enough to see a college built on this farm, into which can be admitted all the classes of the human family, without regard to sex or color.... I want professorships of the highest order.... You see that my wants are so many, and so great, that I have no time to waste, no time to spend in grief.

Though Connecticut repealed the Black Law in 1838, Crandall never resided there again. But four years before her death, at the urging of Mark Twain and others, the Connecticut legislature voted to send her a pension of $400 per year, or about $11,000 in 2016 dollars. The mansion she bought and turned into a school almost two hundred years ago is still there in Canterbury, now the home of the Prudence Crandall Museum. In 1995 Connecticut legislators officially designated her the state heroine. It was belated recognition of her courageous stand against prejudice.

Government Meddling

The Prudence Crandall case was neither the first nor the last time that government attempted to thwart education, and race is only one of many excuses authorities have used to hamper or shut down schools they didn't like.

How would children learn without government? That's a perennial question asked by many who assume, mistakenly, that government is indispensable to the business of education. Prudence Crandall would undoubtedly respond with another query: "How will children get an education *with* government?"

Lessons from Prudence Crandall

Fight prejudice: Prudence Crandall called prejudice "the mother of abominations." Her conscience would not allow her to ignore the educational desires of young black women. To satisfy those desires, she fought both her town and her state.

Remember government's proper place: Education is often thought of as something best provided by government. The Prudence Crandall story, however, is about the vision and courage of a woman who had to fight government to educate young black girls.

11

Harriet Tubman

She Never Lost a Passenger

I n April 2016 the U.S. treasury secretary announced that a woman's image will adorn Federal Reserve currency for the first time. The image will be that of Harriet Tubman. It may, however, be a dubious honor to appear on something that declines so regularly in value. Without a doubt, this woman will impart more esteem to the bill than the bill will to her. Her value is far more solid and enduring.

Slavery was once ubiquitous, and even intellectually respectable. That began to change in the late eighteenth century; by 1807, Britain has ended its slave trade, and in 1834 it liberated the enslaved throughout its jurisdiction. (See chapter 8.) Before the Thirteenth Amendment abolished slavery in America in 1865, American blacks risked everything attempting to escape from their masters, who sometimes pursued them all the way to the Canadian border. Tubman, herself a fugitive slave, became the most renowned "conductor" on the Underground Railroad, a network of trails for escapees from the antebellum South to the North. As many as 100,000 slaves risked life and limb traveling its routes. It was the most dangerous "railroad" in the world.

Strength and Courage

Born Araminta Ross in 1822 on Maryland's Eastern Shore, Tubman survived the brutalities of bondage for twenty-seven years. Three of her sisters had been sold to distant plantation owners. For her entire life she carried scars from frequent whippings. Once, when she refused to restrain a runaway slave, she was bashed in the head with a two-pound weight, causing lifelong pain, migraines, "buzzing" in her ears, and seizures. She bolted for freedom in 1849, making her way to the free state of Pennsylvania and its city of brotherly love, Philadelphia.

"I had crossed the line of which I had so long been dreaming," she later wrote.

> I was free; but there was no one to welcome me to the land of freedom. I was a stranger in a strange land, and my home after all was down in the old cabin quarter, with the old folks and my brothers and sisters. But to this solemn resolution I came: I was free, and they should be free also; I would make a home for them in the North, and the Lord helping me, I would bring them all there. Oh, how I prayed then, lying all alone on the cold damp ground! "Oh, dear Lord," I said. "I haven't got no friend but you. Come to my help, Lord, for I'm in trouble! Oh, Lord! You've been with me in six troubles, don't desert me in the seventh!"

Tubman bravely ventured thirteen times back into slave states to escort at least seventy escapees to northern states and to Canada.

Though schoolchildren across America now learn of Tubman's deeds, biographer Kate Clifford Larson makes a convincing case that the lengths Tubman and her colleagues went to secure freedom for others are underappreciated. In *Bound for the People*, Larson calls Tubman's efforts to free slaves "monumental and dangerous"; the escape missions she organized "reveal intricate planning involving complex networks of black and white supporters." The fact that she so frequently returned to the Eastern Shore on these missions "set Tubman apart from even those brave souls who swelled the routes of the Underground Railroad," Larson writes. "For self-liberators such as Tubman, it was unusual to return to the land of their enslavers, risking capture, reenslavement, or even lynching to help others seek freedom."

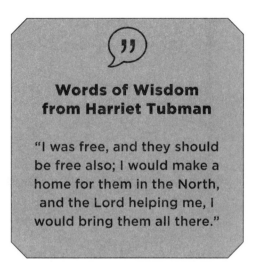

Words of Wisdom from Harriet Tubman

"I was free, and they should be free also; I would make a home for them in the North, and the Lord helping me, I would bring them all there."

Think about what was involved in any one of these missions. Tubman and her associates had to cover perhaps a hundred miles, often by foot, under cover of darkness. Slave catchers and their packs of vicious dogs were a constant threat, but as Larson notes, any number of natural dangers could derail a journey: "Spiny sweet gum burrs, thorny thickets, the sharp needles of marsh grass, and icy paths in the winter all took their toll on the feet and limbs of struggling runaways. The Eastern Shore's numerous rivers, streams, and wetlands presented a serious hindrance, particularly to runaways who could not swim. Wet clothing could draw unwanted attention, and cold weather could seriously debilitate drenched and hungry escapees."

Extraordinary courage was just one of the traits Tubman displayed in leading so many people to freedom. She became a master of disguise, presenting herself as an elderly woman or even a man.

She displayed quick thinking to keep from arousing the suspicions of white travelers she encountered, averting disaster a number of times. Walking at night in the woods, often alone, she displayed an unerring sense of direction; she said she could find her way by the stars and natural signs "as well as any hunter." She saw through her missions despite the seizures she continued to experience.

"I was the conductor of the Underground Railroad for eight years," Tubman famously recounted, "and I can say what most conductors can't say: I never ran my train off the track and I never lost a passenger." Those passengers included her aging parents, her three brothers, their wives, and many of their children.

Working for the Union Army as a cook and nurse during the Civil War, Tubman morphed quickly into an armed scout and spy. She became the war's first woman to lead an armed expedition when she guided the Combahee River Raid, an expedition that liberated more than seven hundred slaves in South Carolina.

For her service to the government—tending to newly freed slaves, scouting into enemy territory, and nursing wounded soldiers—she was treated shamefully and shabbily. She was denied compensation and didn't receive a pension for her war duties until 1899. She took in boarders and worked long hours at odd jobs to make ends meet.

Tubman spent her last decades caring for others, especially the sick and aged. She spoke publicly on behalf of women's right to vote. For relief from her head injury, she endured brain surgery in Boston in the late 1890s. She refused anesthesia, preferring simply to bite down on a bullet. In her words, the surgeon "sawed open my skull, and raised it up, and now it feels more comfortable." She died in 1913 at the age of ninety-one—a real hero to the very end.

Recognition

Recognition of Tubman's heroism came late, but some of her contemporaries appreciated her extraordinary contributions and courage.

The famous abolitionist and former slave Frederick Douglass paid Tubman this tribute in an August 1868 letter:

> Most that I have done and suffered in the service of our cause has been in public, and I have received much encouragement at every step of the way. You, on the other hand, have labored in a private way. I have wrought in the day—you in the night. I have had the applause of the crowd and the satisfaction that comes of being approved by the multitude, while the most that you have done has been witnessed by a few trembling, scarred, and foot-sore bondmen and women, whom you have led out of the house of bondage, and whose heartfelt "God bless you" has been your only reward. The midnight sky and the silent stars have been the witnesses of your devotion to freedom and of your heroism.

In 2014 an asteroid was named for Tubman. In my book, that beats a Federal Reserve note hands down.

Lessons from Harriet Tubman

Don't stop at securing your own freedom: Harriet Tubman escaped from slavery but was not content simply to have her own freedom. She risked her life multiple times to return to slave states and liberate dozens of fellow human beings.

To have real courage, be strong: Tubman's story reminds us that moral courage and physical courage often go hand in hand. Though plagued by seizures, she risked her newfound freedom—even her life—for the freedom of others.

12

Black Entrepreneurs

Models Too Often Forgotten

S ince Black History Month was inaugurated in 1976, Americans have made special note each February of the achievements of black citizens. African Americans have played important and often inspirational roles in shaping the country's history, from the days of slavery through Jim Crow to substantial, if not yet complete, political and social equality today.

It's understandable that in highlighting this important minority group, we heavily emphasize those men and women who escaped bondage or those in more recent decades who led the civil rights movement.

Frederick Douglass, the eloquent abolitionist and former slave, extolled the importance of constructive agitation when he declared in an 1857 speech:

> The whole history of the progress of human liberty shows that all concessions yet made to her august claims have been born of earnest struggle. The conflict has been exciting, agitating, all-absorbing, and for the time being, putting all other tumults to silence. It must do this or it does nothing. If there is no struggle, there is no progress. Those who profess to favor freedom, and yet depreciate agitation, are men who want crops without plowing up the ground. They want rain without thunder and lightning. They want the ocean without the awful roar of its many waters. This struggle may be a moral one; or it may be a physical one; or it may be both moral and physical; but it must be a struggle. Power concedes nothing without a demand. It never did and it never will. Find out just what any people will quietly submit to, and you have found out the exact amount of injustice and wrong which will be imposed upon them; and these will continue till they are resisted with either words or blows, or with both. The limits of tyrants are prescribed by the endurance of those whom they oppress.

Black history in America, however, isn't just about overcoming slavery and discrimination. It's also about the less-familiar names of black citizens who excelled at entrepreneurship, invention, the creation of wealth. They are numerous and deserve greater recognition for their heroism.

McCoy, Reynolds, and Pelham: Inventors and Engineers

Twenty years ago my good friend and favorite historian, Dr. Burton Folsom, told me about three such people—Elijah McCoy, Humphrey H. Reynolds, and Fred Pelham.

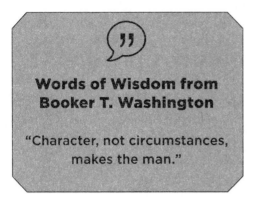

Words of Wisdom from Booker T. Washington

"Character, not circumstances, makes the man."

McCoy (pictured at the beginning of this chapter) was born in 1843 in Colchester in the province of Ontario, Canada, where his parents had settled as fugitives from slavery. The family returned to the United States five years later and settled in Ypsilanti, Michigan. Though they were poor, their hard work and thrifty habits eventually paid off. Elijah was sent to Scotland at age fifteen to study mechanical engineering, and he returned afterward to work for the Michigan Central Railroad.

Locomotives at the time overheated easily, and trains were forced to stop often to apply oil to engine parts to reduce friction. McCoy invented a "lubricating cup" that applied the oil without the need to halt the journey. He secured a patent for it in 1872 and continued to improve the device for years thereafter.

"Others tried to imitate McCoy's invention, but he kept ahead of them with his superior engineering skills," writes Folsom. "His standard of quality was so high that to separate his lubricating cup from cheaper imitations it became known as 'the real McCoy,' which many believe to be the origin of the famous phrase. The grateful management of the Michigan Central promoted McCoy and honored him as a teacher and innovator for the railroad."

That 1872 patent was the first of fifty-seven McCoy picked up during a long and productive life. When he was seventy-seven, he earned one for an improved airbrake lubricator; at age eighty, he patented a vehicle wheel tire. He founded the Elijah McCoy Manufacturing Company in Detroit in 1920 to produce and market his inventions and died in 1929 at eighty-six, a well-loved and celebrated achiever.

While McCoy improved the operation of locomotives at the front of the train, Humphrey H. Reynolds made the rail cars more comfortable in the back. Whether the locomotive burned coal or wood, the windows remained shut in the cars behind so the smoke wouldn't choke the passengers. On hot days, those cars could be unbearable.

Reynolds was a porter for the Pullman Company and knew just how bad the conditions could be. So he did something about the problem. In 1883 he invented a ventilator that permitted air to flow into passenger cars while keeping out the dust and soot. When the Pullman Company tried to grab the patent rights for the idea, Reynolds quit his job and successfully sued for $10,000. He thereby won the right to profit from his own invention, which greatly enhanced the number of Americans willing to ride the rails no matter the weather.

Fred Pelham not only built bridges to people metaphorically; he constructed real ones, too, all over Michigan. Some of them (like his unique "skew-arch bridge" in Dexter) are still standing more than a century after his untimely death in 1895 at age thirty-seven.

Pelham's parents were free blacks in Virginia who left that state in the 1850s on a quest for opportunity in Michigan. Fred excelled in mathematics and civil engineering at the University of Michigan, where he was president of his class in 1887 and the first black man to graduate with an engineering degree. He designed and built at least eighteen bridges, known for their beauty and structural integrity.

Booker T. Washington: The Importance of Character

Booker T. Washington (1856–1915) is still reasonably well known, but he fell out of favor with black leadership in the 1960s. That's when Lyndon Johnson's "Great Society" programs shifted the focus away from black entrepreneurship and ushered in government handouts. The message of Washington, who was born a slave, had always been what he called "self-help" through education, employment, and starting a business. He also stressed personal integrity. "Character," he said, "not circumstances, makes the man."

Washington founded the Tuskegee Institute (now Tuskegee University) in Alabama to educate blacks to develop their talents for

America's industrial society. Business enterprise would be the ticket to progress, he felt. "More and more thoughtful students of the race problem," he said, "are beginning to see that business and industry constitute what we may call the strategic points in its solution."

George Washington Carver: Pioneer

Growing up in the 1950s and '60s, I learned to admire George Washington Carver (1864–1943) as another great black achiever. A pioneering botanist and inventor, he devised techniques for replenishing depleted soils and popularized the peanut. He researched, experimented, and taught at the Tuskegee Institute for forty-seven years. *Time* magazine once dubbed him "the black Leonardo" because of his multiple talents. "When you do the common things in life in an uncommon way," he once advised, "you will command the attention of the world."

Carver was a man of generous spirit, a committed Christian who urged peace, reconciliation, and forgiveness. "Fear of something is at the root of hate for others, and hate within will eventually destroy the hater," he cautioned. "Keep your thoughts free from hate, and you need have no fear from those who hate you." He's buried next to Booker T. Washington on the Tuskegee University campus.

Brown, Bannister, and Walker: Female Entrepreneurs

Black entrepreneurship is not the province of one sex. Many women have made significant contributions in this area.

One of the earliest American examples was Clara Brown, born into slavery in 1800. Set free by her owner in the 1850s, she traveled throughout the West, opening one successful laundry business after another. She settled finally in Colorado and became the first black female businesswoman to cash in on the Gold Rush.

Have you seen the acclaimed 1989 film *Glory*, starring Matthew

Broderick and Denzel Washington? It tells the inspiring story of the Fifty-Fourth Massachusetts Infantry, the first black regiment to fight for the North in the Civil War. Though the movie never mentions her by name, a black woman named Christiana Carteaux Bannister was a major financier of the regiment. An activist for the Underground Railroad, Bannister made her money as the "hair doctress" of Providence, Boston, and Worcester. She started and managed thriving beauty salons in all three New England cities.

Madam C. J. Walker deserves recognition as the first black woman to become a millionaire entirely from her own efforts, not from an inheritance or from a wealthy husband. She built a thriving business selling a line of hair care products and cosmetic creams. She employed some ten thousand women at a time and served millions with her products and services. (For more on Walker, see the next chapter.)

Berry Gordy: Record Mogul

Record producer and songwriter Berry Gordy of Detroit provides us with a still-living example of a black entrepreneur whose work virtually everybody knows and loves, even if they don't recognize his name. He founded Motown Records in 1959. The artists he signed and promoted are legendary: Diana Ross and the Supremes, Marvin Gaye, the Temptations, the Four Tops, Gladys Knight and the Pips, the Commodores, the Jackson 5, and many more.

Gordy started his company in his small Detroit house, which is now a museum. Some years later, the city of Detroit passed an ordinance banning home-based businesses. What could have been a model for many poor but aspiring entrepreneurs in the Motor City—starting a business in your house when you don't yet have the capital to buy or rent a building—became almost impossible. That sad fact is undoubtedly one of many reasons for Detroit's long economic decline.

Remember the Wealth Creators

While the major media today seem to focus inordinately on blacks who are active in politics, academia, and "community organizing" of various forms, black entrepreneurship is alive and well, creating wealth for millions in America and beyond. Do an Internet search for "black entrepreneurs" and you'll find an abundance of names in virtually every industry. That speaks to a degree of economic progress that would have seemed unimaginable a century and a half ago.

So when Black History Month rolls around each February, let's remember—and celebrate—not only the speechmakers but the wealth creators, too.

Lessons from Black Entrepreneurs

Remember that heroes can be found in many fields: Heroes among America's black community certainly include many recent, notable activists in the civil rights movement. But we are in danger of forgetting the entrepreneurs who helped build the country while facing social, economic, and political barriers.

Remember that *entrepreneurs* can be found in many fields: The roster of entrepreneurs considered here includes inventors, engineers, musicians, and educators. Booker T. Washington strongly emphasized that the most productive route for blacks to follow is one that puts their entrepreneurial talents to work and allows them to become as independent as possible.

13

Martha Coston, Hetty Green, and Madam C. J. Walker

Female Pioneers in American Business

Culture isn't always pretty, and like almost everything else in human life, it evolves. At one time or another in every corner of the planet, almost every imaginable grouping of people has faced unequal treatment, legal and institutional discrimination, or outright persecution. As we learn to reject unwarranted prejudice, we recognize that every individual is unique. He (or she) deserves to be judged by the content of his character and to pursue his dreams in the marketplace of free exchange.

America in its first century offered more liberty to more people than any other place in the world, but there was still plenty of room for improvement. It took decades, but we eventually ended the ancient evil of race-based slavery. Decades later, Jim Crow laws were abolished. Pick any immigrant group—Catholics, Irish, Chinese—and to a considerable extent, we've come to see that once-widespread prejudice against that group prevented everyone else from enjoying the benefits of its members' productivity. We've made progress, lots of it, toward the ideal of unshackling peaceful people from the chains of injustice and intolerance.

The philosophy of liberty appeals to me because it says to all people, regardless of race, religion, place of birth, or sex, "If you want to dream, create, build, own, grow, or improve, *go for it!*"

Leonard Read, who started the Foundation for Economic Education (where I now serve as president), expressed the credo of a free society when he called for "no man-concocted restraints against the release of peaceful, creative energy."

Martha Coston, Hetty Green, and Madam C. J. Walker (Walker is pictured at the beginning of this chapter) were pioneering women in American business. Each was born into a culture that assigned the "fairer sex" to home and family life. They couldn't vote because they were female. They weren't supposed to engage in business because, well, that was regarded (as it had been everywhere for centuries) as a "manly" pursuit. Yet each possessed a spirit to break barriers. These women achieved success and respect in private enterprise. They opened doors for millions of other women to enter the marketplace and compete with men in the creation of wealth.

Martha Coston: Inventor, Business Leader, Patriot

"Extreme" describes the highs and lows in the life of the remarkable Martha Coston. Widowed with five children at the age of thirty-two, Coston was just beginning to recover from the unexpected loss of her husband when two of her children and her mother died. She was depressed and penniless, with three surviving children facing a bleak future. Yet she managed to turn adversity into success.

Coston was born Martha Jane Hunt in Baltimore in 1826 and moved to Philadelphia with her mother a decade later when her father died. When she was sixteen, she eloped with twenty-one-year-old Benjamin Coston, a nautical engineer and promising inventor. His work in pyrotechnics and on early gas lighting earned him notable attention, but his life was cut short by a combination of pneumonia and chemical poisoning. Poring over his papers, Martha discovered drawings for a pyrotechnic signal (or "flare") that would allow ships to communicate with the shore or with one another at night or in fog. Benjamin had labored over the idea while at the Washington Navy Yard but never progressed beyond plans on paper.

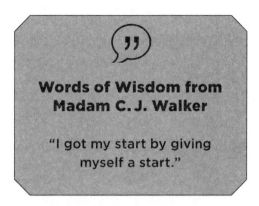

Words of Wisdom from Madam C. J. Walker

"I got my start by giving myself a start."

For ten long years, Coston worked to perfect her late husband's work. She developed the proper "recipe" for flares that burned red, white, and blue, and she created a system (a sort of Morse code) to permit messaging by flare. In her own words:

> The men I employed and dismissed, the experiments I made myself, the frauds that were practiced upon me, almost disheartened me; but despair I would not, and eagerly I treasured up each little step that was made in the right direction, the hints of naval officers, and the opinions of the different boards that gave the signals a trial.

On April 5, 1859, she presented her results to the world: a pyrotechnic signaling flare and code system. It worked beautifully. Reliable ship-to-ship and ship-to-shore communications were now possible.

Inventing something useful, however, doesn't translate into money unless the invention can be marketed, and Coston had no prior experience in business. That didn't stop her from starting her own company, one that lasted for more than 125 years.

To the amazement of many, the widow blossomed into a successful entrepreneur. At first she felt the need to downplay her gender, even using a man's name in initial communications to improve the chance that men would do business with her. In her autobiography she wrote, "We hear much of the chivalry of men towards women; but let me tell you dear reader, it vanishes like dew before the summer sun when one of us comes into competition with the manly sex."

With the coming of the Civil War, Coston found a large and ready market by selling her signaling flares to the U.S. Navy. She traveled around Europe, securing customers in both the government and private sectors. In the late 1860s she struck a lucrative deal with the United States Life-Saving Service, which made her product standard equipment at its lifeboat stations.

Her biggest disappointment in business involved a customer that took advantage of her goodwill and patriotism. To help the Lincoln administration's war effort, Coston sold her flares and signaling system at below cost and sometimes accepted nothing more than a government IOU as payment. Washington ripped her off through its Civil War greenback inflation, eventually compensating her, in real terms, at about a quarter on the dollar. Had it not been for her skill at marketing elsewhere, she would have been bankrupt by war's end.

When Coston died in 1902, she was honored as a great inventor and business leader. She overcame huge challenges to prove that a woman could be just as good in business as any man—and far better than those who defrauded her with their depreciating paper money.

Hetty Green: "One-Woman Federal Reserve"

Martha Coston was rich by any measure, but by the late nineteenth century the title of "richest woman in the world" belonged to Henrietta Howland Robinson Green, better known as Hetty Green.

Born to a Quaker whaling family in 1834 in New Bedford, Massachusetts, Hetty Robinson was regularly reading the financial papers to her father and grandfather by the age of six. "In this way I came to know what stocks and bonds were, how the markets fluctuated, and the meaning of bulls and bears," she later recalled.

When her parents died in the 1860s, Hetty inherited a fortune of about $6 million (about $120 million in 2016 dollars). What she did with it made her a legend as one of the savviest investors and independent financiers ever. Combining a conservative approach with a canny sense of timing, she bought and sold bonds, railroad stocks, and real estate, and over thirty years parlayed her inheritance into what would be well over a billion dollars today. She was her own adviser, her own bank, and what one biographer would later call "a one-woman Federal Reserve." In an arena dominated by men like J. P. Morgan, she dazzled the financial world with her golden touch.

Green loaned so much money to so many people, companies, institutions, and municipalities that headlines would regularly announce "Hetty Cuts Rates" or "Hetty Raises Rates." The City of New York asked her for loans to keep the city from going broke. During the Panic of 1907, she wrote a check to the Big Apple for $1.1 million and took her payment in short-term revenue bonds.

Green kept debtors honest. "She would travel thousands of miles alone—in an era when few women would dare travel unescorted—to collect a debt of a few hundred dollars," writes one observer. Her collection efforts included churches, to whom she often loaned money at below-market rates as a charitable contribution. But when the First Presbyterian Church of Chicago defaulted on a $12,000 loan and the pastor tried to shame her into forgiving the debt by publicly denouncing her as a ruthless capitalist, she told him to pay up or she would foreclose—and that's exactly what she did. Other pastors came to her defense—one of them declaring, "To expect the holder of a church mortgage to cancel it upon the grounds of Christianity, after the money has been lent in good faith, is nothing less than a hold-up."

As Green's riches grew, so did the attacks of the envious. Because she always wore black, she was derided as the "Witch of Wall Street." Rumors of her miserliness circulated widely but were largely debunked in later years by her own family and by the many people and organizations that benefited from her quiet charity. Green explained in a 1913 magazine profile: "One way is to give money and make a big show. That is not my way of doing. I am of the Quaker belief, and although the Quakers are about all dead, I still follow their example. An ordinary gift to be bragged about is not a gift in the eyes of the Lord."

Next to her extraordinary skill at creating wealth, Green's personal lifestyle fascinated people then and biographers to this day. She was the opposite of ostentatious. Her frugality was astonishing in a day when her great wealth could have bought her anything. Home was never more than a modest flat in New York City. When she traveled, she stayed in cheap boardinghouses. She lived the way she wanted to and never bent to any custom of modernity she didn't like. She was, in every sense of the phrase, her own woman.

When Hetty Green died in 1916 at the age of eighty-one, the *New York Times* editorialized:

> If a man had lived as did Mrs. Hetty Green, devoting the greater part of his time and mind to the increasing of an inherited fortune that even at the start was far larger than is needed for the satisfaction of all such human needs as money can satisfy, nobody would have seen him as very peculiar—as notably out of the common. He would have done what is expected of the average man so circumscribed, and there would have been no difficulty in understanding the joys he obtained from participation in the grim conflicts of higher finance. It was the fact that Mrs. Green was a woman that made her career the subject of endless curiosity, comment and astonishment.... She had enough courage to live as she chose and to be as thrifty as she pleased and she observed such of the world's conventions as seemed to her right and useful, coldly and calmly ignoring all the others.

Madam C. J. Walker: Self-Starter

When, in December 1867, Sarah Breedlove was born the sixth child of parents who had been slaves a few years earlier, Martha Coston and Hetty Green were already wealthy Americans ensconced in business. But this enterprising black woman came on fast and strong as a wealth creator before she died at the age of fifty-one in 1919. Biographer John Blundell, in his book *Ladies for Liberty: Women Who Made a Difference in American History*, says: "It is reliably claimed she was the first woman ever to make a million without an inheritance, husband or government intervention. She did it on her own."

Orphaned at seven, married at fourteen, then widowed at twenty with a young daughter to raise, she was determined that her daughter, A'Lelia, would receive a good private education. She took work as a washerwoman, earning about a dollar a day and saving for many years to make her dream a reality.

By the time of her second marriage, to Charles James Walker, her hair had thinned dramatically owing to poor diet, infrequent washing, and the use of damaging hair products. She realized that the market for quality hair products for black women was nonexistent and decided to do something about it.

Learning everything she could about hair and its proper care, she experimented with various concoctions of her own making. In 1905 she formed the Madam C. J. Walker Manufacturing Company, selling a line of hair care products and cosmetic creams.

"I got my start by giving myself a start," Walker later said.

She assigned daughter A'Lelia to run the mail order operation out of Denver while she and her husband traveled the country recruiting saleswomen. Eventually, Walker settled in Indianapolis in 1910, where she built her headquarters, a factory, a laboratory, a hair salon, and a beauty school to train the company's sales agents. By this time her business was selling products in virtually every state as well as throughout the Caribbean. Her vision was to cure scalp and hair problems and empower black women with both beauty and economic opportunity.

Walker's most famous formula included a shampoo and a pomade that "transformed lusterless and brittle hair into soft, luxuriant hair." The women she employed wore uniforms of white shirts and black skirts and carried black satchels of product samples as they made house calls all over the United States and the Caribbean. Her name and image were well known to women both black and white.

For Walker, money was "not an end in itself," John Blundell writes. "It allowed her to become an active philanthropist for black causes," including Booker T. Washington's Tuskegee Institute and the NAACP. In an article about Walker, Blundell expands on her philosophy, pointing out that she believed in "self-respect through self-support, a hand-up not a hand-out." She emphasized her belief in "entrepreneurial, bottom-up, self-help economics" whenever she gave hair care sales training lessons, at the end of which "she showed future agents photo slides of great African-American entrepreneurs to educate and enthuse them."

Toward the end of her life, Walker left the corporate headquarters in Indianapolis to move to New York City. The salon she built in Harlem was "larger than that of Helena Rubinstein or of Elizabeth Arden." Earning a six-figure income—the equivalent of millions today—she was hailed in one newspaper as the "World's Richest Negress." Her company employed ten thousand agents.

Walker died of hypertension in 1919. She left behind a legacy of economic success, generous philanthropy, and political activism on behalf of equality before the law. Millions of black women were inspired by her example, and tens of thousands were directly empowered by working for the company she founded.

Though widespread discrimination against both blacks and women taint stories of early-twentieth-century American life, Madam C. J. Walker's life stands out as a remarkable testament to the spirit of that great civil rights anthem of later years, "We Shall Overcome." She surely did, by any measure.

Lessons from Martha Coston, Hetty Green, and Madam C. J. Walker

Break barriers: In the late nineteenth and early twentieth centuries, women were generally expected not to participate in business or public life. It took pioneers like Martha Coston, Hetty Green, and Madam C. J. Walker to break down barriers.

Make your opportunities: Coston overcame personal and family hardship to become a noted inventor and marketer. Green took a small fortune and, with largely self-taught knowledge of finance, turned it into a big one. And Walker became America's first black female millionaire, earning her fortune from her own talent and hard work.

14

William Ewart Gladstone

A Decades-Long Defense of Liberty

Westminster Abbey, nearly eight hundred years old, is my favorite stop in London. I have visited it so many times now that I've lost count. Each time I walk through the main entrance, my eyes are drawn immediately to the left because of the imposing statue of a man I deeply admire: William Ewart Gladstone, a devoted friend of liberty and the greatest of all British prime ministers.

Biographer Philip Magnus wrote that Gladstone, at the time of his death in 1898, was "the most venerated and influential statesman in the world." A quarter million citizens attended his funeral, one of the largest Britain ever witnessed. No one has ever had a longer or more distinguished career in the British government: Gladstone served sixty-two years in the House of Commons. He was in charge of the nation's finances as chancellor of the exchequer for fourteen budgets in four administrations. He led a major political party (the Liberals) for almost forty years. He was prime minister for four terms (more than anyone else in British history), for a total of twelve years. When he retired in 1894, he was eighty-four years old, the oldest prime minister the country has ever known. He was hailed as the "Grand Old Man" for his leadership and stature, and as England's "Great Commoner" because he refused to accept any titles of nobility.

But a long career in government is not in itself a mark of true greatness. What made Gladstone great was what he *accomplished*. Magnus said that Gladstone "achieved unparalleled success in his policy of setting the individual free from a multitude of obsolete restrictions."

Today, when a citizen gets elected to make government smaller but ends up moderating his positions while in power, conventional wisdom credits him with having "grown in office." Gladstone's philosophy evolved in precisely the opposite direction—from a hodgepodge of statist notions to principled application of liberty.

The principles that Gladstone defended and advanced are perhaps best expressed in this excerpt from a speech he delivered in 1879:

> There should be a sympathy with freedom, a desire to give it scope, founded not upon visionary ideas, but upon the long experience of many generations within the shores of this happy isle—that in freedom you lay the firmest foundations both of loyalty and order; the firmest foundations for the development of individual character; and the best provision for the happiness of the nation at large.

Liberating the Individual

The son of Scottish parents, Gladstone could speak Greek, Latin, Italian, and French as well as English. In 1832, at age twenty-two, he

Words of Wisdom from William Ewart Gladstone

"If the Government takes into its hands that which the man ought to do for himself it will inflict upon him greater mischiefs than all the benefits he will have received or all the advantages that would accrue from them."

entered Parliament as a protectionist, a defender of the state-subsidized Church of England, an opponent of reform, and a protector of the status quo. The eminent British historian Thomas Babington Macauley described him as "the rising hope of the stern and unbending Tories."

By 1850 he had become an ardent free trader, and by 1890 he could look back proudly and take a substantial share of the credit for reducing Britain's tariffs from 1,200 to just 12. As president of the Board of Trade in the ministry of Sir Robert Peel in the 1840s, a young Gladstone saw the disastrous Irish potato famine as a powerful argument against laws forbidding the importation of grain for a starving populace. Gladstone befriended the Anti–Corn Law League's John Bright, became convinced of the logic of free trade, and secured the repeal of the protectionist Corn Laws over the objections of many in his own Conservative or "Tory" Party. The measure split the Conservatives, which paved the way for Gladstone and others a decade later to found the Liberal Party.

"Economy is the first and great article in my financial creed," he wrote in 1859. During his four ministries, he slashed government spending, taxes, and regulations. He was attacked by statists for being miserly with the public's money, but he said that any official not willing to save something even on "candle-ends and cheese-parings" was "not worth his salt." He opposed the introduction of the income tax when it was first proposed in the 1840s and later tried to eliminate it when he was prime minister. In that noble effort he was unsuccessful, but he prevented the tax from becoming "progressive" and beat the rate down from a high of 10 percent to well under 2 percent.

When London hosted the Great Exhibition of 1851, the Royal Commission solicited proposals for a building to house the six-month public exhibition. The project was in danger of foundering amid designs deemed too costly when entrepreneur Joseph Paxton came forth with plans for a monster edifice made entirely of glass panes (nearly a quarter million of them) and the supporting iron framework. Paxton's now-famous Crystal Palace was affordable only because Britain in 1845 had repealed its long-standing and onerous "window tax," reducing the price of glass by 80 percent. Who had engineered the abolition of the window tax? None other than the tax-cutting William Ewart Gladstone.

Gladstone also pushed through reforms that allowed Jews and Catholics to serve in Parliament and that extended the vote to millions of taxpaying workers who had previously been denied it. A devoutly religious man, he extolled the virtues of self-help and private charity. As prime minister, he often walked the streets of London (with no security detail) to find prostitutes to bring back to 10 Downing Street so he and his wife, Catherine, could talk them out of their unseemly occupation.

Gladstone's international reputation soared in 1851 when, after a visit to Naples, he revealed to the world the appalling conditions in Neapolitan prisons. Reformers there were being locked up for speaking out on behalf of freedom. Gladstone's vigorous denunciation reverberated around the globe and later prompted the Italian patriot Giuseppe Garibaldi to credit the British parliamentarian with having "sounded the first trumpet call of Italian liberty."

Gladstone is remembered well in Ireland to this day because of his early efforts to grant more liberty to the Irish and to reform the vestiges of feudalism. He ended state subsidies for the Church of England in Ireland. He fought hard but failed to secure home rule for the Irish; had Parliament been as wise as he on that issue, Ireland today might still be a part of the United Kingdom.

It wasn't the instruction Gladstone received at Oxford that converted him to the liberation of the individual. He later observed:

> I trace in the education of Oxford of my own time one great defect. Perhaps it was my own fault; but I must admit that I did not learn when at Oxford that which I have learned since— namely, to set a due value on the imperishable and inestimable principles of human liberty. The temper which, I think, too much prevailed in academic circles was to regard liberty with jealousy.

Anyone familiar with the prevailing orthodoxy of today's academia would have to conclude that, in this respect, the more things have changed, the more they've stayed the same.

Replacing the Love of Power

In foreign policy, with a painful exception or two that he came mostly to regret, Gladstone practiced nonintervention. He spoke against the Opium War with China as early as 1840. Decades later he opposed his rival Benjamin Disraeli's imperialist policies, saying that he preferred the Golden Rule over adventurism and empire. He once opined, "Here is my first principle of foreign policy: good government at home."

Historian Jim Powell writes: "Gladstone believed the cost of war should be a deterrent to militarism. He insisted on a policy of financing war exclusively by taxation. He opposed borrowing money for war, since this would make it easier, and future generations would be unfairly burdened."

What a contrast to present times, when governments think nothing of spending more for programs at home at the same time they ratchet up military spending for wars abroad, then pile up the debt to cover it all in the short term.

Gladstone firmly believed that the prospects for peace improve when the lust for power recedes. "We look forward to the time," he once declared, "when the power of love will replace the love of power. Then will our world know the blessings of peace."

Liberty's Champion

Though he towered over everyone else in government in his day, including other classical liberals, Gladstone wasn't perfect. Powell touches on one area where he fell: "Having matured in an era when his government had limited power and committed few horrors, Gladstone figured it could do some good. For instance, he approved taxes for government schools." Perhaps the decision reflected the political pressure to spend some of the government revenues that soared after Gladstone had led the push to repeal tariffs and cut taxes.

If the Grand Old Man could have seen where government involvement in education would lead, he might not have yielded on the matter. In my view, this is the only blemish on an otherwise sterling, decades-long career in defense of liberty. He may have sensed his error when he wrote in 1885: "The rule of our policy is that nothing should be done by the state which can be better or as well done by voluntary effort; and I am not aware that, either in its moral or even its literary aspects, the work of the state for education has as yet proved its superiority to the work of the religious bodies or of philanthropic individuals."

In February 1893, in his eighty-third year, Gladstone delivered what one biographer terms "a lucid and brilliant speech" that upheld the sanctity of sound money and the gold standard. Honest men and honest governments don't steal from the people by debasing the currency, Gladstone said. He urged the British people to look to the ideas of America's Founding Fathers for inspiration. The more he reflected on the wisdom of men like Madison and Jefferson, the more he saw them as political and intellectual giants.

In warning against the temptations to grow the size and scope of the state, Gladstone was positively prophetic:

But let the working man be on his guard against another danger. We live at a time when there is a disposition to think that the Government ought to do this and that and that the Government ought to do everything. There are things which the Government ought to do, I have no doubt. In former periods the Government have neglected much, and possibly even now they neglect something; but there is a danger on the other side. If the Government takes into its hands that which the man ought to do for himself it will inflict upon him greater mischiefs than all the benefits he will have received or all the advantages that would accrue from them.

This was a man who embraced activist government in his youth but learned quickly what a snare and a delusion it could be, then set himself on a course to fight it.

"I was brought up to distrust and dislike liberty; I learned to believe in it," he told a friend in 1891. "I view with the greatest alarm the progress of socialism at the present day," he said. "Whatever influence I possess will be used in the direction of stopping it."

We who love liberty often think poorly of politicians. William Ewart Gladstone, however, was one we can embrace as a champion.

Lessons from William Ewart Gladstone

Fight for liberty on many fronts: Gladstone championed free trade, sound money, low taxes, and private property; denounced the idea that "the Government ought to do everything"; fought for religious liberty and Irish home rule; and resisted foreign adventurism.

Question the prevailing orthodoxy in academia: At Oxford, Gladstone encountered a problem that many students face today: a widespread tendency "to regard liberty with jealousy."

15

George Eastman

Genius of Invention and Enterprise

In 2015 a new world record was set: humans recorded fleeting moments of their lives at least one *trillion* times. That's how many photos we snapped over the course of the year, up from 810 billion in 2014, according to *InfoTrends' Worldwide Image Capture Forecast*. About three-quarters of them were taken with smartphones, which didn't even exist a couple of decades ago.

Giants in the field of photography have enriched our lives far beyond the imaginations of the first few generations of Americans. Although the first photographic process—called *daguerreotype*—was introduced commercially in 1839, decades of innovation and investment followed before picture taking was inexpensive enough to make it a national pastime. More than anyone else, the man who ushered in the era of modern photography was George Eastman.

Eastman introduced the Kodak "Brownie" box camera in February 1900. The price tag was one dollar; film sold for fifteen cents a roll. Eastman did for cameras what Steve Jobs would do for computers almost eight decades later: put exciting new technology within the reach of almost every American family.

"Kodak Freaks"

Whether you're a camera buff or not, you probably have seen a Brownie. Nowadays these cameras show up at rummage sales and antique shows, but I can remember when they were still widely used in my childhood during the 1950s. They were simple to operate and took great pictures. I would snap a roll of fewer than twenty photos, reel them back onto the original spool, remove the spool from the camera, and give it to my father. He would drop it off at the camera store on his way to work. A full week of anxious waiting later, my photos would be ready for pickup.

The Brownie was a genuine cultural phenomenon. Millions were sold. Thousands of American youngsters signed up as members of the Brownie Camera Club and entered Kodak photo contests. Famous photographers got their start with Eastman's invention.

In 1871, at the age of seventeen, Eastman bought almost a hundred dollars' worth of photographic equipment and hired a photographer to instruct him in the art. He read everything he could find on the subject and began hauling his equipment everywhere to capture images.

Hauling is the appropriate term. Cameras in the 1870s were as big as microwave ovens are now. The tools of the professional photographer's trade—including a bulky, unreliable camera, a tripod, and various liquid chemicals—were more than a single man could carry, "a pack-horse load," as Eastman described it. He resolved to downsize, simplify, and reduce the burden of taking pictures.

Eastman experimented endlessly and discovered new techniques and processes for producing better film and lighter, less expensive cameras. A self-taught chemist, he ended the era of sloppy, wet-plate photography by inventing a process that used dry chemicals, though not without many disappointments along the way. His Eastman Dry Plate Company almost went bankrupt in

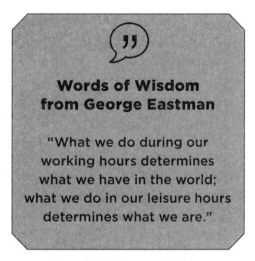

Words of Wisdom from George Eastman

"What we do during our working hours determines what we have in the world; what we do in our leisure hours determines what we are."

the 1880s. But in America's golden age of invention—when taxes were low, rewards for persistence were often great, and government largely left creative people alone—this genius who had dropped out of school at age thirteen built an extraordinarily successful business.

Professional photographers praised Eastman's pioneering work. They called his prints and negatives "the best dry plate work on the market." Journals and newspapers began publishing articles about each Eastman invention and eagerly awaited the next one.

By 1888 Eastman had simplified the camera into a small, easily held box measuring three and three-quarter inches high, three and a quarter inches wide, and six and a half inches long. He needed a name for it, a catchy trademark that could be easily pronounced and spelled. "K" was his favorite letter because, he said, it was "a strong, incisive sort of letter." After toying with various combinations of letters, he hit on one that rang some sort of bell in his mind: "Kodak."

In 1892 Eastman founded the Eastman Kodak Company, in Rochester, New York, the first company to mass produce standardized photography equipment. It also manufactured the flexible transparent film, which proved indispensable to the development of the motion picture industry.

But the first Kodak camera, priced at twenty-five dollars, was still unaffordable for most Americans. Eastman and his team of expert craftsmen worked feverishly to cut costs and improve quality. The result was the Kodak Brownie, a camera that would reach people, in Eastman's words, "the same way the bicycle has reached them."

The Brownie took the world by storm. The first run of five thousand cameras flew off the shelves, and orders piled up at a pace that exceeded the most optimistic projections. Even corner drugstores were selling them.

A new term was coined during a 1905 court trial to describe the millions of people caught up in the craze: "Kodak freaks." In her biography of George Eastman, Elizabeth Brayer quotes the court transcript, which read, "Wherever they go, and whomever they see, and whatever place they have come to, they have got to have a Kodak along for the purpose of getting pictures." In 1904, reports Brayer, when the Dalai Lama fled from his Tibetan palace, he took his Brownie with him.

Inventor, Business Leader, Philanthropist

George Eastman was not only a talented inventor but also a superb businessman. He inspired great loyalty among his employees, in large measure because of what Brayer calls "his countless acts of kindness, his enlightened personnel policies, and his tireless working habits."

This self-made man became one of America's wealthiest citizens and most generous philanthropists. During his lifetime he gave away, usually without fanfare, what today would amount to more than $100 million. He gave the equivalent of $20 million to what is now the Rochester Institute of Technology and millions more to the Massachusetts Institute of Technology. Eastman's giving was a huge financial help to some historically black colleges in the South, including Booker T. Washington's Tuskegee Institute.

Of course, what he gave away didn't make him a hero. That was the easy part. He had to earn a fortune first by serving billions of eager consumers who benefited from his vision and abilities over the decades.

No central planner could have foreseen what Eastman achieved in his time, or what his successors have since achieved in ours. In 2015 the number of cell phones in the world exceeded the earth's population for the first time, and about half of those phones had built-in cameras. Smartphones equipped with high-quality cameras are easily one of the fastest-growing consumer technology marvels in history, and they are direct descendants of the innovations Eastman was responsible for in the nineteenth century. Like Eastman's products, these smartphones improve in quality with every new release—photo resolution has increased exponentially since the first camera phone went on sale in 1996—and prices continue to drop. These developments are tributes to the spontaneous order of a relatively free, entrepreneurial marketplace, unplanned by politicians or bureaucrats. They didn't require a government venture-capital fund, taxpayer-funded subsidies, or job-training grants—only an environment of low taxes, minimal regulation, and freewheeling risk taking by inventors and marketers.

Wealthy citizens played key roles in this story. They were the prime sources of capital to launch inventions like cameras and phones, and they were the ones who could afford to buy the early versions. Those purchases helped cover the initial high costs and enormous risks.

The same is true for almost every other invention. Wealthy people bought the first cameras when they sold for hundreds of nineteenth-century dollars, helping to provide the income and the capital for people like George Eastman to figure out how to cut their price to a comparative pittance.

I'm thankful that these benefactors of humanity never had to pay the 90 percent marginal income tax rate that some would like to reimpose today.

"My Work Is Done"

Eastman's final two years were arduous and painful. Suffering from a degenerative spinal condition, he found it increasingly difficult to stand or walk. On March 14, 1932, at age seventy-seven, he took his own life by way of a single gunshot to the heart. He left a note that read, "To my friends, my work is done. Why wait? —GE."

Successful geniuses of capital and enterprise like George Eastman are viewed with disdain by many in our midst. These critics are the envious, the demagogues, the class warriors, the power lusters, the people who are more eager to steal and redistribute what others create than to bake a bigger pie. The Eastmans of the world, however, will go on bequeathing great gifts to humanity while their detractors, with a little luck, will be forgotten.

Lessons from George Eastman

Free the innovators: George Eastman, not government planners, revolutionized picture taking the world over. He did for photography what Steve Jobs later did for computers: making expensive technologies accessible to the average citizen. When innovators like Eastman are freed from onerous taxation and government meddling, they improve lives by delivering greatly improved products and services, and by creating jobs.

Don't vilify "the rich": The cartoon stereotype of the rich man playing with his gold coins bears no resemblance to Eastman—or to most other rich people, for that matter. This self-made man employed countless thousands worldwide and was one of the most generous philanthropists of his day.

16

Fanny Crosby

Blind but Not Disabled

The most revered woman in late nineteenth-century America is someone you've probably never heard of: Fanny Crosby.

Though barely remembered today, Crosby earned fame and, more important, the respect of people the world over during her long life of achievement. She established a reputation for compassionate service through her charitable work in inner cities. But it was through her songwriting that she really came to prominence. Crosby wrote many popular songs but became best known for her hymns. In fact, she wrote more hymns than any other person who ever lived; many of them are still sung today. She also wrote more than a thousand poems and was a renowned public speaker.

Crosby got to know many of the most prominent figures of the era, including politicians, generals, evangelists, and singers. She probably met more U.S. presidents than any other person, living or dead. She became the first woman to address the U.S. Congress.

What made Crosby's life so remarkable was the handicap she endured and overcame: total blindness. Her family believed that she went blind when she was six weeks old, after mistreatment for an inflammation of her eyes (though modern medical experts say her blindness was probably congenital). She inspired others with her hard work and personal initiative. Crosby was popular as much for her perseverance in the face of a horrific obstacle as for all the many good deeds she performed.

Yankee Values

Born in Putnam County, New York, in 1820, Frances Jane Crosby could trace her ancestry back to Puritans who came to Massachusetts in the seventeenth century. Throughout her life she was, biographer Edith Blumhofer notes, "animated by nostalgic pride in her forebears and uncomplicated devotion to liberty and democracy."

That family pride shaped her character. In *Her Heart Can See*, Blumhofer writes of the Yankee values Crosby admired in her lineage: "independence, sobriety, thrift, morality, hard work, public service, family loyalty, unashamed patriotism, and above all, devotion to duty." Crosby displayed all these traits in her nearly ninety-five years of life.

She would always remember how her mother encouraged her. Her mother often said that two of the world's greatest poets, Homer and John Milton, were blind. Mrs. Crosby also told Fanny that "sometimes Providence deprived persons of some physical faculty in order that the spiritual insight might more fully awake[n]." Fanny Crosby's Christian faith would guide and sustain her throughout her life.

Crosby also was blessed with many talents. She wrote her first poem when she was only eight. Her memory was legendary. By age fifteen, she had memorized the first five books of the Old Testament, the first four of the New (the gospels of Matthew, Mark, Luke, and John), the books of Proverbs and Song of Solomon, and many of the Psalms.

At the same age she became a student at the New York Institution for the Blind. During her decade there she learned to play the guitar, piano, organ,

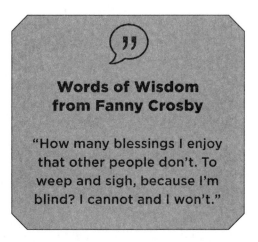

Words of Wisdom from Fanny Crosby

"How many blessings I enjoy that other people don't. To weep and sigh, because I'm blind? I cannot and I won't."

and harp. She also developed her talents as a singer.

In the 1840s, when she was in her twenties, Crosby threw herself into being a mission worker in New York. As thousands fled the city during the cholera epidemic, she stayed behind to nurse the sick. She contracted the disease herself, though she later recovered. In *Satisfied: Women Hymn Writers of the Nineteenth Century*, author Keith Schwanz notes that long after she had gained fame for her compositions, Crosby still thought of herself as a city mission worker.

Hymn Writer

Crosby's first poem was published when she was twenty-one, and soon she began her prodigious output of songs. To start, her songs were mostly popular and patriotic. She transitioned into hymns during the Civil War, when the prominent composer and publisher William B. Bradbury was looking for someone to supply lyrics to his melodies. Looking back on her first collaboration with Bradbury, she recalled, "It now seemed to me that the great work of my life had really begun."

Crosby wrote about nine thousand hymns over the next several decades, a record no one else has ever approached. She became the best-known hymn writer of her day. This was not simply because she was so prolific. She also pioneered a style that became immensely influential. Biographer Bernard Ruffin writes that before Crosby, "many hymns were staid, formal, and rather cold." But Crosby developed "a kind of hymn, in the popular idiom, that appealed to the emotions of the worshipper."

By the late nineteenth century, America's Protestant churches were filled with music from the creative mind of Fanny Crosby. Some of her hymns are still well known and widely sung, from "To God Be the Glory" to "Blessed Assurance" to "Pass Me Not, O Gentle Savior."

Crosby set a personal goal of bringing a million people to Christianity through her hymns. Whenever she wrote one, she prayed it would bring women and men to the faith, and she kept careful records of those reported to have been converted through her works.

Crosby's influence cannot be overstated. She met every single president (in some cases after they served in the White House) from John Quincy Adams to Woodrow Wilson—an astounding twenty-one presidents in all, or nearly half of those who have held the office in our nation's history. In honor of her eighty-fifth birthday, in 1905, churches worldwide celebrated Fanny Crosby Day. In May 1911, at age ninety-one, she spoke to five thousand people in Carnegie Hall after the crowd sang her songs for thirty minutes.

Bernard Ruffin opens his biography with a scene from late in her life. When her cab driver discovers that his passenger is Fanny Crosby, the hymn writer, the young man "takes off his hat and weeps openly," Ruffin writes. When they arrive at her destination, the train station, the driver flags a policeman and asks him to make sure the great Fanny Crosby makes it safely to her train. The policeman, too, weeps upon meeting her.

"Blessed Providence"

Fanny Crosby died in February 1915, just a month short of her ninety-fifth birthday. She had made a remarkable impact in her long and productive life. Through her powerful example and exemplary character, she became one of the most admired women in American history.

Such a trajectory would not have seemed likely when she was starting out in life. But Crosby did not complain about her blindness. Quite the contrary. "It seemed intended by the blessed providence of God that I should be blind all my life," she once observed, "and I thank him for the dispensation. If perfect earthly sight were offered me tomorrow I would not accept it. I might not have sung hymns to the praise of God if I had been distracted by the beautiful and interesting things around me."

She was reported as saying that had it not been for her affliction, she "might not have so good an education or have so great an influence, and certainly not so fine a memory."

If Crosby had only kept quiet about her faith, complained about her plight as a blind person, or declared a right to a federal handout, maybe the writers of our history texts today wouldn't ignore her.

Lessons from Fanny Crosby

Count your blessings: Who, you might ask, could ever see blindness as a blessing? Fanny Crosby did, and her blindness never seemed to slow her down. She overcame a major handicap to gift the world with her hymns, poems, and popular songs. She serves as a model of character and perseverance.

Develop your work ethic: Crosby embodied the famous Thomas Edison maxim "Genius is 1 percent inspiration and 99 percent perspiration." She used her God-given talents to the fullest, displaying a tireless work ethic. She would often write several hymns in a single day.

17

Siegfried Sassoon

Conscience on and off the Battlefield

When you hear the term *war hero*, what do you picture?
Battlefield bravery—charging enemy lines in the face of incoming fire, risking one's life to save friends, enduring injuries without complaint?

You probably don't think of a war hero as one who sticks his neck out to oppose the very war in which he fights.

If we more readily associated heroism in war with the courageous resistance to one's own bellicose government, the world might more often eschew the stupid and jingoistic reasons for which nations frequently shed innocent blood.

Siegfried Sassoon was a hero of both descriptions.

"The Hell Where Youth and Laughter Go"

Born in 1886 in southeast England, Sassoon was the son of an Anglo-Catholic mother and a Jewish father from Baghdad. His last name means "joy" in Hebrew. His first name might suggest a German origin, but his mother named him Siegfried because of her love of Richard Wagner's operas. Otherwise, Siegfried's only connection to Germany was his service to Britain in the tragically misnamed "war to end all wars"—also laughably dubbed the conflict that would "make the world safe for democracy."

More than a century after its start, World War I remains an enigma to people everywhere. We take history courses and still ask, "What was it all about?" and "What could possibly have justified the unimaginable devastation it caused?"

Its main result was to make inevitable an even deadlier conflagration a quarter century later. Perhaps few adventures in history were more absurd in origin, outrageous in duration, and counterproductive in their consequences than the one that began when an obscure Austrian royal was assassinated in Sarajevo in June 1914.

Sassoon was not a likely candidate for future hero status: as the world stumbled into war in the summer of 1914, he was a carefree twenty-seven-year-old, a novelist and an avid cricket player. He didn't wait to be drafted, however. In a gesture of patriotism, he joined the British Army. He was already in service with the Sussex Imperial Yeomanry on August 4 when the United Kingdom declared war on Germany. He was commissioned with the Royal Welch Fusiliers as a second lieutenant in May 1915. In November of that year, his brother was killed in the Gallipoli disaster, and days later Siegfried himself was sent to the front lines in France.

Almost immediately, he inspired the deepest confidence of the men serving under him. On bombing patrols and night raids, he demonstrated stunning efficiency as a company commander. He single-handedly stormed an enemy trench and scattered sixty German soldiers. Nicknamed "Mad Jack" by his men for his near-suicidal

Words of Wisdom from Siegfried Sassoon

"I have seen and endured the sufferings of the troops, and I can no longer be a party to prolong these sufferings for ends which I believe to be evil and unjust."

courage, he was awarded the Military Cross, for which the citation read: "For conspicuous gallantry during a raid on the enemy's trenches. He remained for 1½ hours under rifle and bomb fire collecting and bringing in our wounded. Owing to his courage and determination all of the killed and wounded were brought in."

One of every eight British men who served on the western front in World War I died in the trenches or in the ghastly death zones that separated them. Casualties—the wounded in addition to the killed—totaled a staggering 56 percent. Though it was the first war in which disease claimed fewer men than did combat, that may have resulted not from medical advances as much as from the ruthless precision of machine guns and shell fire and the endless, violent gridlock of trench warfare. It's nearly impossible to convey in words the horrors soldiers witnessed, but Sassoon would be among the few who made the attempt.

Sassoon emerged as one of the best of the "war poets," a group that included Rupert Brooke, Isaac Rosenberg, Ivor Gurney, Charles Sorley, David Jones, Edward Thomas, and Wilfred Owen. These warriors came face-to-face with their own mortality, the squandering of life, the death of close friends, the failure of modernity, and the nightmare of combat. The more Sassoon experienced the agonies of those around him, the more he questioned the purpose—the very sanity—of the enterprise. Astonished at the rate of servicemen taking their own lives, he wrote the poem "Suicide in the Trenches":

I knew a simple soldier boy
Who grinned at life in empty joy,

Slept soundly through the lonesome dark,
And whistled early with the lark.
In winter trenches, cowed and glum,
With crumps and lice and lack of rum,
He put a bullet through his brain.
No one spoke of him again.
You smug-faced crowds with kindling eye
Who cheer when soldier lads march by,
Sneak home and pray you'll never know
The hell where youth and laughter go.

"An Act of Willful Defiance"

Three years into the war, Sassoon had had enough. "In war-time,"
he wrote, "the word patriotism means suppression of truth." After a
period of convalescence from war wounds, he declined to return to
duty and threw the ribbon portion of his Military Cross into the river
Mersey. His conscience compelled him to write this letter to his commanding officer in July 1917:

> I am making this statement as an act of willful defiance of mili-
> tary authority, because I believe that the war is being deliberately
> prolonged by those who have the power to end it. I am a soldier,
> convinced that I am acting on behalf of soldiers. I believe that the
> war upon which I entered as a war of defense and liberation has
> now become a war of aggression and conquest. I believe that the
> purposes for which I and my fellow soldiers entered upon this
> war should have been so clearly stated as to have made it impos-
> sible to change them and that had this been done the objects
> which actuated us would now be attainable by negotiation.
>
> I have seen and endured the sufferings of the troops, and
> I can no longer be a party to prolong these sufferings for ends
> which I believe to be evil and unjust.

I am not protesting against the conduct of the war, but against the political errors and insincerities for which the fighting men are being sacrificed.

On behalf of those who are suffering now, I make this protest against the deception which is being practiced upon them; also I believe it may help to destroy the callous complacency with which the majority of those at home regard the continuance of agonies which they do not share and which they have not enough imagination to realize.

Before the month was out, Sassoon's letter became a sensation across Britain. It was read aloud by a sympathetic member of the House of Commons and printed the next day in London's biggest newspaper, the *Times*.

The country's military and political hierarchy debated how to respond. Sassoon might have been court-martialed and executed, but his reputation both as a poet and on the battlefield pushed the authorities in another direction. They decided he was mentally ill, deranged by neurasthenia ("shell shock"). They sent him for treatment to Craiglockhart Hospital near Edinburgh, Scotland.

At Craiglockhart, Sassoon befriended Wilfred Owen, also remanded to the hospital for shell shock. Owen later credited Sassoon as the inspiration that made him a great poet. Owen would return to the battlefield a few months later and be killed on the eve of the war's end, but Sassoon labored to bring Owen's poetry to the attention of the world. (The friendship between the two men is the subject of Stephen MacDonald's remarkable play *Not about Heroes*.)

The psychiatrist and officer attending to Sassoon, W. H. R. Rivers, soon realized that this principled young man was in full possession of his faculties. Unable to prove that anything was physically or mentally wrong with Sassoon, the British military released him from Craiglockhart and even promoted him to lieutenant. In July 1918, in spite of all he had endured, Sassoon volunteered to return to the western front. He hadn't changed his mind about the war; he simply couldn't stand the thought of not being of assistance to the men in the trenches.

Within days of returning to battle, Sassoon was wounded in the head by a fellow British soldier who mistook him for the enemy. He recovered, but that "friendly fire" took him permanently off the front. The war finally ended four months later. The death toll: more than nine million combatants and seven million civilians.

"The Pity of War"

Siegfried Sassoon lived another half century. In those postwar years he earned his living as a poet, editor, novelist, and public lecturer. He married and fathered a son. When war with Hitler came in 1939, he lamented but supported the fight, believing it a necessity brought on by the folly of the previous war.

It's not uncommon for great issues to elicit an alteration of perspective from even the best man or woman. In time, Sassoon changed his mind regarding the stance that made him famous in 1917. In his autobiography, published in 1945, he expressed the view that fighting on until Germany was defeated seemed in hindsight to be the sounder position. That he had had such second thoughts was a fact that never took hold in the public mind, so his deeds and words during the Great War would forever define his legacy. I prefer to see him in those years as courageous and principled when under fire, no matter what form the fire took.

In 1951 he was named Commander of the Order of the British Empire by King George VI, an honor that recognizes "contributions to the arts and sciences, work with charitable and welfare organizations and public service outside the Civil Service." He converted to Catholicism and took great comfort in his faith in his final years. He died of stomach cancer at age eighty on September 1, 1967.

Sixteen great war poets, including Siegfried Sassoon, are remembered on a slate stone in Westminster Abbey's Poets' Corner. The stone's inscription features the words of Wilfred Owen: "My subject is war, and the pity of war. The poetry is in the pity."

Lessons from Siegfried Sassoon

Act on your conscience: Siegfried Sassoon saw World War I for the political folly it was and said so, both in his published poetry and in what he called his "willful defiance of military authority."

Honor your duty: Despite his outspoken opposition to the war, Sassoon didn't flinch when called to fight. He returned to battle even after his government consigned him to a mental institution for his opposition to the war. He couldn't bear the thought of his friends' sacrificing life and limb without him.

18

Andrew Mellon

Unleashing Wealth Creators

Of the dozens of people who have held the office of secretary of the treasury of the United States, my choice for the best would be Andrew Mellon.

I must admit up front that I have a fondness for Mellon for a personal reason. Like me, he was of Scots-Irish ancestry and grew up in western Pennsylvania (he in Pittsburgh, I in Beaver Falls). But what he stood for is what really stands out.

From 1921 to 1932, Andrew William Mellon served Presidents Warren Harding, Calvin Coolidge, and Herbert Hoover as treasury secretary. Only two individuals in American history held the office longer than his ten years and eleven months. Mellon's business prowess before that was legendary. Never impulsive, he put in long hours of study before making an important decision, displaying a sharp intellect and a quiet thoughtfulness that contemporaries admired. With an uncanny ability to pick cutting-edge technologies and the right entrepreneurs to bet on, Mellon built a financial and industrial empire in steel, oil, shipbuilding, coal, coke, banking, and aluminum.

One of the giant firms he helped found was the Aluminum Company of America, or Alcoa. By the 1920s he was one of the wealthiest men in America. He was also one of the country's most generous philanthropists, not to mention the third highest income tax *payer*, behind only John D. Rockefeller and Henry Ford.

Arguably, Mellon's greatest contribution to America was not the vast wealth he created or the vast wealth he gave away, but rather the vast wealth his fiscal policies allowed millions of *other* Americans to produce. Mellon's riches did not insulate him from the real world; they reinforced in his mind just how the real world works.

The Mellon Plan

When Mellon came to Washington, the federal income tax hadn't yet celebrated its tenth birthday, but the false prophets who had scoffed that the rate could ever get as high as 10 percent had already been shamed by events. The top marginal income tax bracket stood at 73 percent by 1921. Mellon noticed that confiscatory rates were putting scarce capital to flight as investors sought refuge abroad or in tax havens at home. He often pointed to John D. Rockefeller's brother William, who had $44 million in tax-exempt bonds and only $7 million in Standard Oil when he died in 1923.

Mellon's view of the deleterious effect of high tax rates was formed early in life. His grandfather left Ulster to escape a crushing tax burden, and Andrew's father made sure his son understood that. In America the Mellon family practiced thrift and entrepreneurship.

As treasury secretary, Mellon argued that taxes had to be slashed "to attract the large fortunes back into productive enterprise." He added, "It seems difficult for some to understand that high rates of taxation do not necessarily mean large revenue to the Government, and that more revenue may often be obtained by lower rates." Henry Ford, he pointed out, made more money by reducing the price of his cars from $3,000 to $380 and increasing his sales than he would have earned by keeping high the price and profit per car.

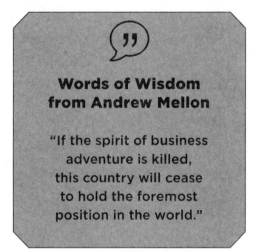

Words of Wisdom from Andrew Mellon

"If the spirit of business adventure is killed, this country will cease to hold the foremost position in the world."

Mellon relentlessly pressed Congress to cut taxes across the board, for all brackets. By 1929, when Congress passed his sixth tax cut of the decade, the top rate had been lowered two-thirds, from 73 percent to 24 percent. Those in the lowest income bracket (earning under $4,000 annually) saw their rates fall by an even greater percentage—from 4 percent to 0.5 percent. So many exemptions were introduced or raised that between 1921 and 1929 the number of Americans who paid federal income taxes fell by one million. Barely 2 percent paid any federal income tax at all by the end of the decade.

Mellon also worked to repeal the federal estate tax, but secured just half the loaf; Congress cut it from 40 to 20 percent. At his urging, the gift tax was abolished.

The Mellon Plan was, as Burton W. Folsom points out in *The Myth of the Robber Barons*, "a startling triumph." The budget was in surplus year after year. Personal income tax revenues soared from $719 million in 1921 to more than $1 billion in 1929. The national debt was halved. The economy grew by 59 percent, America was awash in new inventions, and American wages became the envy of the world.

Soak-the-rich class warriors cried foul anyway. During the debate over the 1926 tax cuts, Senator George Norris of Nebraska charged that if the administration had its way, Mellon himself would reap "a larger personal reduction [in taxes] than the aggregate of practically all the taxpayers in the state of Nebraska." Norris never mentioned that Mellon was *paying* more in taxes than all the people of Nebraska combined.

Senator James Couzens of Michigan, a fellow Republican, fought the Mellon Plan as well. He conducted witch-hunting investigations in an attempt to embarrass Coolidge and Mellon. He publicly charged that the Treasury Department was secretly giving refunds to rich, politically favored businessmen. The effort backfired: the investigation revealed that the refunds were the result of nothing illegal or unethical.

None of Mellon's congressional enemies made much of a dent in the treasury secretary's program in the 1920s. Until President Hoover in 1930 began jacking up tax rates, the great majority of what Mellon wanted he got, and very little of what he opposed ever passed.

Against Wasteful Government Spending

To his further credit, Mellon exerted his influence to constrain government spending. In 1928 total federal expenditures were actually a shade lower than they had been in 1923. Mellon slashed expenses and, according to historian Folsom, he eliminated an average of one treasury staffer per day for every single day during the 1920s. The last significant redesign of American currency was Mellon's doing in the 1920s; he cut the size of our paper notes to save money.

As Mellon's fiscal policies at the Treasury Department unleashed an explosion of productivity, investment, and innovation, the good times were being undermined down the street by unsustainable monetary policies at the Federal Reserve System. Artificially low interest rates, caused by the Fed's inflation of money and credit from 1924 through 1928, endangered an otherwise healthy economy. When the Fed burst the bubble by raising interest rates starting in 1929, the boom gave way to the bust, made worse for a decade by tax and regulatory policies that were the antithesis of what Mellon advocated.

President Hoover wrote in later years that Mellon advised him at the onset of the Depression to pursue policies that would "liquidate labor, liquidate stocks, liquidate farmers, liquidate real estate." The treasury secretary allegedly added: "It will purge the rottenness out of the system. High costs of living and high living will come down. People will work harder, live a more moral life. Values will be adjusted, and enterprising people will pick up from less competent people." No corroborative evidence has ever surfaced to support Hoover's claim. Hoover boasted that he didn't follow the treasury secretary's advice—but he should have. The fact is that the Depression only worsened under Hoover's endless interventions (higher taxes, tariffs, and spending along with bailouts and other failures that President Franklin Roosevelt would expand even more).

If Mellon indeed said what Hoover claimed, he was actually close to the truth. The sooner the economy could slough off the excesses and the unsustainable, artificial investments of the cheap money boom, the sooner it could recover. When the Harding administration had allowed the economy to do just that in 1921, a sharp depression ended in a matter of months.

Finding himself unpopular within the meddling Hoover administration, Mellon resigned his position as treasury secretary in 1932. He then served one year as U.S. ambassador to Great Britain.

FDR Attacks

While campaigning for president in 1932, Franklin Roosevelt declared that "the day of the great promoter or financial titan...is over." As president, he tried to make an example of Mellon, going after him with a frightening vengeance.

FDR's Justice Department charged Mellon with income tax fraud. As Mellon biographer David Cannadine points out, Roosevelt's attorney general took up Mellon's case from the very beginning, "preempting due process" and operating in a manner "wholly without precedent." Despite these high-level efforts and months of intense investigation, Justice couldn't even get a grand jury to indict Mellon.

Cannadine reports that FDR, furious to be thwarted in criminal court, "personally authorized" a civil case against Mellon. Thus began the infamous "Mellon Tax Trial." For two years the Board of Tax Appeals considered fraud charges against the former treasury secretary. On these charges, too, Mellon was exonerated—but not until three months after his death, at age eighty-two, in 1937. Former IRS commissioner David Blair blasted the whole affair as "unwarranted abuse by high officials of the government." It was one of many sorry episodes that exposed a nasty side of FDR that his idolaters rarely admit to.

To score political points, FDR attacked rich people like Mellon for their "greed." Never mind that Mellon created wealth and gave much of it away through his generous philanthropy. He almost single-handedly created the National Gallery of Art in Washington, D.C., donating his substantial art collection, plus millions for construction and endowment. To the National Gallery alone he gave hundreds of millions in today's dollars, and that was just one of his many charitable causes.

Roosevelt, meanwhile, was a child of privilege who accomplished relatively little in private life before he became a politician. He received a monthly allowance from his mother until her death in 1941—when FDR was fifty-nine and in his third term as president.

Even more important than how these two men handled their personal wealth is how they approached wealth through their public policy. As treasury secretary, Mellon didn't carve out favors for "the rich"; his across-the-board tax cuts benefited Americans of *every* class and unlocked the potential of the free American economy to create jobs and wealth. As president, FDR either stifled or swiped wealth, squandering much of it on government boondoggles and misguided programs that generations later would yield destructive dependency and debt. By executive order he once imposed a *100 percent* tax rate on all incomes over $25,000; Congress overturned that order but still approved a confiscatory tax rate of 94 percent on the highest incomes.

Andrew Mellon was John Galt from *Atlas Shrugged* in every sense but one: though he endured shameless abuse for his success, he never disappeared to a hideaway in the Colorado Rockies. But you couldn't blame him if he had, given how Roosevelt and his henchmen vilified him. H. L. Mencken was spot-on when he wrote that the president was surrounded by "an astonishing rabble of impudent nobodies," "a gang of half-educated pedagogues, non-constitutional lawyers, starry-eyed uplifters and other such sorry wizards." The New Deal, Mencken said, was a "political racket," a "series of stupendous bogus miracles," with its "constant appeals to class envy and hatred," treating government as "a milch cow with 125 million teats." And, I might add, it didn't cure the Great Depression; it prolonged it by at least seven years.

Mellon's Legacy

The Roosevelt administration failed in its efforts to convict Andrew Mellon of tax fraud. Its efforts to besmirch his character didn't succeed either. In 1955, to commemorate the hundredth anniversary of his birth, the federal post office honored the vindicated Mellon by placing his image on the three-cent postage stamp.

Still, statist historians to this day are prone to ignore or attack the achievements of Mellon. After all, he was one of those "rich" guys we're supposed to dislike. Andrew Mellon, however, is worthy of so much more than all but a few of his critics ever were. He was a successful "one-percenter" who did more for the other 99 percent than all those critics combined.

Lessons from Andrew Mellon

Don't succumb to the temptations of class warfare:
President Franklin Roosevelt, born of great wealth, used
to great effect a political ploy popular in our own time:
attacking "the rich." Andrew Mellon's achievements
remind us how misguided such attacks usually are. As a
business leader, Mellon created jobs and brought better
products to more consumers at lower prices. As a philanthropist, he gave many millions of dollars to charitable causes. And as treasury secretary, Mellon encouraged investment and employment.

Get the government out of the way: As treasury secretary under three presidents, Mellon achieved policy
changes we can only dream of today. Whereas many of
his successors have tried to use government powers to
control the economy, Mellon dramatically reduced government spending, taxation, and debt—and the economy flourished.

19

J. Gresham Machen

God's Forgotten Libertarian

Of the Presbyterian theologian J. Gresham Machen (1881–1937), Pulitzer Prize–winning novelist and Nobel laureate Pearl S. Buck declared: "The man was admirable. He never gave in one inch to anyone. He never bowed his head. It was not in him to trim or compromise, to accept any peace that was less than triumph. He was a glorious enemy because he was completely open and direct in his angers and hatreds. He stood for something and everyone knew what it was."

Lest you be tempted to dismiss Buck's praise as biased—because, after all, she was raised by Presbyterian missionaries living in China—consider the view of H. L. Mencken.

Mencken was known for his caustic criticisms of Christians in general and ministers in particular. He described the Creator as "a comedian whose audience is afraid to laugh" and once wrote, "Shave a gorilla and it would be almost impossible, at twenty paces, to distinguish him from a heavyweight champion of the world. Skin a chimpanzee, and it would take an autopsy to prove he was not a theologian."

And yet Mencken pronounced great admiration for Machen:

> Dr. Machen is surely no mere soap-boxer of God, alarming bucolic sinners for a percentage of the plate. On the contrary, he is a man of great learning.... His moral advantage over his Modernist adversaries, like his logical advantage, is immense and obvious. He faces the onslaught of the Higher Criticism without flinching, and he yields nothing of his faith to expediency or decorum.

When Machen died, Mencken compared him to another prominent Presbyterian, politician William Jennings Bryan, with these words: "Dr. Machen was to Bryan as the Matterhorn is to a wart."

I present Machen as a hero not because he best represents my personal perspective on Christ, the Bible, and Christianity—though I enthusiastically admit that he does. I do so, rather, because he exhibited a remarkable degree of courage and logical consistency that I wish were far more common within Christian leadership. His convictions were deep and thoroughly reasoned. When he faced opposition, as he often did, he didn't retreat to his sitting room; instead, he created institutions to advance his principles. He saw liberty as God's intention for humanity and would not abide the presumptuous claims of earthly governments to diminish it for our own good. This was a man who was confident, persuasive, and fearlessly principled.

Challenging Intellectual Corruption

Machen was born in Baltimore in 1881 to an Episcopalian father, but it was his Presbyterian mother who exerted the greater influence.

By the time Machen enrolled as an undergraduate Classics major at Johns Hopkins University, he was Presbyterian to the core. Having distinguished himself as a first-rate scholar at Hopkins, he went on to Princeton, where he focused on theology at the seminary and philosophy at the university. After a year at a German university, he returned to America in 1906 to teach at Princeton Seminary.

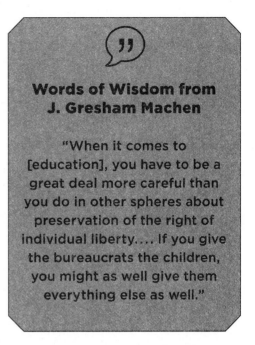

Words of Wisdom from J. Gresham Machen

"When it comes to [education], you have to be a great deal more careful than you do in other spheres about preservation of the right of individual liberty.... If you give the bureaucrats the children, you might as well give them everything else as well."

Machen resolved to defend conservative Reformed theology against the growing influence of the modernists, the theological wing of the "progressive" movement that watered down traditional Christian beliefs and elevated moral relativism and activist government. He proved a worthy antagonist to the religious left. It wouldn't be correct to consider him a theological "fundamentalist" because he was too scholarly for that; fundamentalism was often anti-intellectual, whereas Machen was a deeply intellectual Christian. He appreciated science as a tool for unraveling the mysteries of an ordered and logical universe. His best-known books were systematic and thorough defenses of Christianity (for example, *The Origin of Paul's Religion* and *What Is Faith?*) and devastating critiques of modernist revisionism (e.g., *Christianity and Liberalism*) that remain influential nearly a century later.

Princeton was one of many seminaries infected by progressive ideology. Machen butted heads with Princeton's increasingly leftist faculty until he had had enough. In 1929, after twenty-three years of teaching, he resigned from the university. Rather than seek employment at another established school, he started his own—

Westminster Theological Seminary near Philadelphia—and put it on a path to international fame as one of the most rigorous and respected theological institutions in the world.

In 1933 Machen's simmering concern about religious progressivism (or "liberalism," as he generally termed it) in the Presbyterian mission field motivated him to form the Independent Board for Presbyterian Foreign Missions. The move prompted the mainline Presbyterian Church to excommunicate him, so in 1936 he created what later became known as the Orthodox Presbyterian Church. He was, in many ways, a Presbyterian Martin Luther—a man who boldly challenged the intellectual corruption of the very church that had become a central part of his own life.

"Radical Libertarian"

Machen didn't much care for politics. He saw it as inherently stifling and anti-individual. The idea that true Christianity was to even a small degree compatible with any form of statism—socialism, communism, or fascism—was, to Machen, a dangerous fiction. Historian George Marsden, in his book *Understanding Fundamentalism and Evangelicalism*, labels Machen's political views "radical libertarian" because the theologian "opposed almost any extension of state power." Machen might have been happy with the description, but he would have seen it as a natural extension of the teachings of Christ, who advocated character building and spiritual renewal, not state power.

Although Woodrow Wilson had been a close family friend dating back to their Princeton days, Machen spoke out against U.S. involvement in World War I and condemned the subsequent Versailles Treaty as "an attack on international peace" that would produce war after war "in a wearisome progression." He deemed Wilson's overseas interventions as starry-eyed adventurism. He denounced conscription, arguing that the draft was an assault on freedom and a "brutal interference" with the individual and with family life.

When a proposed child labor amendment to the Constitution grabbed headlines in the 1920s, Machen slammed it as "one of the most cruel and heartless measures that have ever been proposed in the name of philanthropy." He understood the economics of a measure outlawing any employment for children under the age of eighteen: it would either drive child labor underground and into deplorable conditions or relegate poor families to even greater poverty. More important to Machen was what the amendment represented: a federal usurpation of a matter more properly left to the states, localities, and families.

At a time when the overwhelming majority of Presbyterians supported alcohol prohibition, Machen fought it. Scripture cautions against inebriation, he argued, but nowhere does it suggest government coercion as the solution.

He objected to Bible reading and prayer in public schools because they mixed politics with faith; Christians, he said, should form their own schools. He believed it was foolish to think that government would be anything but a soul-crushing, collectivist mediocrity in the classroom:

> Place the lives of children in their formative years, despite the convictions of their parents, under the intimate control of experts appointed by the state, force them to attend schools where the higher aspirations of humanity are crushed out, and where the mind is filled with the materialism of the day, and it is difficult to see how even the remnants of liberty can subsist.

In 1979 President Jimmy Carter signed the bill that cursed the country with the U.S. Department of Education. If Carter, a Sunday school teacher, had read Machen's warnings from more than a half century earlier, he might have avoided that colossal mistake. In 1926 Machen testified before Congress against a proposal to create such a federal department. His remarks, positively prophetic in light of more recent history, deserve an extensive excerpting here:

The department of education...is to promote uniformity in education. That uniformity in education under central control it seems to me is the worst fate into which any country can fall....

It is to be opposed...because it represents a tendency which is no new thing, but has been in the world for at least 2,300 years, which seems to be opposed to the whole principle of liberty for which our country stands. It is the notion that education is an affair essentially of the State; that the children of the State must be educated for the benefit of the State; that idiosyncrasies should be avoided, and the State should devise that method of education which will best promote the welfare of the State....

The principle of this bill, and the principle of all the advocates of it, is that standardization in education is a good thing. I do not think a person can read the literature of advocates of measures of this sort without seeing that that is taken almost without argument as a matter of course, that standardization in education is a good thing. Now, I am perfectly ready to admit that standardization in some spheres is a good thing. It is a good thing in the making of Ford cars; but just because it is a good thing in the making of Ford cars it is a bad thing in the making of human beings, for the reason that a Ford car is a machine and a human being is a person. But a great many educators today deny the distinction between the two, and that is the gist of the whole matter....

I do not believe that the personal, free, individual character of education can be preserved when you have a federal department laying down standards of education which become more or less mandatory to the whole country....

I believe that in the sphere of the mind we should have absolutely unlimited competition.... A public education that is not faced by such competition of private schools is one of the deadliest enemies to liberty that has ever been devised.... I think that when it comes to the training of human beings, you have to be a great deal more careful than you do in other spheres about preservation of the right of individual liberty and the principle of individual responsibility; and I think we ought to be plain about this—that unless we preserve the principles of liberty in this department there is no use in trying to preserve them anywhere else. If you give the bureaucrats the children, you might as well give them everything else as well.

"Faithful unto Death"

In December 1936 Machen traveled to North Dakota for several speaking engagements. In the exceptional cold, he contracted pleurisy, which then developed into pneumonia. He died on New Year's Day, 1937. He was only fifty-five.

Machen is buried in a cemetery in his hometown of Baltimore, where the modest stone over his grave declares simply his name, degree, dates, and the phrase "Faithful unto Death" in Greek.

Lessons from J. Gresham Machen

Don't avoid intellectual combat: J. Gresham Machen was a man of both intellect and principle. He spoke out against the policies of family friend Woodrow Wilson, fought what he regarded as theological apostasy among his colleagues, and challenged religious progressivism even when his critiques led to excommunication.

Oppose extensions of state power: Machen was one of those all-too-rare Christian thinkers who understood that Christians should actively resist unwarranted encroachments by the earthly state on matters of spirituality and personal choice.

20

Marie Curie

Trailblazing Scientist

S he was the first woman to win a Nobel Prize—in fact, to this day she remains the only woman to win two—and the first person of either sex to win Nobel Prizes in two different sciences. These achievements make it all the more noteworthy that her undergraduate education took place at an illegal private institution.

When I learned that the Polish-born and naturalized French scientist Marie Curie attended an "underground" university in the 1880s in Warsaw, I immediately recalled a personal experience. In 1986, while embedded with the antigovernment resistance in communist Poland, I met people who were taking classes at such a place, as well as others who had received their illegal degrees at underground commencement exercises. Little did I know then that Poles have a storied history in what could be termed "educational independence."

A hundred years before my visit to Poland, Curie's college years began at the so-called Flying University (sometimes known as the Floating University). The nation of Poland had formally disappeared in 1795, partitioned for the next 123 years into regions of Russia, Austria-Hungary, and Prussia. Warsaw was under Russian occupation when the Flying University began there in 1885. Poles wanted to avoid "Russification" and desired to teach ideas that the Russian authorities officially censored, so they did what daring people do: they published books and created educational programs and institutions without government approval.

Both sides of Marie Curie's family were involved in resistance movements against occupiers and suffered property seizures and hassles with the police for years, which probably explains her lifelong skepticism of central authority and claims of "consensus." Her father, a teacher and scientist, was punished and demoted by the Russians for holding views contrary to the powers that be. You can understand, then, why she felt compelled after attending the Flying University to emigrate to France at the age of twenty-four and earn her graduate degrees in a freer country. This was a young woman determined to pursue her passion for scientific truth no matter what the regime or consensus imposed. She once said:

I am among those who think that science has great beauty. A scientist in his laboratory is not only a technician: he is also a child placed before natural phenomena which impress him like a fairy tale. We should not allow it to be believed that all scientific progress can be reduced to mechanisms, machines, gearings, even though such machinery also has its beauty. Neither do I believe that the spirit of adventure runs any risk of disappearing in our world. If I see anything vital around me, it is precisely that spirit of adventure, which seems indestructible and is akin to curiosity.

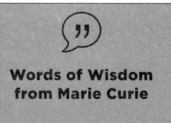

Words of Wisdom from Marie Curie

"Life is not easy for any of us. But what of that? We must have perseverance and, above all, confidence in ourselves."

Perseverance and Confidence

In 1893, two years after her arrival in Paris, the brilliant but penniless Marie Skłodowska (Curie's maiden name) earned the first of two master's degrees at the University of Paris. It was in physics; she would collect the second, in mathematics, a year later. Over the next forty years she would earn a PhD in physics from the University of Paris and receive almost twenty honorary doctorates from prestigious institutions in half a dozen countries on both sides of the Atlantic.

Apparent to all who came to know her was her insatiable drive to excel and achieve. "Life is not easy for any of us. But what of that?" she said. "We must have perseverance and, above all, confidence in ourselves. We must believe that we are gifted for something, and that this thing, at whatever cost, must be attained."

In 1894 she met a young scientist named Pierre Curie, and in 1895 they married. When a friend offered to gift her a dress for the occasion, she instructed: "I have no dress except the one I wear every day. If you are going to be kind enough to give me one, please let it be practical and dark so that I can put it on afterwards to go to the laboratory." She wore that dark blue dress in the lab for many years.

When it came time to settle on an area of research for her PhD, Curie decided to explore the source of the recently discovered "radiance" or energy emitted by the rare element uranium. What was the nature of these rays (which she would ultimately call *radioactivity*)? To what purposes might they be employed?

Biographer Robert William Reid notes that though Pierre later put aside his own work and assisted Marie in her initial discoveries, she set the agenda:

The [research] idea was her own; no one helped her formulate it, and although she took it to her husband for his opinion she clearly established her ownership of it. She later recorded the fact twice in her biography of her husband to ensure there was no chance whatever of any ambiguity. It [is] likely that already at this early stage of her career [she] realized that...many scientists would find it difficult to believe that a woman could be capable of the original work in which she was involved.

Her task required the acquisition of a large quantity of uranium ore known as *pitchblende* from mines in Bohemia. That posed a seemingly insurmountable cost problem, but Marie overcame it through shrewd bargaining and the use of her and Pierre's meager savings. Their daughter Eve Curie would later write of this pivotal moment in her parents' lives:

They were not so foolish as to ask for official credits [or subsidies].... If two physicists on the scent of an immense discovery had asked the University of Paris or the French government for a grant to buy pitchblende residue, they would have been laughed at. In any case, their letter would have been lost in the files of some office, and they would have had to wait months for a reply, probably unfavorable in the end.

The "lab" in which the Curies worked was nothing more than a shed that had once been a medical school dissection room. It leaked when it rained and offered no more ventilation than the single door would provide. But it was there that Marie, with the aid of Pierre, began her work on the sacks of imported ore. In the process, she proved that the radiation came from the uranium atom itself and not from an interaction between uranium and something else. She then discovered that other elements, such as thorium, emitted radiation, too.

Curie was convinced that elements as yet unidentified were also sources of radioactivity within the pitchblende ore. In 1896 she ascertained the presence of one and named it *polonium* in honor of her native Poland. The existence of the other, which she detected and called *radium*, remained to be proven. In 1902 she succeeded in isolating a decigram of pure radium—a scientific breakthrough of massive significance. Before the year was out, she also announced a finding that would have implications for the next century of medical treatment: when exposed to radium, cancer cells were more vulnerable than normal cells.

In June 1903 Marie was awarded her doctorate from the University of Paris. That same month, she and Pierre were invited to present a paper on radioactivity at the Royal Institution in London, but as a woman she was required to be silent while Pierre spoke for them both. Six months later, the couple were declared joint winners, along with a third scientist, of a Nobel Prize in Physics "in recognition of the extraordinary services they have rendered by their joint researches on the radiation phenomena."

In 1906 tragedy struck when Pierre was killed in an accident with a horse-drawn carriage, leaving Marie with two small children. The University of Paris had been ready to offer Pierre a teaching position. They gave it to Marie instead. She was determined to use it to pay tribute to her late husband.

The Business of Saving Lives

No doubt Pierre would have been proud of Marie's subsequent achievements. Her work grew immensely in international stature. She founded and headed the Radium Institute, which advanced scientific study of radium specifically and radiation in general. She was awarded a second Nobel in 1911 "in recognition of her services to the advancement of chemistry by the discovery of the elements radium and polonium, by the isolation of radium and the study of the nature and compounds of this remarkable element."

Curie did not keep her discoveries confined to the laboratory. When World War I broke out, the two-time Nobel Prize winner developed mobile x-ray units to bring this vital medical equipment right to the front. Her mobile devices treated more than a million wounded soldiers during the war, saving many thousands of lives.

Marie Curie died in 1934 at the age of sixty-six. The cause of death was a form of anemia brought on by exposure to the very radiation she had discovered. To this day her papers from the 1890s—and even her cookbook—are so contaminated that they're stored in lead boxes to be viewed only by scientists in protective clothing.

Curie's discoveries set physics in a new direction by opening the door to atomic energy and the controlled use of radiation for medical treatment. With good reason she is regarded as one of the greatest scientists of the modern age.

Lessons from Marie Curie

Persevere with confidence: A tireless, driven achiever, Marie Curie was responsible for some of the greatest scientific discoveries of the modern age. She won two Nobel Prizes at a time when science was almost exclusively the province of men. She had the confidence to overcome all obstacles.

Put your gifts to work for others: Curie advised that "we must believe that we are gifted for something." Her scientific findings led to profound advances in medical treatments, and she personally developed mobile x-ray units that saved thousands of lives during the First World War.

21

Prohibition's Foes

Still Teaching Lessons Today

Barely a century ago, the hatchet-wielding "temperance" fanatic Carrie Nation smashed bars and saloons in Kansas and Texas. She was arrested at least thirty times for her self-described "hatchetations." Some of the targets of her rage posted signs in their establishments that read, "All Nations Welcome Except Carrie."

Nation died in 1911. Less than a decade later, her "good intentions" were realized when the federal government attempted to accomplish with guns and police what she had so eagerly pursued with a hatchet.

Carrie Nation was not a hero. Years before she appeared on the scene, former president Rutherford B. Hayes wisely rejected the violent tactics of the temperance movement in an 1883 diary entry: "Personally I do not resort to force—not even the force of law—to advance moral reforms. I prefer education, argument, persuasion, and above all the influence of example—of fashion. Until these resources are exhausted I would not think of force."

So if not Carrie Nation, who is the real hero of this story? Not one person but many: all those Americans who *opposed* Prohibition and thereby paved the way for its repeal after almost fourteen years of futility and violence. We have much to learn from them today.

The Futility of Prohibition

It took a constitutional amendment (the Eighteenth) and a law of Congress (the Volstead Act) to outlaw the "manufacture, sale, or transportation of intoxicating liquors" in January 1920 and another constitutional amendment (the Twenty-First) to undo them in December 1933. In the intervening years, Americans paid an awful price for a fruitless effort to stamp out alcohol. No one disputes that some people will abuse just about anything, even the freedom of speech. But the answer to the sins of the irresponsible few isn't to outlaw the private, personal, and peaceful choices of the many.

Historian Lisa Andersen describes how ineffective Prohibition was:

> People who could afford the high price of smuggled liquor flocked to speakeasies and gin joints.... Working-class consumption largely moved from saloons into the home. "Bathtub gin" and moonshine took the place of mass-produced liquor, and hosts might use additives to turn grape juice into wine for their guests. Americans who sought to remain in the liquor business found ways to redistill the alcohol in perfume, paint, and carpentry supplies.... Criminal organizations profited from Americans' insatiable desire for liquor, and then defended those profits by murdering hundreds of their competitors and infiltrating legitimate businesses, labor unions, and government.

Words of Wisdom from Clarence Darrow

"As long as the world shall last there will be wrongs, and if no man objected and no man rebelled, those wrongs would last forever."

President Woodrow Wilson opposed Prohibition before it became law. He defended his administration's enforcement of it, but he and his wife took their stash of booze from the White House when he left the presidency in March 1921. His successor, Warren G. Harding, brought his own large supply with him to the White House immediately after his inauguration.

Such double standards were widely practiced, prompting gangster Al Capone to say, "When I sell liquor, it's called bootlegging; when my patrons serve it on Lake Shore Drive, it's called hospitality." Capone's rise to the pinnacle of the crime world stemmed directly from Prohibition; he happily supplied the booze while the government pummeled his competition.

Economist Mark Thornton, in a 1991 policy analysis paper for the Cato Institute, noted that Prohibition reversed what had been a gradual decline in serious crime since the late nineteenth century. During the 1920s the homicide rate increased 78 percent over the pre-Prohibition period. "More crimes were committed," Thornton wrote, "because prohibition destroys legal jobs, creates black-market violence, diverts resources from enforcement of other laws, and greatly increases the prices people have to pay for the prohibited goods."

One of Prohibition's more colorful dissenters was commentator H. L. Mencken, who wrote in 1925:

Five years of Prohibition have had, at least, this one benign effect: they have completely disposed of all the favorite arguments of the Prohibitionists. None of the great boons and usufructs that were to follow the passage of the Eighteenth Amendment has come to pass. There is not less drunkenness in the Republic, but more. There is not less crime, but more. There is not less insanity, but more. The cost of government is not smaller, but vastly greater. Respect for law has not increased, but diminished.

Mencken understood that it wasn't government's function to make war on people over their personal, private, and peaceful choices. As long as we do no harm to others, each of us possesses an inherent, natural right to our own lives and property—and that includes our bodies. Prohibition assumes *everybody* who touches the prohibited stuff deserves to be treated as a criminal, and that just isn't so. If you take a book and beat somebody over the head with it, you may rightfully be charged with assault. But if you do nothing more than read the text, even if it's a book as offensive as *The Communist Manifesto*, only a fool or a tyrant would ban the book and throw you in prison.

Honorable Resistance

Though evidence suggests that the ban did cut alcohol consumption temporarily—we'll never know by how much, because bans drive the prohibited behavior behind closed doors—the benefits of Prohibition were dwarfed by the harm it did. Those with the courage to say so and to work to change the law are the heroes in this otherwise sorry saga.

Women took lead roles in the crusade for repeal, as documented in Kenneth D. Rose's 1996 book, *American Women and the Repeal of Prohibition*. One example was M. Louise Gross, who created the New York City–based Molly Pitcher Club in 1922 to campaign for repeal.

Another was Pauline Sabin, an influential Republican Party official, who founded the Women's Organization for National Prohibition Reform. Sabin "found the hypocrisy of Prohibition intolerable," according to one biographer, and "was repelled by politicians who voted dry and then turned up at her dinner table expecting a drink."

My personal favorites among Prohibition's foes were the many jurors who simply refused to convict defendants accused of buying, selling, or drinking illegal booze. They were exercising what legal scholars term the right of "jury nullification." When jurors acquit an accused person they know is guilty of breaking the law because they object to the law itself, at least in that individual case they are "nullifying" it. Though controversial among members of the legal community, the practice commands considerable precedent in common law dating back as far as the thirteenth century.

In their highly regarded and frequently referenced 1966 book, *The American Jury*, Harry Kalven Jr. and Hans Zeisel wrote, "The Prohibition era provided the most intense example of jury revolt in recent history." They reported that the acquittal rate for liquor violations for 8,078 trials in the federal system from 1929 to 1930 was 26 percent. In the Second District of New York it was an astonishing 60 percent. Kalven and Zeisel quoted a judge's note, "Difficult generally to convict bootleggers." Another judge wrote, "A very great number of persons maintain the belief that the law against selling alcoholic drinks should not be enforced, and it is extremely difficult to get a conviction no matter how strong the evidence may be."

The typical nullification case did not involve the accused abusing alcohol and then, under the influence, doing harm to another person or his property. Jurors almost always voted to acquit in cases where there were no victims or in cases where, if there was a victim, it was the accused himself through his own voluntary choice. Those jurors were, in a way, echoing the sentiments of Henry David Thoreau: "If...the machine of government is of such a nature that it requires you to be the agent of injustice to another, then I say, break the law."

Kirsten Tynan directs the Fully Informed Jury Association (FIJA), an organization formed to educate Americans about the jury nullification concept. She brought to my attention a January 1928 *New York Times* article headlined "Jurors Go on Trial, Drank Up Evidence." The story revealed that the prosecution's main exhibit in its case against one George Beven, accused of an alcohol violation, was a pint of liquor. Left alone with the pint for three hours during deliberation, the jurors "sampled" the evidence until it was gone, claiming they did so to determine if it was in fact alcohol. They found Beven not guilty.

In honoring this heroic resistance, are we endorsing lawlessness?

In the words of the famous lawyer Clarence Darrow, "As long as the world shall last there will be wrongs, and if no man objected and no man rebelled, those wrongs would last forever."

When bad law conflicts with good conscience, nullification is an honorable option.

Prohibition Today

After nearly fourteen years of bad law and its tragedies, Prohibition was repealed on December 5, 1933—just in time for some legal Christmas cheer. Newly elected president Franklin Roosevelt had pushed for repeal mainly to shore up declining federal revenues by taxing legal alcohol. The real heroes of the repeal effort were the men and women who wrote and spoke against Prohibition, who formed organizations to educate for personal choice, and who refused to enforce the law even when judges never advised them they had that right.

What does all this imply about the wisdom of today's laws against the possession, use, or sale of the most ubiquitous illegal substance, marijuana, which results in far fewer deaths each year than swimming pool accidents do?

The evidence is stark. Our marijuana laws are a colossal and expensive failure. Practically anybody who wants the stuff can get it, easily. Ironically, those who have the toughest time securing it are those who would benefit from its pain-reducing qualities but are averse to breaking the law. The war against it is no more effective or desirable than was alcohol Prohibition.

Thanks largely to marijuana prohibition, we prop up Capone-like drug cartels with billions in artificial profits. The associated violence on both sides of the border with Mexico kills and maims thousands more in any one year than marijuana has in the past hundred years. More than forty thousand people—virtually all nonviolent offenders—are languishing in U.S. jails and prisons on marijuana charges, at an average cost to taxpayers of at least $20,000 per inmate.

What do we have to show for it all? Mostly pain, sorrow, and billions of dollars down the drain—not to mention the liberties we've lost because of property forfeitures and other intrusive police powers. Someday, thanks to those like FIJA's Kirsten Tynan who are working to enlighten us, problems of substance abuse will be widely recognized not as criminal issues but as personal and medical ones.

In recent years, juries have nullified in marijuana cases in states as diverse as New Jersey, Montana, and New Hampshire. In 2013 Reason TV interviewed a medical marijuana patient who escaped conviction and up to ten years in prison through jury nullification. The jurors who freed him from a life ruined by jail time for a victimless crime are real heroes. So are the voters who have supported legalization at the polls. And so are the many other men, women, and organizations speaking out against the insanity of present-day marijuana laws.

I salute the heroic foes of prohibitions past and present, and I'm grateful I can raise a glass of beer or wine in their honor without fear of jail time.

Lessons from Prohibition's Foes

Have the courage to resist unjust laws: Prohibition was a predictable disaster of social experimentation. The heroes were those who spoke up and organized against Prohibition, making repeal possible.

Remember that good intentions alone don't make good government policy: Even many well-intentioned government policies do more harm than good. Government shouldn't make war on people over their personal, private, and peaceful choices.

22

Four Justices

Liberty's Saving Hands

"We want a Supreme Court," declared President Franklin Roosevelt in March 1937, "which will do justice *under* the Constitution—not *over* it. In our courts, we want a government of laws and not of men."

A month earlier, the very same FDR had announced his plan to "pack" the Supreme Court with enough additional justices to accomplish precisely the opposite. The last thing FDR wanted was a court that defended the Constitution; he preferred one that would meekly sanctify the centralizing nonsense of his New Deal.

Four justices in particular drew FDR's wrath in the 1930s. They did the job they were sworn to do: uphold the Constitution as it was written against all attempts to subvert it or the liberties of the people it protected. They were respected legal scholars of the first order. Unlike Roosevelt, they didn't think it was their duty to torture the Constitution until it confessed to federal powers never dreamed of by those who designed it. Power and political expediency were not among their priorities. These four heroes were George Sutherland, Willis Van Devanter, James Clark McReynolds, and Pierce Butler.

In few law schools today are these four defended as heroes. They are commonly vilified as legal Neanderthals who stood in the way of FDR's vast expansion of federal power to deal with the Great Depression.

Progressive intellectuals in the 1930s labeled them with the epithet the "Four Horsemen"—comparing them to the biblical harbingers of the Apocalypse. But I count Sutherland, Van Devanter, McReynolds, and Butler as four of the most principled and courageous people ever appointed to the Supreme Court.

The New Deal's Attacks on the Constitution

None of these men was perfect. Sutherland defended sugar tariffs as a Utah congressman and supported much of Theodore Roosevelt's progressive agenda as a senator. Van Devanter of Indiana suffered from chronic writer's block and wrote few opinions in his twenty-six years on the court. Kentucky's McReynolds could be cantankerous and even bigoted. It's hard to find more than a minor flaw, however, in the life or writings of Minnesota's Butler—a perfect gentleman and a constitutional stalwart who cast the lone dissent in a 1927 eugenics decision upholding the right of states to sterilize forcibly the "feeble-minded."

Sutherland, Van Devanter, McReynolds, and Butler teamed up many times in the two decades they served together on the court—almost invariably to restrain the federal government in its pursuit of powers not granted to it in the Constitution. They also protected individual liberties against encroachments by state governments. In 1925 Sutherland, Van Devanter, McReynolds, Butler, and the rest of the court struck down an Oregon law that outlawed private schools and mandated attendance by all Oregon students at government schools. McReynolds wrote the opinion in that case, *Pierce v. Society of Sisters*, declaring that children were not "mere creatures of the State." The freedom to choose a private education, he wrote, was protected by the Constitution (the Fourteenth Amendment in particular).

When Franklin Roosevelt's New Deal came along, no one

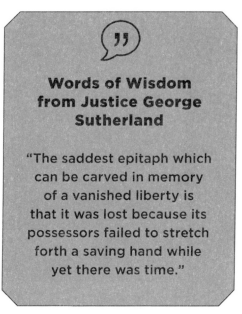

Words of Wisdom from Justice George Sutherland

"The saddest epitaph which can be carved in memory of a vanished liberty is that it was lost because its possessors failed to stretch forth a saving hand while yet there was time."

opposed its dubious legal assumptions with more vigor and impact than these four men. In academia, it's still fashionable today to support the New Deal's federal power grabs as essential and effective, but they were neither. The measures expressly intended to remedy the Depression actually prolonged it and were mostly abandoned or repudiated later. And regardless of whether they were effective, many of the New Deal programs were constitutional quackery, as Sutherland, Van Devanter, McReynolds, and Butler wisely saw.

With the Four Horsemen leading the way in 1935, the Supreme Court voted unanimously to overturn FDR's centerpiece: the National Industrial Recovery Act, a price-fixing artifice aimed at cartelizing American industry and forcing prices up at a time of widespread poverty and unemployment. The specific case involved a poultry company and whether consumers had the legal right to choose the chickens they wanted to buy. The government's lawyers claimed they didn't, prompting derisive laughter during oral arguments before the court.

In 1936 Chief Justice Charles Evans Hughes and Justice Owen Roberts joined the four in tossing out FDR's ludicrous Agricultural

Adjustment Act. The law imposed a tax on agricultural processors and used the revenue to pay for the destruction of healthy crops and cattle so as to raise prices. The court held that the tax was not constitutional because the payments from its revenues to farmers were coupled with coercive contracts. The justices couldn't find any nook or cranny in the Constitution that authorized subsidies to farmers for destroying or reducing their crops. (I can't, either.)

Justice Sutherland, who once flirted with progressive ideology, defended the Constitution in these and other cases with the ferocity of a strict constructionist. In the 1934 case of *Home Building & Loan Association v. Blaisdell*, he wrote, "If the provisions of the Constitution be not upheld when they pinch as well as when they comfort, they may as well be abandoned."

The four's reverence for the Constitution was on brilliant display in the 1936 case *Carter v. Carter Coal Company*, when, joined by a fifth justice, they refused to treat the Commerce Clause like a piece of taffy. That a commodity might in the future be sold in interstate commerce does not grant the federal government the power to regulate it before it ever leaves a state, the court ruled. The law the justices threw out required mines to pay a tax on coal to support a commission established to fix wages, prices, hours, and other elements of production and trade—a proposition so constitutionally dubious that it should have been laughed out of Congress in the first place.

Sadly, the four were outnumbered in the very important Gold Clause Cases of 1935. Two years earlier, FDR had issued an executive order demanding that American citizens surrender all gold coins, bullion, and gold certificates within a month or face penalties of $10,000 and/or up to ten years in prison. Congress followed up with a resolution that canceled all clauses in private and public contracts that called for payment in gold. In blatant disregard for private property and agreements, the court upheld the seizures by a narrow 5–4 margin. Americans would not be allowed to own gold again until 1974.

In his blistering dissent in the Gold Clause Cases decision, Justice McReynolds wrote:

Just men regard repudiation and spoliation of citizens by their sovereign with abhorrence; but we are asked to affirm that the Constitution has granted power to accomplish both. No definite delegation of such a power exists, and we cannot believe the far-seeing framers, who labored with hope of establishing justice and securing the blessings of liberty, intended that the expected government should have authority to annihilate its own obligations and destroy the very rights which they were endeavoring to protect. Not only is there no permission for such actions, they are inhibited. And no plenitude of words can conform them to our charter.

The four were pilloried in the pro-FDR media and in the progressive ivory towers of academia. Whipped up by Democratic partisans, some communities even hanged them in effigy. The four justices were the principal (and principled) figures FDR had in mind when he sneered at "those nine old men" on the Supreme Court.

But Roosevelt failed in his court-packing contrivance, intended to circumvent the Four Horsemen. Even the president's own party turned against the scheme. The proposal failed by better than a two-to-one margin in Congress.

Soon, however, Roosevelt would find openings to put his ideological allies on the court. Justice Van Devanter retired later that year; Justice Sutherland, in 1938; Justice Butler, in 1939; and Justice McReynolds, in 1941.

To Preserve Liberty

In Utah today, a think tank named for one of the four justices—George Sutherland—labors to make liberty and limited, constitutional government the lodestars of public policy in that state. Stan Rasmussen is the director of public affairs for the Sutherland Institute. He regards the organization's namesake as a man who evolved into "a devoted protector of individual freedom." Rasmussen is fond of quoting these words of Sutherland's, spoken a year before his passing in 1942:

> Good character does not consist in the mere ability to store away in the memory a collection of moral aphorisms that runs loosely off the tongue.... Character to be good must be stable—must have taken root. It is an acquisition of thought and conduct which have become habitual—so firmly fixed in the conscience, and indeed in the body itself, as to insure unhesitating rejection of an impulse to do wrong.

Perhaps it was Sutherland's emphasis on the importance of character that led him to appreciate liberty, which, I've argued, is the other side of the same coin. In his dissenting opinion in the 1937 case that upheld extraordinary coercive powers for organized labor, he penned this eloquent appeal:

> Do the people of this land...desire to preserve those [liberties] so carefully protected by the First Amendment: liberty of religious worship, freedom of speech and of the press, and the right as freemen peaceably to assemble and petition their government for a redress of grievances? If so, let them withstand all beginnings of encroachment. *For the saddest epitaph which can be carved in memory of a vanished liberty is that it was lost because its possessors failed to stretch forth a saving hand while yet there was time* [emphasis added].

George Sutherland, Willis Van Devanter, James Clark McReynolds, and Pierce Butler—four justices who endured ridicule from the highest places and from men far less principled—defended the Constitution as their oaths required. That's rare enough to earn them hero status.

Lessons from the Four Justices

Defend the Constitution even when its provisions "pinch": Some people felt that the Great Depression warranted drastic government measures, even if Franklin Roosevelt's New Deal policies might be unconstitutional (never mind that they were often of dubious economic value). But Supreme Court justices George Sutherland, Willis Van Devanter, James Clark McReynolds, and Pierce Butler refused to sanction a breach of the nation's most important governing document for the sake of ideology or convenience.

Do the job you're called to do: These four justices endured derision from FDR and his allies and even threats to their authority with Roosevelt's court-packing scheme. But rather than succumbing to the political pressure, they honored their oaths and did their jobs according to their best judgment.

Katharine Atholl

A Modern-Day Cassandra

Some people can smell a rat a mile away. Others don't notice even when the odor wafts right under their noses.

Olfactory proficiency by itself doesn't make you a hero. But if you're among the first to pick up the scent and warn others, and then you put your political future on the line to save society, you've got something that makes you heroic. C. S. Lewis wrote in *The Magician's Nephew*, "What you see and hear [and smell] depends a good deal on where you are standing: it also depends on what sort of person you are."

Katharine Stewart-Murray, Duchess of Atholl, combined courage and character with a great nose for rats. She warned the world about

Soviet communism and Hitler years before most others had recognized the threats. She had principles and the guts to stand by them.

Exposing the "Ruthless" Soviet Regime

Born of Scottish noble blood in Edinburgh in 1874, Katharine "Kitty" Ramsay was an accomplished composer and pianist. She married John Stewart-Murray in 1899 and became the Duchess of Atholl when her husband succeeded his father as the Duke of Atholl in 1917. Author Lynne Olson, in her superb book *Troublesome Young Men* (about the Tory upstarts in the 1930s who challenged their elder and leader, Prime Minister Neville Chamberlain), describes her as a "diminutive woman with large, expressive blue eyes... cultured, diffident, and unworldly, with little interest in calling attention to herself." For a time the duchess even opposed giving women the right to vote.

She was startled, then, when former prime minister David Lloyd George suggested she stand for a seat in Parliament. But with her husband's support, she agreed to run, and in 1923 she won her race. She became just the third woman elected to the House of Commons, and the first from Scotland. Soon she became the first female Conservative member of Parliament to hold ministerial office: Prime Minister Stanley Baldwin appointed her to a junior post in education.

The men in government assumed that Atholl would be quiet and do the womanly thing: whatever she was told. Even Winston Churchill snubbed her at first, telling her, "I find a woman's intrusion into the House of Commons as embarrassing as if she burst into my bathroom." Churchill would come to appreciate her greatly.

Over time, Atholl's principles deepened, and her courage blossomed. In 1935 she resigned from the leadership position of whip for the Conservative Party largely over the India Bill, believing that it did not provide adequate safeguards for peace and democracy in the subcontinent. She also spoke out against what she derisively labeled the government's "national socialist tendencies" in its domestic agenda.

**Words of Wisdom
from Katharine Atholl**

"[I stand] for a great cause,
the particular essence of
which rested on freedom
and goodwill—freedom
for the fullest possible
development of private
initiative and industry, as
opposed to a system that
would give the State control;
freedom of career for the
development of the individual
as opposed to a system
which would make for a rigid
uniformity in all persons."

The first big rat to catch Atholl's attention was in Moscow. After the Bolshevik Revolution, the Soviet experiment attracted naive acolytes in the West. Reporter Lincoln Steffens famously wrote after his 1919 visit to the USSR, "I have seen the future, and it works." One of the worst of the "useful idiots" was *New York Times* reporter Walter Duranty, who, at the height of the Stalin-induced famine in Ukraine that killed millions, denied that there was a hunger problem.

The Duchess of Atholl was no such fool.

In 1931 Atholl published *The Conscription of a People*, a blistering, well-documented indictment of the savage collectivization of life in the Soviet Union. She wrote:

> Russia has carried through revolution on a scale which knows no parallel, and which, even after thirteen years, is as ruthless as in its early days. She has undermined marriage and is rapidly breaking up family life. She wages ceaseless war on all religion. She is responsible for the most comprehensive and continuous experiment in the nationalization of industry, banking and trade that has ever been seen.

Atholl's book was one of the earliest and most detailed critiques of the communist regime from a high-level British official. Forced labor, the liquidation of the kulaks, mass seizures of property, an extensive secret police network, and an unprecedented diversion of resources to the military meant one thing: the Bolsheviks were a menace to their own people and a growing threat to world peace.

The duchess decried the British government's extension of credit to Moscow. "Can those in any country who value liberty regard such a position with equanimity?" she asked. "Are the citizens of the United Kingdom in particular to tolerate any longer the guaranteeing by taxpayers' money of a system so utterly repugnant to British traditions?"

The rats in Moscow were alarmed at Atholl's denunciations. Who was this Scottish Cassandra who dared so publicly to question the subsidies coming their way from the government of her own party? (In Greek mythology, Cassandra was given the gift of prophecy but was cursed never to be believed. In *The Fall of Troy*, by Quintus Smyrnaeus, Cassandra desperately tried to warn the Trojan people about the peril of a certain large wooden horse.)

Denouncing Appeasement

After 1933, Atholl's wrath turned against the rats in Berlin. When she read Hitler's *Mein Kampf* in 1935, she entertained no illusions about where the führer was headed. "Never can a modern statesman have made so startlingly clear to his reader his ambitions," she later said.

In Lynne Olson's words, this formerly "diffident" woman was becoming "the boldest Tory rebel of all." Many now think of Winston Churchill as the sage who opposed Neville Chamberlain's policy of appeasement, but Atholl helped stiffen his spine. She sent Churchill both the original German edition of *Mein Kampf* and the English translation. The translation, she showed him, was a whitewash—barely a third the length of the German original, cutting out what Olson calls "Hitler's most inflammatory statements, particularly his expressions of hatred for Jews." Atholl sent Churchill similar passages from Hitler's speeches that had not been reported outside Germany.

Those "troublesome young men" in Chamberlain's Conservative Party—including Churchill, Anthony Eden, and Harold Macmillan—did oppose appeasement, but at first they focused exclusively on Hitler. They sought to placate Mussolini in Italy and Franco in Spain. Atholl saw all fascist dictators the same way she saw all communist dictators: as evil men not to be trusted, let alone subsidized. She was a constant thorn in the side of men in power who wanted to cut deals with unsavory thugs. Biographer Sheila Hetherington notes that by 1935, Atholl "had become seriously worried not only about Britain's defences, but about the attitude of mind of the country's leaders: their supineness, their complacency, their willingness to overlook the brutality of fascism and, while making public speeches deploring the actions of the dictators, making no move to deter them and even making friendly overtures to them."

Chamberlain's September 1938 Munich Agreement with Hitler has become synonymous with appeasement: it allowed Hitler to incorporate forcibly the Sudetenland (a Czech region along the border with Germany) into the Third Reich. But when Chamberlain waved the agreement on the tarmac on returning to London and declared, "Peace in our time," much of the world breathed a sigh of relief. War seemed to have been averted. Atholl's husband and others strongly advised her to endorse the Munich accord. The duchess not only refused to do so; she also wrote and widely distributed a pamphlet that castigated the agreement.

Prime Minister Chamberlain reacted furiously. He strong-armed the local Conservative Party officials in Scotland to select a new candidate for Parliament to replace Atholl. She resigned from the party and announced she would run as an Independent in the special by-election set for December 1938. The country's attention was riveted by the fierce campaign that ensued. The prime minister saw to it that Atholl's opponent received showers of cash and endorsements, and he employed every trick possible to stop the duchess. In the words of one historian, it was "one of the dirtiest by-election campaigns of modern times."

Facing threats from Chamberlain and the party whip, even anti-appeasement Conservatives wouldn't go to Scotland to campaign for the duchess. Churchill first accepted an invitation to speak on her behalf but then, under pressure, rescinded. As Olson reports in her book, he instead sent a letter of endorsement that she distributed before the voting. Churchill wrote:

> You are no doubt opposed by many Conservatives as loyal and patriotic as yourself, but the fact remains that outside our island, your defeat at this moment would be relished by the enemies of Britain and of freedom in every part of the world. It would be widely accepted as another sign that Great Britain...no longer has the spirit and willpower to confront the tyrannies and cruel persecutions which have darkened this age.

She lost by a heartbreakingly slim margin. Chamberlain was delighted, even if the razor-thin margin of victory hardly counted as a ringing endorsement of his appeasement policy.

When Hitler invaded Poland less than nine months later, Kitty Atholl was vindicated. A humiliated Chamberlain sulked through the remaining few months of his tenure.

Sounding the Alarm

The Duchess of Atholl never returned to government. She spent the war years working mightily to relieve the awful conditions of European refugees. She died in 1960 at age eighty-five.

Hardly remembered today, Katharine Atholl smelled danger and said so, years before the elite of her own political party mustered similar courage. She took brave stands for principle and for her nation's security even when those positions threatened her career.

How different might history have been if there were more people like her?

Lessons from Katharine Atholl

See something, say something: Katharine Atholl never harbored any illusions as to what the world was facing from Nazi Germany or the Soviet Union. She had the courage to speak out about the threats even when doing so threatened her own career. Putting your principles ahead of your self-interest is easier said than done; Atholl models how to put principles into practice.

Enlist allies in your cause: Winston Churchill is honored today as an implacable foe of Hitler and of appeasement. Atholl, now little remembered, was ahead even of Churchill in this regard, and she was wise enough to enlist him and others in the cause of decrying the Nazi threat. The copies of *Mein Kampf* she sent him proved eye-opening for Churchill.

24

Jesse Owens

"Character Makes the Difference When It's Close"

J ames Cleveland "Jesse" Owens famously won four gold medals at the 1936 Olympic Games in Berlin, Germany. But he did more than win races: this son of a sharecropper and grandson of a slave fought a lifelong struggle against racism in his own country and almost single-handedly exploded the Nazi myth of Aryan supremacy.

At the time of Owens's death in 1980 at age sixty-six, President Jimmy Carter paid this tribute to him:

> Perhaps no athlete better symbolized the human struggle against tyranny, poverty, and racial bigotry. His personal triumphs as a world-class athlete and record holder were the prelude to a

career devoted to helping others. His work with young athletes, as an unofficial ambassador overseas, and a spokesman for freedom are a rich legacy to his fellow Americans.

Carter's words were especially fitting in light of an unfortunate fact in Owens's life: unforgivably, a previous American president had given him the brush-off.

Dedication and Determination

Born in Alabama in 1913, James Owens at the age of nine moved with his family to the town in Ohio that bore his middle name, Cleveland. His first school teacher there asked him his name. With a deep southern twang he replied, "J. C. Owens." She heard "Jesse," so that's what she wrote down. The name stuck for the next fifty-seven years.

Owens displayed his talent for track and field early on. He broke junior high school records in the high jump and broad jump. In high school he won every major track event in which he competed, tying or breaking world records in the 100-yard and 220-yard dashes and setting a new world record in the broad jump. Universities showered him with scholarship offers, but he turned them all down and chose Ohio State, which wasn't extending track scholarships at the time. Owens loved Ohio, the state that had been his home since age nine, and his junior and senior high school coaches helped sell him on Ohio State.

Imagine it. You come from a relatively poor family. You could go to any number of colleges for next to nothing, but you pick one you have to pay for. At twenty-one, you have a wife to support as well. So what do you do? If you are Jesse Owens, you work your way through school as a gas station attendant, a waiter, a night elevator operator, a library assistant, even a page in the Ohio legislature.

Owens was the living embodiment of advice he gave others: "We all have dreams. But in order to make dreams come into reality, it takes an awful lot of determination, dedication, self-discipline, and effort."

At Ohio State he not only had to juggle his work, studies, on-field practice, and family; he also needed to battle racial discrimination. Ohio in the mid-1930s wasn't a paradise of racial equality. The university required Owens and other black athletes to live together off campus. They had to order carry out or eat at "black-only" restaurants and stay in segregated hotels when traveling with the team.

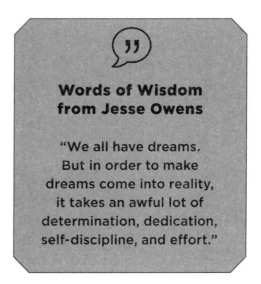

Words of Wisdom from Jesse Owens

"We all have dreams. But in order to make dreams come into reality, it takes an awful lot of determination, dedication, self-discipline, and effort."

Through it all he continued to set records. In fact, during the 1935 Big Ten Championships, he set or tied four world records in only forty-five minutes. And he did it with an injured back; he had to lobby his coach just to be able to compete.

A little more than a year later, Owens would become internationally famous for his exploits at the Berlin Olympics. But that spectacular day at the Big Ten Championships endures as well. *Sports Illustrated* called it "the greatest single-day performance in athletic history," saying that Owens's achievements that May afternoon have "no parallel" in any sport.

Triumph at Berlin

The eyes of the world were focused on Berlin in early August 1936. Five years earlier—before the Nazis came to power—the German capital had been selected as the site for the 1936 Summer Olympics. An effort to boycott them because of Hitler's racism fizzled. It would be a few more years before events convinced the world of the socialist dictator's evil intentions.

Jesse Owens entered the competition with Americans thrilled at his prospects but wondering how Hitler would react if "Aryan superiority" fell short of his expectations. But Owens didn't go to Berlin with a political axe to grind. "I wanted no part of politics," he said. "And I wasn't in Berlin to compete against any one athlete. The purpose of the Olympics, anyway, was to do your best. As I'd learned long ago…, the only victory that counts is the one over yourself."

If a hundred years from now only one name is remembered among those who competed in Berlin, it will surely be that of Jesse Owens.

Owens won the 100-meter sprint, the long jump, the 200-meter sprint, and the 4 x 100 sprint relay. He became the first American to claim four gold medals in a single Olympiad. In the process, he set or equaled three world records.

Legend has it that Hitler snubbed Owens. That's not quite true: Hitler didn't shake Owens's hand, but contemporaneous accounts show (and Owens himself confirmed) that the American athlete waved at Hitler and Hitler waved back. Still, this did not mean the führer suddenly admired Owens or other African American athletes. According to fellow Nazi Albert Speer, Hitler was "highly annoyed" by Owens's victories and said that blacks should never be allowed to compete in the Olympics again. Jeremy Schaap, in his account of Owens's performance at the 1936 games, notes that the American athlete "stood up to [the Nazis] at their own Olympics, refuting their venomous theories with his awesome deeds."

A side story of Owens's Berlin experience was the friendship he made with a German competitor named Luz Long. A decent man by any measure, Long exhibited no racial animosity and even offered tips to Owens that the American found helpful during the games. Of Long, Owens would later tell an interviewer: "It took a lot of courage for him to befriend me in front of Hitler…. You can melt down all the medals and cups I have and they wouldn't be a plating on the 24-karat friendship I felt for Luz Long at that moment. Hitler must have gone crazy watching us embrace. The sad part of the story is I never saw Long again. He was killed in World War II."

Snubbed by FDR

Back home, ticker-tape parades feted Owens in New York City and Cleveland. Hundreds of thousands of Americans came out to cheer him. Letters, phone calls, and telegrams streamed in from around the world to congratulate him. From one important man, however, no word of recognition ever came. As Owens later put it, "Hitler didn't snub me; it was our president who snubbed me. The president didn't even send a telegram."

Franklin Roosevelt, leader of a major political party with deep roots in racism, couldn't bring himself to utter a word of support, even though he hosted a number of white Olympians at the White House. The snubbing may have been a factor in Owens's decision to campaign for Republican Alf Landon in the 1936 presidential election.

"It all goes so fast, and character makes the difference when it's close," Owens once said about athletic competition. He could have taught FDR a few lessons in character, but the president never gave him the chance. Owens wouldn't be invited to the White House for almost twenty years—not until Dwight Eisenhower named him "Ambassador of Sports" in 1955.

Life after the Olympics wasn't always kind to Jesse Owens. When he wanted to earn money from commercial endorsements, athletic officials yanked his amateur status. Then the commercial offers dried up. He was forced to file for bankruptcy. When a dinner was held in his honor at New York's Waldorf-Astoria Hotel, Owens felt the sting of racial discrimination again: he was forced to take the freight elevator to his own celebration.

But for the last thirty years of his life, until he died in 1980 of lung cancer, he found helping underprivileged teenagers to be even more personally satisfying than his Olympic gold medals. In the 1950s he served on the Illinois Youth Commission and organized the Junior Olympic Games for teenage athletes. The website of the Jesse Owens Trust notes that Owens "was an inspirational speaker, highly sought after to address youth groups, professional organizations, civic meetings, sports banquets, PTAs, church organizations, brotherhood and black history programs, as well as high school and college commencements and ceremonies."

Ten years after his death, Owens was awarded one of America's highest civilian honors, the Congressional Gold Medal. Presenting the medal to Owens's widow, President George H. W. Bush recognized her husband's "humanitarian contributions in the race of life." Owens was not simply an Olympic hero, Bush said; he was "an American hero every day of his life."

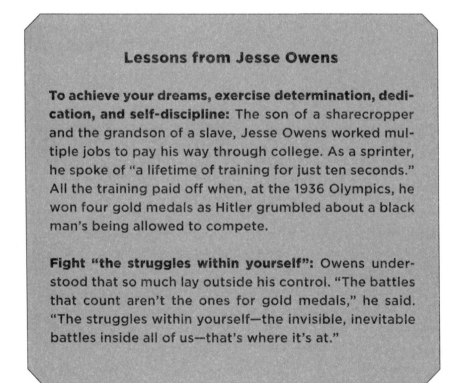

Lessons from Jesse Owens

To achieve your dreams, exercise determination, dedication, and self-discipline: The son of a sharecropper and the grandson of a slave, Jesse Owens worked multiple jobs to pay his way through college. As a sprinter, he spoke of "a lifetime of training for just ten seconds." All the training paid off when, at the 1936 Olympics, he won four gold medals as Hitler grumbled about a black man's being allowed to compete.

Fight "the struggles within yourself": Owens understood that so much lay outside his control. "The battles that count aren't the ones for gold medals," he said. "The struggles within yourself—the invisible, inevitable battles inside all of us—that's where it's at."

25

Nicholas Winton

The Humblest Hero

The truest hero does not think of himself as one, never advertises himself as such, and does not for fame or fortune perform the acts that make him a hero. Nor does he wait for government to act if he senses an opportunity to fix a problem himself.

On July 27, 2006, in the quiet countryside of Maidenhead, England, my colleague Ben Stafford and I spent several hours with a true hero: Sir Nicholas Winton. His friends called him "Nicky."

In the fall of 1938, many Europeans were lulled into complacency by British prime minister Neville Chamberlain, who thought he had pacified Adolf Hitler by handing him a large chunk of Czechoslovakia at Munich in late September. Winston Churchill was among the wise and prescient who believed otherwise. So was Nicholas Winton, then a twenty-nine-year-old London stockbroker.

Having made many business trips to Germany, Winton was well aware that Jews were being arrested, harassed, and beaten there. The infamous Kristallnacht of November 9–10, 1938—in which Nazi thugs destroyed Jewish synagogues, homes, and businesses while murdering scores of Jews across Germany—laid to rest any doubts about Hitler's deadly intentions. The führer's increasingly aggressive anti-Semitism and Germany's occupation of the Sudetenland in October 1938 spurred a tide of predominantly Jewish refugees. Thousands fled to as-yet-unoccupied Czechoslovakia, with many settling into makeshift refugee camps in appalling conditions.

Winton had planned a year-end ski trip to Switzerland with a friend, but at the last moment the friend convinced him to come to Prague instead because he had "something urgent to show him"—the refugee problem. When Winton visited the freezing camps, what he saw aroused deep feelings of compassion within him: orphans and children whose parents had been arrested, and families desperate to get at least their children out of harm's way. Jewish parents who were lifetime residents and citizens in the country were also anxious to send their children to safety. They, like Winton, sensed that the Nazis wouldn't rest until they had taken the rest of the country, and perhaps all of Europe as well. The thought of what could happen to them if the Nazis devoured the rest of Czechoslovakia was enough to inspire this good man to action.

It would have been easy to assume that there was nothing a lone foreigner could do to assist so many trapped families. Winton could have ignored the situation and resumed his vacation in Switzerland, stepping back into his comfortable life. Surely most other people in his shoes would have walked away. But despite the talk of "peace in our time," Winton knew that these refugees needed help, and quickly.

The next steps he took ultimately saved 669 children from death in Nazi concentration camps.

Swinging into Action

Getting all the children who sought safety to a country that would accept them seemed an impossible challenge. Back in London, Winton wrote to governments around the world, pleading for an open door, only to be rejected by all (including the United States) but two: Sweden and Great Britain. He

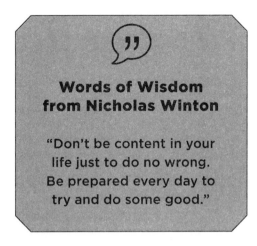

Words of Wisdom from Nicholas Winton

"Don't be content in your life just to do no wrong. Be prepared every day to try and do some good."

assembled a small group of volunteers to assist with the effort. Even his mother pitched in.

The London team's counterpart in Prague was a Brit named Trevor Chadwick. He gathered information from parents who wanted their children out, then forwarded the details to Winton, who used every possible channel in his search for foster homes. Five thousand children were on the list. At no charge, British newspapers published Winton's advertisements to stir interest and highlight the urgent need for foster parents. When enough homes could be found for a group of children, Winton submitted the necessary paperwork to the Home Office. He assisted Chadwick in organizing the rail and ship transportation needed to get them to Britain.

Winton also took the lead in raising the funds to pay for the operation. The expenses included the 50 British pounds the Home Office required for each child (the equivalent of $3,500 in today's dollars) to cover any future costs of repatriation. But hopes that the danger would pass and the children could be returned soon evaporated.

Picture the scene at the Prague railway station: Anguished parents loaded their children onto trains and said what would be, for most, their final good-byes. Boys and girls, many younger than five, peered out the windows wondering about their uncertain future. None of the children knew whether they would ever be reunited with their families.

The first twenty of "Winton's children" left Prague on March 14, 1939. Hitler's troops overran all of Czechoslovakia the very next day, but the volunteers kept working, sometimes forging documents to slip the children past the Germans. By the time World War II broke out on September 1, the rescue effort had transported 669 children out of the country in eight separate groups.

That day, a ninth batch of 250 more children—the largest group of all—was stuck on the train at the Prague station; the outbreak of war prompted the Nazis to stop all departures. Sadly, none of those children lived to see the Allied victory less than six years later. Pitifully few of the parents did either.

While we celebrate the 669 children Winton saved, Nicky's conscience was always stung by the 250 who almost made it but didn't. Hundreds more were on his list waiting for a chance to get out.

Humility

So why did Nicky Winton do it?

It certainly was not for the plaudits it might bring him. He never told anyone about his efforts for a half century. Not until 1988, when his wife stumbled across a musty box of records and a scrapbook while cleaning their attic, did the public learn of Winton's story. The scrapbook, a memento put together by his volunteers when the operation shut down, was filled with documents and pictures of Czech children.

The year the scrapbook was discovered, a television show seen across Britain, *That's Life*, told the Winton story to a large audience and brought Nicky together with many of his "children" for the first time since those horrific days of 1939. For all the intervening decades, the children and the families who took them in knew little more than that some kind soul, some guardian angel, had saved their lives. But for two decades after that show, Nicky was in regular correspondence with, and was often visited by, many of them—a source of joy and comfort, especially after his wife, Grete, passed away in 1999.

Vera Gissing, one of the children Winton saved, put the rescue mission in perspective: "Of the 15,000 Czech Jewish children taken to the camps, only a handful survived. Winton had saved a major part of my generation of Czech Jews."

Vera's story is an especially poignant one. She was ten years old when she left Prague on the fifth train on June 30, 1939. Two of her cousins were on the ninth train that never made it to freedom. Her mother died of typhus two days after the liberation of the concentration camp to which she had been sent. Her father was shot in a Nazi death march in December 1944. Vera has no doubt about her own fate had it not been for Nicholas Winton. Like the other "Winton children" who came to know him, Vera reminded him frequently that she owed her very life to him.

So humble was Nicky Winton that others had to tell him, over his objections, just what an uncommon man he was.

Interviews with many of the adult "Winton children" have revealed a deep appreciation not only for the man whose initiative saved them but also for living life to its fullest. Many expressed a life-long desire to help others as a way of honoring the loved ones who made the painful choice to trust the young stockbroker from Britain. "We understand how precious life is," Vera told us. "We wanted to give something back to our natural parents so their memory would live on."

Years after coming to Britain, Vera asked her foster father, "Why did you choose me?" His reply sums up the spirit of the good people who gave homes to the 669: "I knew I could not save the world and I knew I could not stop war from coming, but I knew I could save one human soul."

"I Thought I Could Help"

I kept returning to the same question: What compelled this man to take on a challenge almost everyone else ignored?

I asked Nicky that very question at our meeting in 2006, the first of many over the next nine years.

In a matter-of-fact fashion, Winton replied, "Because it was the right thing to do and I thought I could help."

Nicky Winton was a quiet, humble man—a reminder of Aristotle's "great-souled man." In the *Nicomachean Ethics* Aristotle said that the great-souled person is "the sort to benefit others but is ashamed to receive a benefaction...[and] is disposed to return a benefaction with a greater one." You never heard boasting from Nicky, no words designed to put any special focus on what he did. One can't help feeling drawn to a man for whom doing good for its own sake seems to come so naturally.

In *The Power of Good*, an International Emmy Award–winning documentary from Czech producer Matej Mináč, Nicky said he kept quiet about the rescue mission because "it was such a small part of my life." The operation spanned only eight months, while he was still working at the stock exchange, and it was prior to his marriage. Still, to Ben Stafford and me, the explanation seemed inadequate. We pressed him on the point.

"When the war started and the transports stopped," Nicky explained, "I immediately went into the RAF [Royal Air Force], where I stayed for the next five years. When peace came, what was a thirty-five-year-old man to do, traverse the country looking for boys and girls?" At the end of the war, Nicky was busy restarting his own life. What he did to save so many others just six years earlier was behind him, and over. For all that he knew, the children might have returned to their homeland (as some did). "Wherever they were, I had good reason to assume they were safe and cared for," he said. Indeed, among their ranks in later life would be doctors, nurses, therapists, teachers, musicians, artists, writers, pilots, ministers, scientists, engineers, entrepreneurs, and even a member of the British Parliament. Today they and their children, grandchildren, and great-grandchildren number more than six thousand.

That's six thousand people who owe their lives to Nicky Winton.

"British Schindler"

When news of Winton's heroic acts finally spread, governments honored Nicky with dozens of awards and recognition he never sought. The queen conferred a knighthood upon him. The Czech Republic recognized him with its highest honor. President George W. Bush wrote him in early 2006, expressing gratitude for his "courage and compassion." Winton became known as the "British Schindler" (after the German Oskar Schindler, the subject of the Academy Award–winning film *Schindler's List*).

In our effort to add to the chorus of friends and admirers who wanted Nicky Winton to understand just how we felt about him, Ben Stafford and I told him this: "You did not save only 669 children. Your story will elevate the moral eloquence of lending a loving hand when lives are at stake. Someday, somewhere, perhaps another man or woman will confront a similar situation and will rise to the occasion because of your example. This is why the world must know what you did and why we think of you as a hero even if you do not."

Winton's daughter, Barbara, said it well when she wrote of her father, "His wish is not that his story should promote hero worship but that, if anything, it might inspire people to recognise that they too can act ethically in the world and make a positive difference to the lives of others."

And that's exactly what Nicky Winton's story does. In a world wracked by violence and cruelty, his selfless acts in 1939 should give us all hope. It's more than a little comfort to know that in our midst are men and women like Nicky Winton whose essential decency can, and did, triumph over evil. Winton often shared his motto, which should inspire us all: "If it's not impossible, there must be a way to do it."

In the nine years I knew Nicky Winton personally, I visited him many times. Friends I would bring with me were in awe of the man, who never thought of himself as anything special. My last visit was to mark his 106th birthday in May 2015. He passed away two months later. I'll never forget him; nor will countless others.

Lessons from Nicholas Winton

Remember that character not only enriches lives; sometimes it can save them, too: Nicholas Winton rescued people in a desperate situation. He didn't save those children to earn personal fame or fortune; he did it because that's what good people of solid character do almost by second nature.

Don't simply "do no wrong"; "try and do some good": More than 6,000 people owe their lives to this one humble man. Winton didn't stop at expressing compassion for the plight of the Jewish refugees he saw; he swung into action, organizing voluntary efforts that saved 669 children from the Nazis.

26

Witold Pilecki

Bravery Beyond Measure

In this great mortuary of the half-living—where nearby someone was wheezing his final breath; someone else was dying;
another was struggling out of bed only to fall over onto the floor;
another was throwing off his blankets, or talking in a fever to his
dear mother and shouting or cursing someone out; [while still
others were] refusing to eat, or demanding water, in a fever and
trying to jump out of the window, arguing with the doctor or
asking for something—I lay thinking that I still had the strength
to understand everything that was going on and take it calmly
in my stride.

That was on a relatively *good* day at the infamous Auschwitz concentration camp in 1942, in the words of the only person ever known to have volunteered to be a prisoner there. His name was Witold Pilecki. His story is one of history's most amazing accounts of boundless courage amid bottomless inhumanity.

Powerful emotions gripped me when I first learned of Pilecki. I felt rage toward the despicable regimes that put this honorable man through hell. I welled up with admiration for how he dealt with it all. Here you have a story that depicts both the worst and the best in men.

To label Pilecki a "hero" seems hopelessly inadequate.

Resistance

Olonets is a small town northeast of Saint Petersburg, Russia, seven hundred miles from present-day Poland. It's where Witold Pilecki was born in 1901, but his family was not there by choice. Four decades earlier, when many Poles lived under Russian occupation, the czarist government in Moscow forcibly resettled the Pileckis in Olonets for their part in an uprising.

At the conclusion of World War I, Poland was reconstituted as an independent nation for the first time since 1795, but it immediately became embroiled in war with Lenin's Russia. Pilecki joined the fight against the Bolsheviks when he was seventeen, first on the front and then from behind enemy lines. For two years he fought gallantly and was twice awarded the prestigious Cross of Valor.

In the eighteen years between the end of the Polish-Russian war in 1921 and the beginning of World War II, Pilecki settled down, married, and fathered two children with his wife, Maria. He rebuilt and farmed his family's estate, became an amateur painter, and volunteered for community and Christian charities—work that earned him the Silver Cross of Merit. And, after extensive officer training, he earned the rank of second lieutenant in the Polish army reserves. He probably thought his combat days were over.

But in August 1939 Hitler and Stalin secretly agreed to divide Poland between them. On September 1 the Nazis attacked the country from the west, and two weeks later the Soviets invaded from the east. The world was at war again—and so was Pilecki.

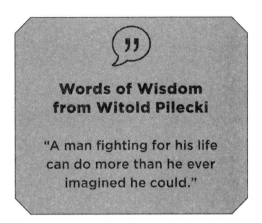

Words of Wisdom from Witold Pilecki

"A man fighting for his life can do more than he ever imagined he could."

Pilecki and Jan Włodarkiewicz cofounded the Secret Polish Army (*Tajna Armia Polska*). This resistance force and other elements of a growing underground movement carried out numerous raids against both Nazi and Soviet forces. In September 1940 Pilecki proposed a daring plan that in hindsight appears nearly unimaginable: he would arrange to be arrested in the hope that the Nazis, instead of executing him, would send him to Auschwitz, where he could gather information and form a resistance group from the inside.

If he could survive arrest, Pilecki figured, Auschwitz would probably be where the Germans incarcerated him. It was nearby (in southern Poland), and many Polish resistance fighters were imprisoned there. It wasn't yet the death camp for Jews that it would soon become, but there were murmurings of executions and brutality that the Polish resistance wanted to investigate so they could inform the world.

On September 19, Pilecki kissed his wife and two young children good-bye. Equipped with forged identity papers and a new name, he walked into a Nazi roundup of some two thousand civilians. Two days and a few beatings later, he was Auschwitz inmate number 4859.

A Dangerous Game

Viktor Frankl, an Auschwitz survivor, had men like Pilecki in mind when he wrote in his powerful book *Man's Search for Meaning*:

The way in which a man accepts his fate and all the suffering it entails, the way in which he takes up his cross, gives him ample opportunity—even under the most difficult circumstances—to add a deeper meaning to his life. It may remain brave, dignified and unselfish. Or in the bitter fight for self-preservation he may forget his human dignity and become no more than an animal. Here lies the chance for a man either to make use of or to forgo the opportunities of attaining the moral values that a difficult situation may afford him. And this decides whether he is worthy of his sufferings or not.

Fired by a determination that almost defies description, Pilecki made the most of every opportunity during his thirty-month imprisonment at Auschwitz. Despite bouts of typhus and pneumonia, lice infestations, stomach ailments, backbreaking toil hauling rocks, extremes of heat and cold, relentless hunger, and cruelties at the hands of German guards, he formed an underground resistance group, the Union of Military Organization (*Związek Organizacji Wojskowej*, or ZOW). His initial reports of conditions within Auschwitz were smuggled out and reached Britain in November 1940, just two months after his detention began. Using a radio transmitter that he and his fellow ZOW conspirators built, in 1942 he broadcast information that convinced the Allies the Nazis were engaged in genocide on an unprecedented scale. What became known as "Witold's Report" was the first comprehensive eyewitness account of the Holocaust.

"The game which I was now playing in Auschwitz was dangerous," Pilecki later wrote. "This sentence does not really convey the reality; in fact, I had gone far beyond what people in the real world would consider dangerous." Even that is an understatement. He was surrounded by a camp staff of seven thousand Nazi SS troops, each of whom possessed life-and-death power over every inmate. It was a hell on earth—one where no moral rules applied.

More than two million people died at Auschwitz. As many as eight thousand per day were gassed with the deadly chemical Zyklon-B, while others died of starvation or disease, from forced labor, or through hideous "medical" experimentation. Smoke from the ovens that burned the corpses could be seen and smelled for miles. Pilecki saw it, wrote about it, broadcast news of it, and even prepared for a general uprising of inmates against it—all under the noses of his captors.

By spring 1943, the Germans knew that an extensive resistance network was at work in Auschwitz. Many ZOW members had been identified and executed, but Pilecki's identity as the ringleader hadn't yet been discovered. Then, on the night of Easter Sunday 1943, Pilecki accomplished what only 143 other people in the history of Auschwitz ever could. He escaped, bringing with him incriminating documents that he and two fellow inmates had stolen from the Germans.

Going Undercover Again

If this were the end of the story, Witold Pilecki would already be a major figure in the history of World War II. Incredibly, there's more to tell—and it's every bit as stunning as what you've read so far.

Avoiding detection, Pilecki made his way from Auschwitz to Warsaw, a journey of some two hundred miles. There he reestablished connections with the underground in time to assume a commanding role in the Warsaw Uprising, the largest single military offensive undertaken by any European resistance movement in World War II.

For sixty-three days fighting raged between the Polish resistance and Nazi forces. No one came to the rescue of the brave Poles—not even the Soviets, who by then had broken ties with Hitler's Germany. The Soviet army had been advancing from the east but halted just short of Warsaw and watched the slaughter. The city was demolished, the rebellion was put down, and Pilecki found himself in a German POW camp for the remaining months of the war. If the Nazis had realized who he was, summary execution surely would have followed.

Germany's surrender in May 1945 resulted in the immediate liberation of its prisoners. For Pilecki in particular, it meant a brief respite from conflict and confinement. Stationed in Italy as part of the Second Polish Corps, he wrote a personal account of his time at Auschwitz.

But as the summer turned into fall, it was becoming apparent that the Soviets were not planning to leave Poland. In October, Pilecki accepted yet another undercover assignment—to go back to Poland and gather evidence of growing Soviet atrocities. His activities led the pro-Soviet Polish puppet regime to mark him as an enemy of the state.

In May 1947, two years to the day after Nazi Germany capitulated, Witold Pilecki's cover was blown. He was arrested and tortured for months before a sham public trial in May 1948, where he was found guilty of espionage and given a death sentence.

His last words before his execution on May 25 were "Long live free Poland!" He was forty-seven.

"Beacon of Hope"

Are you wondering why you've never heard of this man before?

For decades the leaders of the postwar, Soviet-installed Polish regime buried information about Pilecki. They couldn't recount his anti-Nazi activities without telling of his anticommunist work as well. The communist government monitored Pilecki's family for decades, forbidding anyone from mentioning his name in public.

But the fall of the Iron Curtain brought the release of previously classified or suppressed documents, including Pilecki's complete reports. His superhuman exploits are finally becoming known around the world. American film producer David Aaron Gray began working on a movie about Pilecki's life.

Jarek Garlinski, introducing his English translation of Pilecki's 1945 report (published as *The Auschwitz Volunteer: Beyond Bravery*), summarizes the extraordinary character of Witold Pilecki:

> Endowed with great physical resilience and courage, he showed remarkable presence of mind and common sense in quite appall-

ing circumstances, and a complete absence of self-pity. While most inmates of Auschwitz not slated for immediate death were barely able to survive, he had enough reserves of strength and determination left to help others and to build up an underground resistance organization within the camp. Not only that, he managed to keep a clear head at all times and recognize what he needed to do in order to stay alive.

Pilecki's reports from the death camp, Garlinski writes, did more than advance Allied intelligence against the Nazis. They also represented a "beacon of hope"—demonstrating that "even in the midst of so much cruelty and degradation there were those who held to the basic virtues of honesty, compassion, and courage."

In March 2016 I visited Witold Pilecki's eighty-five-year-old son, Andrzej, in his flat in Warsaw. "What makes you happy these days?" I asked. His response: "My father's memory, which finally the world is coming to know."

Lessons from Witold Pilecki

Have the courage to resist oppression: Courage is indispensable to the preservation of liberty. The world is full of people who would be happy to take your liberty—and full of timid people who would let that happen. Witold Pilecki was not timid. He volunteered to go to Auschwitz, the notorious Nazi concentration camp.

Hold fast to your virtues: Pilecki's story underscores the importance of what one commentator calls "the basic virtues of honesty, compassion, and courage." Amid the horrors of Auschwitz, Pilecki retained "the strength to understand everything that was going on and take it calmly in [his] stride."

27

Anne Frank

Gratitude in Adversity

German-born Anne Frank is surely the most unusual bestselling teenage author of the twentieth century. She penned but one volume, a diary, while hiding from the Nazis during the German occupation of the Netherlands.

"How wonderful it is," she wrote in that tiny hideaway, "that no one has to wait, but can start right now to gradually change the world."

Imagine it. Living each day for two years crammed in a secret annex behind a bookcase, knowing that without notice you might be found and hauled off to near-certain death at a concentration camp. Barely a teenager, she managed to write those words and many other remarkable passages before she and her family were discovered in

August 1944. They were sent to the Bergen-Belsen camp, where Anne died in March 1945, three months before her sixteenth birthday and only a month before the Allies liberated the camps.

How is it possible for a youngster to see so much light in a dark world, to find within herself so much hope and optimism amid horror? What insight! What power! That's been the magic of Anne Frank for the past seven decades.

The Diary

When Anne was four, her parents fled Germany. That was in 1933, the year the Nazis came to power. The Franks, who were Jewish, sought refuge in Amsterdam but were trapped there when Hitler occupied the Netherlands in May 1940. Two years later, with persecution of Jews escalating, they went into hiding.

Eight days into her diary, on June 20, 1942, Anne wrote this reflective note about her undertaking: "Writing in a diary is a really strange experience for someone like me. Not only because I've never written anything before, but also because it seems to me that later on neither I nor anyone else will be interested in the musings of a thirteen-year-old schoolgirl."

Little did she know that she would be immortalized once her writings were found and published after the war as *The Diary of a Young Girl*. That's not only because of her remarkable eloquence at such a young age but also because of her unconquerably positive attitude. It was one of optimism, hope, service to others, and, perhaps most important of all, *gratitude* for the good she saw in a war-torn world.

This entry from April 5, 1944, just four months before she penned the last thing she would ever write, will touch almost anybody's heart: "I don't want to have lived in vain like most people. I want to be useful or bring enjoyment to all people, even those I've never met."

Her diary is full of such uplifting sentiments. One would expect to find endless tales about the privations and claustrophobia of

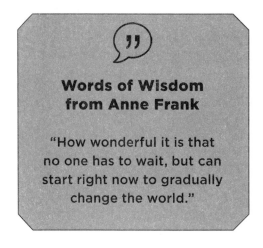

Words of Wisdom from Anne Frank

"How wonderful it is that no one has to wait, but can start right now to gradually change the world."

confinement, fearing discovery at any moment. Not from this girl. Yes, there are dark moments and candid admissions of disappointment and doubt, but just when you think she's down and out, she offers observations like "In spite of everything I still believe that people are really good at heart."

The Power of Gratitude

In the 2007 book *Thanks! How Practicing Gratitude Can Make You Happier*, Dr. Robert A. Emmons reveals groundbreaking research into the emotion we call *gratitude*. As Emmons defines the term, gratitude is the acknowledgment of goodness in one's life and the recognition that the source of this goodness lies at least partially outside oneself. I think this was the secret to Anne Frank's character.

Years of study by Emmons and his associates show that "grateful people experience higher levels of positive emotions such as joy, enthusiasm, love, happiness, and optimism, and that the practice of gratitude as a discipline protects a person from the destructive impulses of envy, resentment, greed, and bitterness."

A grateful attitude enriches life. Emmons believes it elevates, energizes, inspires, and transforms. The science supports him: research shows that gratitude is indispensable to happiness (the more of it you can muster, the happier you'll be) and that happiness adds as many as nine years to life expectancy.

Gratitude is much more than a warm and fuzzy sentiment. And it does not come automatically, unthinkingly. Some people feel and express it all too rarely. And as grateful a person as you may think you are, chances are you can develop an even more grateful attitude.

Doing so carries ample rewards that more than compensate for the task's moral and intellectual challenges. If Anne Frank could do it with all that was going on around her closeted world for two years, you and I have few excuses for failing to muster gratitude as well.

The English writer and philosopher G. K. Chesterton once said, "I would maintain that thanks are the highest form of thought; and that gratitude is happiness doubled by wonder."

Think about that, especially Chesterton's use of the word *wonder*. It means "awe" or "amazement." The least-thankful people tend to be those who are rarely awed or amazed.

A shortage of wonder is a source of considerable error and unhappiness in the world. What should astonish us all, some take for granted or even expect as an entitlement.

We enjoy an endless stream of labor-saving, life-enriching inventions. We're surrounded by abundance in markets for everything from food to shoes to books. We travel in hours distances that required weeks or months of discomfort for our recent ancestors.

In America, life expectancy at age sixty is up by about eight years since 1900, while life expectancy at birth has increased by an incredible thirty years. The top three causes of death in 1900 were pneumonia, tuberculosis, and gastrointestinal infections. Today we live healthier lives and live long enough to die mainly from illnesses (such as heart disease and cancer) that are degenerative, aging-related problems.

Technology, communications, and transportation have all progressed so much in the past century that hardly a library in the world could document the stunning accomplishments. I still marvel every day that I can call a friend in China from my car or find the nearest coffee shop by using an app on my phone. I'm in awe every time I take a coast-to-coast flight, while the guy next to me complains that the flight attendant doesn't have any ketchup for his omelet.

None of these things that should inspire wonderment were inevitable, automatic, or guaranteed. Some see it all and are amazed and grateful. Others see it and are jaded and unappreciative.

Which are you?

A Message of Hope

Anne Frank's message will be remembered for many decades to come—forever, I hope. It reminds us that, no matter the circumstances, we can brighten our lives and those of others. We don't have to sink into despair. We can find good in the smallest of things even as we confront the biggest of evils. Our attitude, the old saying goes, determines our altitude. If you want to make a better world, start by making a better self; it's the one thing you have considerable control over in almost any situation.

Anne Frank didn't live long enough to see or possess very much. But because she found within herself an undying gratitude for what she had—and an awesome ability to communicate it—we can be thankful that she inspires millions to this day. No matter how old you are, you can learn some critical life lessons from this brave teenage heroine.

Lessons from Anne Frank

Practice gratitude: What could Anne Frank have been grateful for? For two years the teenager hid in a secret annex, knowing that at any moment the Nazis could find her and send her to a concentration camp (as eventually happened). Yet her diary inspires us with its optimism and gratitude for the good she saw even amid the evils of the Holocaust. Scientific research has shown that gratitude "protects a person from the destructive impulses of envy, resentment, greed, and bitterness."

If you want to make a better world, start by making a better self: Anne Frank was not blind to the horrors of the Holocaust. But her diary offers us a sustained reminder that our own attitude is the one thing we have considerable control over in almost any situation.

28

Althea Gibson

A Winning Attitude

Baseless prejudice sooner or later meets its match when it runs into indomitable will and exceptional talent. Jackie Robinson proved it in baseball, as did Jesse Owens in track (see chapter 24) and Joe Louis in boxing (see chapter 31).

In the world of tennis, the biggest winner of note was a black woman named Althea Gibson.

Life's victories don't always go to the stronger or faster woman; Gibson demonstrated that eventually the woman who wins is the one who believes she can.

Proving It

Althea Gibson was three years old when, in 1930, her family moved from a sharecropper's shack on a South Carolina cotton farm to New York City's Harlem in search of a better life. In elementary school, playing hooky was her first love. "School was too confining and boring to be worthy of more than cameo appearances," according to her biographers Francis Clayton Gray and Yanick Rice Lamb in *Born to Win*.

When she wasn't fidgeting in the classroom, Gibson was exploring the Big Apple—riding the subway, shooting hoops, sneaking into movie theaters, and beating anybody who dared play her at Ping-Pong. At the age of twelve, in 1939, she was New York City's female table tennis champion, and tennis on the big courts beckoned. Her Harlem neighbors went door to door, raising donations in mostly dimes and quarters to pay for her membership and tennis lessons at the Cosmopolitan Tennis Club. Within a year she won her first tournament, the New York State Championship of the American Tennis Association (ATA).

All through the 1940s, Gibson won title after title. "I knew that I was an unusual, talented girl, through the grace of God," she later wrote. "I didn't need to prove that to myself. I only wanted to prove it to my opponents." Off the court, she was both confident and gracious, never overbearing or condescending. On the court, she was fiercely competitive. Her determination and her athletic, five-foot-eleven frame intimidated opponents right from the start of a match.

Gibson was so skilled at tennis that she earned a full athletic scholarship to attend Florida A&M University. But she was denied the opportunity to display her talents against white players. Tennis was a segregated sport at the time; the ATA was organized expressly in response to the U.S. Lawn Tennis Association's policy banning blacks from its tournaments.

Gibson's situation changed in 1950, largely owing to the courage of another woman, Alice Marble.

The Jackie Robinson of Tennis

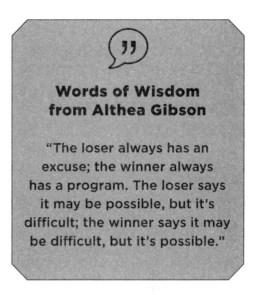

Words of Wisdom from Althea Gibson

"The loser always has an excuse; the winner always has a program. The loser says it may be possible, but it's difficult; the winner says it may be difficult, but it's possible."

Alice Marble had been the world's number one female tennis player, winner of eighteen Grand Slam championships. Her opinion on anything could make headlines. In 1950 she wrote an open letter published in *American Lawn Tennis* magazine challenging the U.S. Lawn Tennis Association for its discriminatory practices. Specifically, she condemned the tennis community for not allowing Althea Gibson to play at the U.S. National Championship (now the U.S. Open):

> If tennis is a game for ladies and gentlemen, it's also time we acted a little more like gentlepeople and less like sanctimonious hypocrites.... If Althea Gibson represents a challenge to the present crop of women players, it's only fair that they should meet that challenge on the courts.... She is not being judged by the yardstick of ability but by the fact that her pigmentation is somewhat different.... She is a fellow human being to whom equal privileges ought to be extended.

If Gibson were not given the opportunity to compete, Marble wrote, "then there is an ineradicable mark against a game to which I have devoted most of my life, and I would be bitterly ashamed."

Marble's letter made an immediate impact. "All of a sudden, the dam broke," Gibson later wrote. She soon received invitations to play in tournaments, including the U.S. National Championship. On her twenty-third birthday, she became the first black player, male or female, to play in the sport's national championship.

Gibson's matches attracted huge crowds, and she endured heck-ling and racial slurs. But she was unflappable. She later said, "I made a vow to myself: 'Althea, you're not going to look around. You're not going to listen to any calls or remarks. All you are going to do is watch the tennis ball.'" Gibson advanced to the tournament's second round, losing a hard-fought match to Louise Brough, who had won two Grand Slam titles that year.

One journalist, Lester Rodney, captured the importance of her breakthrough when he wrote: "No Negro player, man or woman, has ever set foot on one of these courts. In many ways, it's even a tougher personal Jim Crow–busting assignment than was Jackie Robinson's when he first stepped out of the Brooklyn Dodgers dugout."

Number One

Gibson drove herself to heights of excellence. The Grand Slam titles did not come right away. In 1951, the year she became the first black player at Wimbledon, she won her first title, the Caribbean Championship. The following year she reached number seven in the national rankings.

But by the mid-1950s she was considering giving up the game. After graduating from Florida A&M in 1953, she began teaching physical education at Lincoln University in Missouri. Major tennis in those days was an amateur sport, which meant no tournament prize money and no endorsements. Needing more money to support her-self, she came close to joining the military. Then, in 1955, she joined a State Department goodwill tour of Asia. Playing exhibitions with and against other top players, men and women, boosted her confidence and inspired her to push on with her tennis career.

It was a good decision. In 1956 she won the French Open, becom-ing the first black tennis player to win a Grand Slam singles cham-pionship. Before the year was out she had also won the Wimbledon doubles championship, the Italian national championship, and the Asian championship.

The next year, 1957, she defended her doubles title at Wimbledon and also claimed the singles championship, the first black competitor to take the title in the tournament's eight-decade history. Queen Elizabeth personally presented the trophy to an awestruck Gibson. "Shaking hands with the Queen of England," she said, "was a long way from being forced to sit in the colored section of the bus."

When she returned to America, Gibson became the second black American (the first being Jesse Owens) honored by a ticker-tape parade down Broadway in New York City. More than a hundred thousand people cheered their approval.

Later in 1957, Gibson won the Nationals. In 1958 she successfully defended her Wimbledon and U.S. titles while also winning the Australian Open, giving her three of the four Grand Slam titles that year. In 1957 and in 1958, Althea Gibson was the number-one-ranked woman tennis player in the world. Honored as the Associated Press Female Athlete of the Year in both years, she also became the first black woman to appear on the covers of *Sports Illustrated* and *Time*.

Here she was, the world's greatest tennis player, and the financial constraints imposed by amateur sports prevented her from supporting herself. "Being a champ is all well and good," she said, "but you can't eat a crown."

At the top of her game, Gibson retired.

But she wasn't finished achieving athletic excellence or breaking down racial barriers. In 1964 she achieved another milestone when she became the first black woman to golf professionally. Back in college she had been good enough to play on the men's golf team, and now, at the age of thirty-seven, she joined the Ladies Professional Golf Association.

Gibson encountered discrimination in the golfing world just as she had in tennis. Some tournament organizers took to calling their competitions "invitationals" so they could invite whomever they wanted—and, more important, *not* invite Gibson. Even when she was allowed to compete, she might be refused access to a course's clubhouse or bathrooms. She took it in stride. "I don't want to go where

I'm not wanted," she said. "I'm trying to be a good golfer, I have enough problems as it is."

"I Always Wanted to Be Somebody"

"I always wanted to be somebody," Gibson wrote in her autobiography. "If I made it, it's half because I was game enough to take a lot of punishment along the way and half because there were a lot of people who cared enough to help me."

But there was more to it than that. Althea Gibson had drive, determination, and a winning attitude. She summed up that lifelong attitude with these words: "The loser always has an excuse; the winner always has a program. The loser says it may be possible, but it's difficult; the winner says it may be difficult, but it's possible."

Lessons from Althea Gibson

Have the drive to overcome adversity: Like elite performers in other fields, Althea Gibson didn't make it to the top on talent alone. With her indomitable will, she overcame racial discrimination, financial hardship, and other obstacles to become the best tennis player in the world. As she put it, she was "game enough to take a lot of punishment along the way."

Have a winning attitude: As Gibson put it, "The loser always has an excuse; the winner always has a program." She blocked out racial taunts to remain focused on her objectives. Part of her winning attitude was her graciousness; she understood that she reached such heights "because there were a lot of people who cared enough to help."

29

Ludwig Erhard

Architect of a Miracle

How rare and refreshing it is for the powerful to understand the limitations of power and actually repudiate its use, in effect giving it back to the individuals who make up society.

George Washington was such a leader. Cicero (see chapter 1) was another. So was Ludwig Erhard, who did more than any other person to denazify the German economy after World War II.

"In my eyes," Erhard confided in January 1962, "power is always dull, it is dangerous, it is brutal and ultimately even dumb."

By every measure, Germany was a disaster in 1945—defeated, devastated, divided, and demoralized—and not only because of the war. The Nazis, of course, were socialist (the name derives from

National Socialist German Workers Party), so for more than a decade the German economy had been "planned" from the top. It was tormented with price controls, rationing, bureaucracy, inflation, cronyism, cartels, misdirection of resources, and government command of important industries. Producers made what the planners ordered them to. Service to the state was the highest value.

Ludwig Erhard reversed those practices, and in doing so he gave birth to a miraculous economic recovery.

Classical Liberal

Born in Bavaria in 1897, Ludwig Erhard was the son of a clothing and dry goods entrepreneur. Erhard's father was, in the words of biographer Alfred C. Mierzejewski, "by no means wealthy" but "a member of the solid middle class that made its living through hard work and satisfying the burgeoning consumer demand of the period, rather than by lobbying for government subsidies or protection."

As a teenager, Ludwig heard his father argue for classical-liberal values in discussions with fellow businessmen. Young Ludwig resented the burdens that government imposed on honest, independent businessmen like his father. He developed a lifelong passion for free-market competition because he understood what F. A. Hayek would express so well in the 1940s: "The more the state 'plans,' the more difficult planning becomes for the individual."

The younger Erhard's classical-liberal values were strengthened by his experience in the bloody and futile First World War. While serving as an artilleryman in the German army, he was severely wounded by an Allied shell in Belgium in 1918. He began studying economics as tumultuous hyperinflation gripped Germany, rendering savings, pensions, and investments worthless and wiping out the German middle class.

Erhard earned his PhD in 1925, took charge of the family business, and eventually headed a marketing research institute, which gave him opportunities to write and speak about economic issues.

Hitler's rise to power in the 1930s deeply disturbed Erhard. He refused to have anything to do with Nazism or the Nazi Party and quietly supported resistance to the regime. The Nazis saw to it that he lost his job in 1942, when he wrote a paper outlining his ideas for a free postwar economy. He spent the next few years as a business consultant.

Erhard's ideas received a new hearing after the Allies defeated the Nazis. In 1947 he became chair of an important monetary commission. It proved to be a vital stepping-stone to the position of director of economics for the Bizonal Economic Council, a creation of the American and British occupying authorities. There he could finally put his views into practice and transform his country in the process.

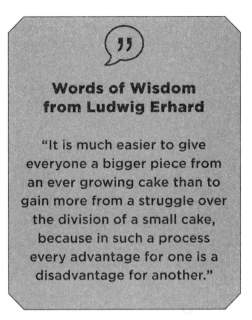

Words of Wisdom from Ludwig Erhard

"It is much easier to give everyone a bigger piece from an ever growing cake than to gain more from a struggle over the division of a small cake, because in such a process every advantage for one is a disadvantage for another."

Turnaround Artist

Erhard's beliefs had by this time solidified into convictions. Currency must be sound and stable. Collectivism was deadly nonsense that choked the creative individual. Central planning was a ruse and a delusion. State enterprises could never be an acceptable substitute for the dynamism of competitive, entrepreneurial markets. Envy and wealth redistribution were evils.

"It is much easier to give everyone a bigger piece from an ever growing cake," he said, "than to gain more from a struggle over the division of a small cake, because in such a process every advantage for one is a disadvantage for another."

Erhard advocated a fair field and no favors. His prescription for recovery? The state would set the rules of the game and otherwise leave people alone to restart the German economy. In June 1948 he "unilaterally and bravely issued a decree wiping out rationing and wage-price controls and introducing a new hard currency, the Deutsche-mark," in the words of the economist William H. Peterson. Erhard did so "without the knowledge or approval of the Allied military occupation authorities" and made the decree "effective immediately." Peterson continues:

> The American, British, and French authorities, who had appointed Erhard to his post, were aghast. Some charged that he had exceeded his defined powers, that he should be removed. But the deed was done. Said U.S. Commanding General Lucius Clay: "Herr Erhard, my advisers tell me you're making a terrible mistake." "Don't listen to them, General," Erhard replied, "my advisers tell me the same thing."

General Clay protested that Erhard had "altered" the Allied price-control program, but Erhard insisted he hadn't altered price controls at all. He had simply abolished them.

In 1949 Erhard won a seat in the Bundestag (the German parliament) in the first free elections since 1933. In the subsequent government of Chancellor Konrad Adenauer, he was appointed the first economics minister of the newly constituted West German republic, a role he would hold until 1963.

In that position he issued a blizzard of deregulatory orders. He slashed tariffs. He raised consumption taxes, but more than offset them with a 15 percent cut in income taxes. By removing disincentives to save, he prompted one of the highest saving rates of any Western industrialized country. West Germany was awash in capital and growth, while communist East Germany languished. Economist

David Henderson writes that Erhard's motto could have been "Don't just sit there; *undo* something."

The results were stunning. Writing in the December 1988 issue of *The Freeman*, Robert A. Peterson (not to be confused with the afore-mentioned William H. Peterson) explained:

> Almost immediately, the German economy sprang to life. The unemployed went back to work, food reappeared on store shelves, and the legendary productivity of the German people was unleashed. Within two years, industrial output tripled. By the early 1960s, Germany was the third greatest economic power in the world. And all of this occurred while West Germany was assimilating hundreds of thousands of East German refugees.

The pace of growth dwarfed that of European countries that received far more Marshall Plan aid than Germany ever did.

The Principles of Liberty

The incredible turnaround of the 1950s became widely known as the "German economic miracle," but Erhard never thought of it as such. In his 1958 book, *Prosperity through Competition*, he wrote: "What has taken place in Germany...is anything but a miracle. It is the result of the honest efforts of a whole people who, in keeping with the principles of liberty, were given the opportunity of using personal initiative and human energy."

The temptations of the welfare state in the 1960s derailed some of Erhard's reforms. His three years as chancellor (1963–66) were less successful than his tenure as economics minister. But his legacy was forged in that decade and a half after the war's end. He forever answered the question "What do you do with an economy in ruins?" with the simple, proven recipe: "Free it."

Lessons from Ludwig Erhard

Want a strong economy? Free it: After years of National Socialism followed by stifling government controls under Allied occupation, Germany in the late 1940s was impoverished. Ludwig Erhard knew the solution was not more government planning but freedom and free markets. He ended price controls, rationing, and other hallmarks of central planning. Freed of all that, Germans went to work and produced an "economic miracle."

Value principles over power: Erhard rose to Germany's highest political office but had little interest in power for its own sake. "In my eyes," he said, "power is always dull, it is dangerous, it is brutal and ultimately even dumb." He was committed instead to the principles of liberty, which meant handing to the people the power he could have hoarded for his government.

30

Gail Halvorsen

The Candy Bomber

n his 1986 bestselling book, *All I Really Need to Know I Learned in Kindergarten*, Robert Fulghum mused:

Maybe we should develop a Crayola bomb as our next secret weapon. A happiness weapon. A beauty bomb. And every time a crisis developed, we would launch one. It would explode high in the air—explode softly—and send thousands, millions, of little parachutes into the air. Floating down to earth—boxes of Crayolas. And we wouldn't go cheap either—not little boxes of eight. Boxes of sixty-four, with the sharpener built right in. With silver and gold and copper, magenta and peach and lime, amber and umber and all the rest. And people would smile and get a little funny look on their faces and cover the world with imagination instead of death. A child who touched one wouldn't have his hand blown off.

Something akin to what Fulghum imagined actually happened almost forty years earlier. The man responsible for it is Gail Halvorsen, known in history as the "Candy Bomber."

Checking Stalin

I first learned of Colonel Halvorsen in late 2013. I was watching a DVD of the Mormon Tabernacle Choir's annual Christmas concert from the year before. NBC's Tom Brokaw narrated a segment about a U.S. Air Force officer who dropped candy from C-47 and C-54 cargo planes during the 1948–49 Soviet blockade of Berlin. Then across the stage strolled Colonel Halvorsen himself, smiling and still robust at ninety-two.

Halvorsen undertook his remarkable venture in the wake of the Nazi surrender, when Germany was divided and occupied by the United States, Britain, France, and the Soviet Union. Berlin lay deep within Soviet territory, but it, too, was carved up into zones. Joseph Stalin hoped the Western Allies would leave the entire city under Soviet control. Tension over the future status of Berlin produced the first major confrontation of the Cold War.

That crisis began after another hero, Ludwig Erhard (see chapter 29), introduced a new currency. For the three years from the end of the war until the spring of 1948, the Soviets handled the printing of Reichsmarks for all of occupied Germany. They promptly overprinted, knowing that currency debasement would thwart economic recovery. That fit right into Stalin's plans to keep Germany vulnerable to Soviet domination. By 1948, Germans were using cigarettes as money instead of the depreciating paper Reichsmark.

When Erhard, the economics director appointed by the British and Americans, ended rationing and price controls and introduced a new, sounder currency, the deutsche mark, on a Sunday in June, the Soviets reacted by cutting all land connections (including electricity) between Berlin and the sectors of Germany occupied by the Western Allies. A hundred miles inside the Soviet sector, West Berlin was suddenly inaccessible by road, river, canal, or railway.

Words of Wisdom from Gail Halvorsen

"Without hope, the soul dies."

Stalin offered to lift the blockade if the deutsche mark were abandoned, and he introduced his own new currency, the Ostmark, in the Soviet zone. But Germans en masse began using the deutsche mark and rejecting the Ostmark, even in East Berlin. Erhard and the Western Allies held firm against Stalin. They organized a campaign of airlifts to ferry food, water, fuel, and other supplies to the besieged city. It was called "Operation Vittles." Pilots and crews from the United States, Britain, Canada, Australia, New Zealand, and South Africa flew more than 200,000 flights over the next year, bringing West Berliners up to nine thousand tons of vital provisions every day.

Although Stalin undoubtedly feared the ramifications of shooting down unarmed aircraft on humanitarian missions, the airlift didn't go unchallenged. Soviet harassment took the form of shining searchlights at the pilots as they attempted landings and takeoffs and using Soviet planes to "buzz" Allied aircraft. Communist propaganda, especially by radio, constantly warned Berliners that collapse was imminent. Stalin calculated that the West's resolve would weaken, but within weeks it was clear that the airlift was working. Berliners organized mass protests against Soviet actions, which only strengthened the world's moral and material support for the Western relief effort. Finally, at one minute after midnight on May 12, 1949, the Soviets ended the blockade.

Gail Halvorsen of Utah was one of the thousands of airlift pilots who saved West Berlin in the eleven months of the airlift. He performed his duty ably, but that wasn't what made him a hero. Compassion, creative thinking, and initiative led him to truly heroic acts.

"Operation Little Vittles"

While on the ground at Berlin's Tempelhof airport between flights, Halvorsen noticed some local children observing the planes from behind a fence. He approached them and offered his only two sticks of gum. Grateful, the children broke the gum into pieces to share with one another; those who didn't get any sniffed the empty wrappers.

Halvorsen was struck by what the kids told him. "Don't give up on us," they said. "If we lose our freedom, we'll never get it back."

"American-style freedom was their dream," Halvorsen later recalled. "Hitler's past and Stalin's future were their nightmare."

Halverson promised the children he'd come back with more and told them that they would know his plane from the others because he would "wiggle" his wings. A day later, he did just that as he dropped chocolate bars attached to parachutes made from handkerchiefs.

Those few chocolate bars were just the beginning. Halvorsen made additional drops of candy that he gathered up from fellow airmen who sacrificed their rations. The crowds of anxious children grew. Kids sent letters to the air base addressed to "Uncle Wiggly Wings." In his book *Candy Bomber: The Story of the Berlin Airlift's Chocolate Pilot*, Michael O. Tunnell recounts an especially poignant episode:

> By October of 1948 Peter Zimmerman must have decided he'd never score a candy parachute unless he took matters into his own hands. So he sent a letter—in English—to the man he hoped would soon be his Chocolate Uncle. He also tucked a map and a crude homemade parachute into the envelope. "As you see," he wrote, "after takeoff fly along the big canal to the second high-

way bridge, turn right one block. I live in the bombed-out house on the corner. I'll be in the backyard every day at 2 p.m. Drop the chocolate there."

Halvorsen followed the instructions, but poor Peter Zimmerman kept missing out on the candy drops. Young Zimmerman wrote again to Halvorsen, complaining, "Didn't get any gum or candy, a bigger kid beat me to it." After several more drops that failed to reach him, Zimmerman sent an impatient letter to Halvorsen: "You are a pilot?" he wrote. "I gave you a map. How did you guys win the war?" He offered to build a fire so Halvorsen would know exactly where he was.

To make sure Zimmerman wasn't disappointed again, Halvorsen boxed up some gum and chocolate and mailed him the package.

When news of the unauthorized candy drops broke in the international media, Halvorsen feared he would be disciplined by his superiors. But instead they approved. Halvorsen's two sticks of gum blossomed into a full-blown campaign: "Operation Little Vittles."

Soon he was attracting donations and volunteers from all over the globe. The National Confectioners Association in America contributed massive amounts of candy. Children and their parents donated candy and provided homemade parachutes by the tens of thousands. By the time the Soviets finally relented and ended the blockade, Operation Little Vittles had dropped at least twenty-three tons of sweets on Berlin. It was a huge factor in kindling the goodwill and close ties that still exist between the German people and those of America and its allies.

Freedom, Integrity, and Hope

In the decades since the airlift, Gail Halvorsen has been honored many times in many countries for his initiative and humanitarianism. In 2002 he wrote *The Berlin Candy Bomber*, a moving account of his experiences in those critical months of 1948–49. Full of photos and copies of letters he received from German children, it's a gem of a read.

Why did he do it? Why did he risk being disciplined by his superiors to help the children of West Berlin? Surely his attitudes about freedom, integrity, and hope shaped his perspective. Colonel Halvorsen has offered a series of maxims we should all remember: "The desire for freedom is inborn in every human soul, no matter on which side of the border he or she is born"; "Keep your word; integrity begets hope, faith, trust, peace of mind, and confidence for yourself and others"; "Give service to others if you seek genuine fulfillment; a happy person has goals that include others"; "Seek a positive outlook on life, and the world will be manageable, even if difficult; attitude is not everything, but it does affect everything"; and "It is never so good or never so bad that the existing situation cannot be improved with patience, determination, love, and hard work."

Thank you, Gail Halvorsen, for your inspiration. People like you—helping other people from the goodness of their hearts—are truly a beautiful thing. You and the other heroes of the Berlin airlift saved a city of more than two million.

Lessons from Gail Halvorsen

"Give service to others if you seek genuine fulfillment": Gail Halvorsen did not stop at serving the people of Berlin through the airlift. Moved by the German children's gratitude and longing for freedom, he became the "Candy Bomber," leading a massive aid effort.

"Keep your word": Halvorsen kept his promise to Berlin children by starting his unauthorized candy operation. Though he sensed that his superiors would discipline him for it, he understood that keeping your word "begets hope, faith, trust, peace of mind, and confidence for yourself and others."

31

Joe Louis

Fighter on Many Fronts

If you remember the famous 1938 fight for the world heavyweight boxing title between Detroit's Joe Louis and Germany's Max Schmeling, you've been around a while. If you don't, there's a good chance you've heard about it from your father or grandfather. It was a rematch that Louis, known as the "Brown Bomber," won in just 124 seconds.

Joe Louis was a hero not only for whom and what he fought but also for maintaining his integrity along the way. He dealt personally with poverty and racism. He overcame a speech impediment and the loss of his father at an early age. He took on the best boxers of his day. He battled the Nazis. He crossed swords with the Internal Revenue Service. When he died at age sixty-six in 1981, he was widely revered as a champion of character and was beloved by good people of every color.

"One-Man Triumphs"

The grandson of slaves, Joseph Louis Barrow was born in 1914 in LaFayette, Alabama. He barely spoke until he was in the second grade. At age twelve, he moved with his mother, his stepdad, and his seven siblings to Detroit after a scare from the Ku Klux Klan. To his credit, the young man never viewed the racism of a few as indicative of the many. He judged men and women the way he wanted them to judge him: namely, by what Martin Luther King would call "the content of their character."

In spite of his mother's desire that he pursue either cabinetmaking or the violin, he showed an early penchant for pugilism. He dropped "Barrow" and became simply "Joe Louis" when he started competing in the ring as a teenager, apparently because he didn't want his mom to know he was boxing. She soon found out, as did the rest of the world.

The Great Depression was in full swing when Louis fought the first big match of his amateur career, in 1932. He lost to a future Olympian. Undaunted, he went on to win all but three of his next fifty-three fights (forty-three by knockout) and caught the attention of boxing promoters. He went pro in 1934.

One of the most famous dates in boxing history is June 22, 1937. That's when Louis went up against heavyweight titleholder James Braddock, knocking him out in the eighth round. Americans black and white stayed up all night across the country in celebration, but the joy was especially pronounced in black communities. Here's how author Langston Hughes described Louis's influence:

> Each time Joe Louis won a fight in those depression years, even before he became champion, thousands of colored Americans on relief or WPA, and poor, would throng out into the streets

all across the land to march and cheer and yell and cry because of Joe's one-man triumphs. No one else in the United States has ever had such an effect on Negro emotions—or on mine. I marched and cheered and yelled and cried, too.

In seventy-two professional fights, Louis scored fifty-seven knockouts and lost only three matches. For twelve years (1937–1949), he held the heavyweight championship—the longest stretch in the sport's history. He successfully defended his title twenty-five times, also a record for heavyweights; at one point he fought seven times in seven months. His closely watched 1938 defeat of Max Schmeling embarrassed the Third Reich because it said to the world, "This Aryan superiority thing is nothing more than propaganda."

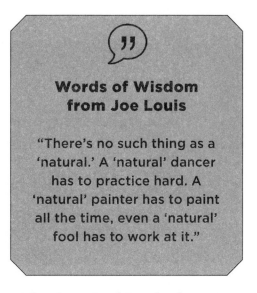

Words of Wisdom from Joe Louis

"There's no such thing as a 'natural.' A 'natural' dancer has to practice hard. A 'natural' painter has to paint all the time, even a 'natural' fool has to work at it."

Breaking Barriers

A month after Pearl Harbor, Louis enlisted in the U.S. Army and went off for basic training with a segregated cavalry unit at Fort Riley, Kansas. Asked why he would be willing to serve a country where blacks still did not enjoy equal rights, he replied, "There's nothing wrong with America that Hitler can fix."

The army used Louis to cheer up the troops by sending him some twenty thousand miles for ninety-six boxing matches in front of two million soldiers. He was eventually given the Legion of Merit for his "incalculable contribution to the general morale." It was in the army that he befriended Jackie Robinson, the future major league baseball player. Louis persuaded a commanding officer to drop charges against Robinson for punching out a fellow soldier who called him the N-word.

Nobody who ever really knew Joe Louis, it seems, had an unkind word for him. Perhaps the worst ever said was actually spoken in jest, by fellow boxer Max Baer: "I define fear as standing across the ring from Joe Louis and knowing he wants to go home early."

You may not think of Louis in connection with the game of golf, but he made an impact there as well. Golf was his longtime hobby. In 1952, as an amateur, he received a sponsor's exemption to play at a PGA Tour event in San Diego. Only one problem: the PGA had a "Caucasian-only" clause in its bylaws. As Bob Denney of the PGA of America reports, when Louis found out about the discriminatory rule, he and others sent a petition to the governor of California. The governor said that the clause was unconstitutional. The PGA wouldn't remove the rule until 1961, but it did agree to give Louis an exemption to compete in the tournament. Thus he became the first black American to play in a PGA Tour event.

Just as Jackie Robinson broke the color barrier in baseball, Joe Louis broke it in golf. His appearance as an amateur paved the way for black golfers like Calvin Peete to play on the pro tour. According to the Golf Channel's Rich Lerner, Louis also helped "black professionals like Bill Spiller, Teddy Rhodes, Howard Wheeler, Clyde Martin, and Charlie Sifford make their way in a white man's sport."

Battling the IRS

A very different fight that Louis waged is less well known than his boxing. It was with the Internal Revenue Service. As we do in our day, Louis had to contend with a president whose fingers itched to get into the pockets of wealthy Americans. I first learned of this story from historian Burton Folsom, author of the superb book *New Deal or Raw Deal?*

In 1935 President Franklin Roosevelt pushed Congress to raise the top income tax rate to 79 percent, then later to 94 percent during and after World War II. In the war years, Joe Louis donated money to military charities, but the complicated tax laws wouldn't allow him to deduct those gifts. Although Louis saw almost none of the money he won in charity fights, the IRS credited the full amounts as taxable income paid to Louis. He had even voluntarily paid back to the city of Detroit all the money he and his family had received in welfare years earlier, but that counted for nothing with the feds.

Louis retired as heavyweight champion in 1949. But he couldn't remain out of the ring long. In 1950 the IRS ruled that his tax debt, with penalties and interest included, stood at more than $500,000 (nearly $5 million in 2016 dollars). The federal government sometimes reached settlements in such situations; Folsom recounts how, in 1944, FDR had personally halted an IRS investigation into a young but politically valuable congressman named Lyndon Johnson. Louis received no accommodations. His debt would accumulate interest each year.

Although he showed obvious signs of physical deterioration after so many punishing fights, Louis felt compelled to come out of retirement in 1950 to fight Ezzard Charles, the new champion. After he lost the fight, his mother begged him to stop. "She couldn't understand how much money I owed," he said. "The government wanted their money, and I had to try to get it to them."

The next year, Louis fought Rocky Marciano and lost. The fight earned him $300,000. That sounds like a great opportunity to pay off what he owed the government—until you remember that the tax rate on high incomes stood at 91 percent. He could barely make a dent in the debt with interest compounding. When his mother died in 1953, the IRS swiped the $667 she left him in her will. By 1960 his debt had soared to more than $1 million.

According to Folsom, "Louis refereed wrestling matches, made guest appearances on quiz shows, and served as a greeter at Caesars Palace in Las Vegas—anything to bring in money to keep the tax man at bay."

The drug kingpin Frank Lucas was so disgusted with the IRS's treatment of Louis that he once paid a $50,000 tax lien against the boxer. Even Max Schmeling came to the rescue, assisting with money when Louis was alive and then paying funeral expenses when the boxer died.

Louis's tax troubles finally eased somewhat when the IRS settled with him in the early 1960s. The agreement didn't make him debt free; it simply limited what he had to pay the IRS thereafter to a fixed portion of his annual income. He was, in fact, in debt to the federal government until his dying day.

Belated Honors

Joe Louis, a decorated army veteran and world-class athlete, remained a symbol of black achievement in spite of his difficulties with the IRS. Biographer Chris Mead notes that Louis "was the first black American to achieve lasting fame and popularity in the twentieth century." More than that, he opened doors for fellow black Americans. Louis faced only one black boxer during his forty-three fights before World War II; by the time he retired as champion in 1949, the leading contenders for the title were black. When Jackie Robinson integrated baseball in 1947, he cited Louis as his role model: "I'll try to do as good a job as Joe Louis has done.... He has done a great job for us and I will try to carry on." "Louis had broken the ground," Mead writes. "He had opened sports to blacks and made athletics a cutting edge of the civil rights movement."

When Louis died, President Ronald Reagan waived the eligibility rules to allow him to be buried in Arlington National Cemetery with full military honors. Joe Louis was a man who fought on many fronts and emerged as a great example to people of all races.

Lessons from Joe Louis

Put in the work: Before he became heavyweight champion, Joe Louis was quoted as saying, "If I reach the goal I have set for myself...I'll walk out and leave the other fellows to argue over the spoils." Louis set goals and achieved them by putting in the work, whether training relentlessly to defend his title a record twenty-five times or taking on whatever work he could to pay off his tax debt.

Remember that "a good name is better than money": Louis credited his mother with instilling this lesson in him. He generously donated to military charities. He was a genuine American patriot who served his country and earned the Legion of Merit. In his 1938 fight against the German Max Schmeling, he had "the burden of representing all of America" against the Nazis, as he put it. His own government treated him shabbily, but he did whatever he could to repay his debts.

32

Peter Fechter

Death at the Wall

From 1961 to 1989, the ghastly palisade known as the Berlin Wall divided the city of Berlin. It sealed off the only escape hatch for people in the communist East who wanted freedom in the West.

No warning was given before August 13, 1961, when East German soldiers and police first stretched barbed wire and then began erecting the infamous wall.

In my home hangs a framed copy of a photo from that sad day. The image shows a young, apprehensive East German soldier glancing about as he prepares to let a small boy pass through the emerging barrier. No doubt the boy had spent the night with friends and found himself the next morning on the opposite side of the wall from his family.

But the communist regime ordered its men to let *no one* pass. The photo's inscription explains that, at this very moment, a superior officer noticed what the soldier was doing and immediately detached him. "No one knows what became of him," the inscription reads.

Only the most despicable tyrants could punish a man for letting a child get to his loved ones, but in the Evil Empire, that and much worse happened all the time.

By one estimate, 254 people died at the Berlin Wall during the twenty-eight years it stood. Most of them were killed in the infamous "death strip" next to the main barrier, which the East Germans packed with guard towers, dog runs, explosive devices, and trip-wire machine guns. The communist regime cynically referred to the barrier as the "Anti-Fascist Protection Wall."

Like millions of others, a strapping eighteen-year-old bricklayer named Peter Fechter yearned for so much more than the stifling dreariness of socialism. He had the courage to risk his own life to surmount that hideous barrier.

"Murderers!"

The Berlin Wall had been up for only a year when Fechter and his friend Helmut Kulbeik hatched a plan to escape. The two young men decided to conceal themselves in a carpenter's woodshop near the wall and watch for an opportune moment to jump from a second-story window into the death strip. They would then run to and climb over the six-and-a-half-foot-high concrete barrier, laced with barbed wire, and emerge in freedom on the other side.

They set the plan in motion on August 17, 1962. When the moment came that guards were looking the other way, Fechter and Kulbeik jumped. Seconds later, during their mad dash to the wall, guards began firing. Amazingly, Kulbeik made it to freedom. Fechter was not so lucky. In plain view of witnesses numbering in the hundreds, he was hit in the pelvis. He fell to the ground, screaming in pain.

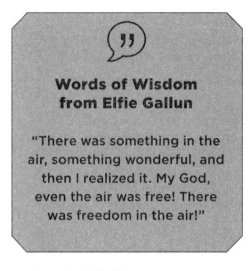

Words of Wisdom from Elfie Gallun

"There was something in the air, something wonderful, and then I realized it. My God, even the air was free! There was freedom in the air!"

No one on the East side, soldiers included, came to his aid. Westerners threw bandages over the wall, but Fechter couldn't reach them. Bleeding profusely, he died alone an hour later. Demonstrators in West Berlin shouted, "Murderers!" at the East Berlin border guards, who eventually retrieved his lifeless body.

An Awful Chapter

Decades later, after the Berlin Wall came down, Peter Fechter's family pushed for justice at last. Fechter's sister Ruth charged former East German guards with her brother's death. In 1997 two former guards were found guilty of manslaughter. They received sentences of twenty and twenty-one months in prison, though their sentences were suspended.

The trial revealed that the Fechter family's ordeal had not ended with the horrifying death of their only son. In *The Victims at the Berlin Wall, 1961–1989*, Christine Brecht writes that during the trial Ruth "movingly described how she and her family experienced the tragic death of her brother and had felt powerless to act against his public defamation." The Fechters "had been sworn to secrecy, an involuntary obligation that put the family under tremendous pressure." Ruth herself said: "We were ostracized and experienced hostile encounters daily. They were not born of our personal desire, but were instead imposed on us by others."

The world must never forget this awful chapter in history. Nor should we ever forget that these heinous acts were committed in the name of a system that declared its "solidarity with the working class" and professed its devotion to "the people."

We who embrace liberty don't believe in shooting people because they don't conform, and that is ultimately what socialism and communism are all about. We don't plan other people's lives, because we're too busy at the full-time job of reforming and improving our own. We believe in persuasion, not coercion. We solve problems at penpoint, not gunpoint. We're never so smug in our beliefs that we're ready to dragoon the rest of society into our schemes.

All this is why so many of us get a rush every time we think of Ronald Reagan standing in front of the Brandenburg Gate in 1987 and demanding, "Mr. Gorbachev, *tear down this wall!*" This is why we were brought to tears in the heady days of 1989 when thousands of Berliners scaled the wall with their hammers, picks, and fists and pummeled that terrible edifice and the Marxist vision that fostered it.

Peter Fechter and the 253 others who died at the Berlin Wall are real heroes. They deserve to be remembered.

Postscript

Elfie Gallun is among the four people to whom this book is dedicated. A decade before the Berlin Wall rose, at barely the same age Peter Fechter was, she risked life and limb to flee her native East Germany. Somehow she made it and later married another hero of mine, Ned Gallun, a successful Wisconsin entrepreneur.

In 1984 Elfie wrote to President Reagan and described the moments after her daring escape, moments that were denied to Peter Fechter:

There was something in the air, something wonderful, and then I realized it. My God, even the air was free! There was freedom in the air! Only 50 yards and yet the air smelled so different. I wanted to shout, "I am free! I am free!" but no words came from my lips because by then my heart was in my throat. There I stood in silence, having no one else to share that moment with me, and being lost in the wonder of Freedom.

In a little town just behind a hill two miles away, the lights were turned on. The Olympic fireworks of 1984, as spectacular as they were, could not compare to what I saw that dark night. Then I turned East toward Communism and it was so very dark, not one light. I had come out of the dark into the light.

President Reagan wrote back to Elfie a few weeks later. She and Ned cherish his letter to this day. It reads in part:

Those of us who were born free and have known freedom all our lives sometimes forget what a precious blessing it is. Your experience in a totalitarian country has given you a special appreciation of the God-given gift of freedom, an appreciation you can share with others. One look around the globe is enough to remind us how rare and fragile a thing freedom is, and how each generation is called upon to make the necessary sacrifices to safeguard it. Examples like yours shine therefore like a beacon of hope for others. That path you followed from darkness to light is truly the way to the future for all mankind. I pray that some-day soon all nations may travel it together.

Lessons from Peter Fechter

Don't take freedom for granted: "How rare and fragile a thing freedom is," Ronald Reagan said. It's easy to take our liberty for granted, but Peter Fechter and millions of others who have suffered under tyranny know how right Reagan was.

Don't fall for claims that coercive efforts are done for "the people": Communism was sold to the world as creating a "workers' paradise." But lovers of liberty understand that if an idea truly works, it doesn't need to be advanced at gunpoint.

33

Norval Morey

Wealth Creation Through Entrepreneurship

How is it that we recognize someone as great? Is it by how often his or her name appears in the newspapers? Is it by how much he gives away, or by how many public offices she has held, or by how many degrees he lists after his name?

Greatness isn't any of those things. It's something that springs from *character*, the critical, self-determined stuff that defines a person. A great man or woman is one who does great things from the heart and doesn't care whether it makes the news. Giving to worthy causes is a noble thing, but having the wisdom and the drive to do what it takes to earn it in the first place is what's *really* great.

A person can become great in public office, but America is not a country whose strength and vitality come from government. As Ronald Reagan said, "We are a nation that has a government—not the other way around." And having a collection of degrees after your name doesn't say anything about what you've done to put any of that to good use.

Norval K. Morey didn't make his mark in public office or by racking up degrees (except for an honorary degree Harvard University awarded him). But he rose from practically nothing to extraordinary heights, thanks to his character, work ethic, and entrepreneurial spirit. This is why Morey—"Nub" to those of us who knew him—was a great man, the quintessence of the American Dream.

Humble Beginnings

Norval's start in life was as humble as humble gets. So was his formal education, which ended with the sixth grade. Even that understates the matter. Perhaps the most truant kid in the public schools of Isabella County, Michigan, he didn't learn much from a teacher after the fourth grade. Half a century later, he was awarded that honorary degree from Harvard after delivering a speech there on environmental harvesting.

Biographer Rich Donnell explains that the Great Depression was Norval's "ticket out of the seventh grade." Nub loved relating the story about how, after a couple of days in his seventh-grade class, his teacher told him he was smarter than her so he didn't need to come back. So he quit. He spent the first half of the 1930s working the family farm, cutting and hauling wood, and taking on every odd job he could find. He then moved to Idaho to work as a logger near Lewiston. Returning to Michigan at the start of World War II, he labored in defense plants in Detroit until he was drafted by the U.S. Army in 1942. He faced danger head-on as a combat squad leader in northern Italy. Back in his home state after the war, he became a sawmill operator. Wood was his passion and his career for the next four decades.

In 1957, at age thirty-seven, Norval took a big chance. He designed a portable device to strip bark from pulp wood and launched the Morbark Debarker Company in the tiny village of Winn, Michigan. The company made only one product. The payroll: two people.

When Norval died forty years later, head of the company to the last, Morbark was a 1.5-million-square-foot manufacturing complex with nearly five hundred employees producing hundreds of heavy-equipment designs for sale around the world. The company builds high-performance machines for customers in the forestry, recycling, sawmill, biomass, landscaping, irrigation, and tree care markets. It helps customers harvest, process, and convert organic materials into valuable, usable, and environmentally sound products.

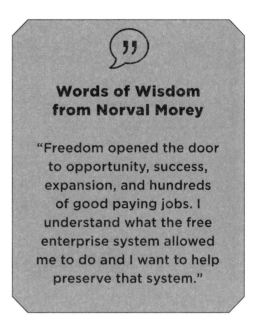

Words of Wisdom from Norval Morey

"Freedom opened the door to opportunity, success, expansion, and hundreds of good paying jobs. I understand what the free enterprise system allowed me to do and I want to help preserve that system."

Planting Flowers

In seventy-seven years of life, Norval Morey journeyed farther than most of us ever will if we live to be one hundred. He was a pioneering inventor, an entrepreneurial genius, a job creator, a benefactor of education. Not bad for a guy whose formal education ended on the third day of the seventh grade. He knew the truth of what advertising guru Leo Burnett once said: "When you reach for the stars you may not quite get one, but you won't come up with a handful of mud either."

Here was a man who had achieved great wealth and could have sat back at the age of sixty and said, "I quit; I've earned a life of leisure now." No one would have begrudged him for that. But he went on for another seventeen years—working, creating, employing, growing a company, even building a school for hundreds of Isabella County children.

Norval not only knew what it takes to make a successful company tick; he knew what it takes to make a successful *country* tick as well. He spoke out in favor of individual liberty and free enterprise. He supported candidates who came down squarely in favor of those principles. One of those candidates, in fact, was me. He was my staunchest supporter when I ran for Congress in the primary and general elections of 1982. He wasn't like so many businesspeople today, easily browbeaten by the left and afraid to defend the free markets that allowed them to succeed.

Those who didn't have the pleasure of knowing Norval well could be forgiven for thinking that he was a little "different." He could be cantankerous, but that was because he didn't suffer fools gladly. He could be impatient, but that was because he wanted to get things done. He didn't exactly speak the King's English, but that never mattered because he always made eminently good sense. He never cared for kings anyway. Nub was a down-to-earth, no-pretense guy whose least concern was whether or not he impressed you. I never once heard him say anything boastful.

Framed and sitting on my office desk is a quotation from a president of the United States that just as easily could have come from Norval Morey: "Die when I may, I want it said of me by those who know me best, that I always plucked a thistle and planted a flower when I thought a flower would grow."

Postscript

Over the years I have come to know many fine entrepreneurs like Norval Morey. In many ways, he reminds me of another longtime friend and one of those to whom this book is dedicated, Ron Manners.

Born in 1936 in Kalgoorlie, Australia, Ron assumed the management of his family's mining business before he was twenty, building it into a major concern. He founded other natural resource companies as well and in 2011 was inducted into the Australian Prospectors and Miners Hall of Fame as a "living legend." In an age when too many businesspeople are afraid to be "controversial" by defending freedom and free markets, Ron (like Norval Morey) does so actively and publicly. In 1997 he founded the Mannkal Economic Education Foundation, which, I am proud to say, supports freedom-loving organizations like my own all over the world. He and his charming wife, Jenny, live in Perth, Australia.

Lessons from Norval Morey

Risk failure: The right to start a business is a key element of the American Dream. So is the right to fail. When Norval Morey founded his company with only one product and one other employee, success was hardly foreordained. Norval had the work ethic, entrepreneurial spirit, and winning ideas to achieve success—but he also had the courage to risk failure.

Don't bash the wealth creators: It's popular to bash the "One-Percenters" for their wealth. But what of those people who built their wealth and in the process created jobs and wealth for so many others? Morey parlayed a grade school education into a major business that employed five hundred people and created valuable products. His efforts and genius helped other people far more than they helped him.

34

Jerzy Popiełuszko

Witness to Truth and Freedom

More than a century ago, in *Life and Destiny*, ethicist Felix Adler reflected on what the lives of the deceased can teach the living:

> Let us live truly while we live, live for what is true and good and lasting. And let the memory of our dead help us to do this. For they are not wholly separated from us, if we remain loyal to them. In spirit they are with us. And we may think of them as silent, invisible, but real presences in our households.

All across Poland, the life and words of Father Jerzy Popiełuszko still resonate in millions of households more than thirty years after the priest's murder by the communist secret police. I first visited Father Popiełuszko's Saint Stanislaus Kostka Church in Warsaw on a chilly Sunday in November 1986, just two years after his death. It was an oasis amid a desert of communist oppression, a place where Poles renewed their strength by recalling the man who had led them not so long before. The walls of the church were adorned with pictures of him—offering Communion, boating with his dog, encouraging steelworkers, comforting children. Though I am not Catholic, the memory of those few hours evokes powerful emotions to this day.

Unlikely Hero

Jerzy Popiełuszko was an unlikely hero. Born in the small village of Okopy in northeastern Poland in September 1947, he was short, frail, sickly, introverted, and of average intellect. At seventeen he traveled to Warsaw intent on studying for a quiet life in the priesthood. He would live only another twenty years, but before he died, his country's communist regime came to see him as the most dangerous man in Poland. To millions of other Poles, he became a beacon of hope; his only weapons were the truth and his courage.

After one year at seminary, Popiełuszko had to interrupt his studies to begin compulsory military service, a two-year requirement of all young men at the time. Such service was especially difficult for seminary students. The atheistic regime routinely mistreated seminarians and subjected them to humiliating ridicule. The military also segregated them within special units to diminish their influence. Prayer and Bible study were strictly prohibited.

Popiełuszko demonstrated a steely defiance that surprised even those who knew him best. He openly disdained the army's coercive atheistic indoctrination. Obedient he was—but not to communist authorities.

For refusing to relinquish the cross he wore around his neck, he was ordered to stand all night at attention, barefoot in the snow.

Words of Wisdom from Jerzy Popiełuszko

"It is not enough for a Christian to condemn evil, cowardice, lies, and use of force, hatred, and oppression. He must at all times be a witness to and defender of justice, goodness, truth, freedom, and love."

From such frequent cruelty, he emerged with his health permanently damaged but his spirits higher than ever. The experience reinforced his life's mission: to serve God by resisting evil, to comfort and encourage victims of oppression, and ultimately to free his country.

He returned to the seminary, and in May 1972, at the age of twenty-four, he was ordained.

Call to Action

In the 1970s the Soviet Union seemed to be winning its battle with a demoralized West. Its Eastern European empire, though occasionally restive, was cowed by the 1968 invasion of Czechoslovakia. At the close of the decade, the Soviet army rolled into Afghanistan. American leadership was reeling from the Watergate scandal, the Vietnam fiasco, and stagflation; the Soviets boasted that communism represented the world's future.

Then, in 1978, the first non-Italian ascended to the papacy. Cardinal Karol Józef Wojtyła of Wadowice, Poland, became Pope John Paul II. The news electrified Poland.

Before the end of his first year in Rome, the pope returned triumphant to his native land. Communist authorities were at first hesitant to allow the visit. They relented in the belief that they could limit its effects and turn them to the state's advantage. This was a profound miscalculation by men who arrogantly believed themselves capable of "planning" society.

Poles turned out by the millions to welcome John Paul. They heard him declare, "Be not afraid!" and they knew what his message was. Father Jerzy, who assisted in the planning for the visit, took the message as a call to action. He resolved to step up his public opposition to the regime, declaring one Sunday, "Justice and the right to know the truth require us from this pulpit to repeatedly demand a limit on the tyranny of censorship!"

Poles had put up with communism since the Soviets imposed it on them after World War II. The tyranny of a one-party political monopoly was compounded by the stifling effects of socialist central planning—environmental destruction, stagnant living standards, inflation, long lines for simple foodstuffs and toiletries. It was a dreary, claustrophobic existence. In clever and sometimes subtle language, John Paul II told them they could and should resist.

The pope's historic visit led directly to the legalization of the Solidarity organization, which Popiełuszko endorsed and assisted—publicly and privately, legally and illegally. The visit proved to be the galvanizing moment when Poles by the millions began to lose their fear of the regime and contemplate the real possibility of freedom from their oppressors.

Poles ventured into open opposition. Workers went on strike with demands that pertained not simply to wages or working conditions but to political, economic, and social freedoms as well. Rumors grew that the Soviets might put an end to it all with an invasion, just as they had done to Czechoslovakia a decade earlier.

Martyr

In 1980 Cardinal Stefan Wyszyński was the revered primate of Poland, the highest-ranking Catholic in the country, with a long history of antagonism toward the communists. When striking steelworkers begged him to send a priest into the huge Huta Warszawa steel mill, he chose thirty-three-year-old Jerzy Popiełuszko.

It was a daring move, the first time a priest even entered a state-owned enterprise of such size, let alone one who so openly denounced the government. From that moment until his death, Father Jerzy was known as the favorite priest of both Solidarity in Poland and John Paul II in Rome. Perhaps he already knew it, but his life was on the line. In *The Priest and the Policeman*, biographers John Moody and Roger Boyes write:

> He was stalked like a game animal in the last years of his life, hunted by agents...who knew that the priest had to be silenced. Murder was not the only solution. It would have been enough to persuade the Church to transfer him to an obscure rural parish, or bring him to Rome. It would have sufficed to put him on trial and sentence him to prison for his political preaching, or to strain his delicate health to the breaking point, so that his death could be passed off, in the words of one agent [of the secret police], as "a beautiful accident." The police tried all these methods but found it was impossible to silence the priest, who declared modestly, "I am only saying aloud what people are thinking privately."

All through 1981, Poles kept pushing the dictatorship to grant basic liberties. The world watched the unfolding events with mixed emotions—hopeful for freedom in Poland but fearful of a backlash.

The backlash came on December 13, when Moscow's puppets in Warsaw imposed martial law. In a massive crackdown, the communist regime jailed thousands of dissidents and banned Solidarity and other pro-freedom groups.

Father Jerzy didn't retreat. He summoned every ounce of energy his ailing body would allow. He denounced martial law and aided the underground resistance. His sermons were routinely broadcast by Radio Free Europe, making him famous throughout the Eastern Bloc for his uncompromising stance against the communists.

The secret police planted weapons in his apartment, then staged a raid for the television cameras to "prove" that he was a subversive revolutionary. He was arrested several times, but pressure from the clergy helped each time to secure his release. As soon as he got out, he would renew his pleas for freedom.

People traveled from all over the country to hear him speak every Sunday at Saint Stanislaus Kostka Church; they even packed into the nearby streets by the thousands to hear his words broadcast over loudspeakers. He was granted permission to leave Poland to visit a beloved aunt in Pittsburgh, Pennsylvania, and then went right back home to resume the struggle.

"It is not enough for a Christian to condemn evil, cowardice, lies, and use of force, hatred, and oppression," he once declared. "He must at all times be a witness to and defender of justice, goodness, truth, freedom, and love. He must never tire of claiming these values as a right both for himself and others."

A visiting Western journalist asked Father Jerzy in 1984 how he could continue to speak so boldly without fear of retaliation. The priest replied: "They will kill me. They will kill me." But, he went on, he could not remain silent as members of his own congregation were jailed, tortured, and even killed for nothing more than wanting to be free. "We must conquer the bad through the good," he often implored.

In October 1984 the communist secret police contrived a scheme to take out the young priest in what would look like a car accident, but the plot failed. Less than a week later, while riding with his driver back to Warsaw from priestly duties in Bydgoszcz, Father Jerzy was ambushed. He endured torture so fierce that one of the secret police agents would later remark, "I never knew a man could withstand such a beating."

Tied to a heavy stone, the mangled and lifeless body of Father Jerzy was tossed unceremoniously into the Vistula River, where it was recovered eleven days later. Poles were heartbroken, but in keeping with the spirit of the martyred priest, they continued the fight for freedom.

A Prophecy Fulfilled

In early 1989 the communist regime announced to the world that Poland had become "ungovernable." Hardly anyone paid much attention anymore to its edicts and decrees. Even many government employees were thwarting their bosses and joining the underground.

Free elections were held in June, for the first time in all the decades of communist rule. The communists lost every seat, fulfilling Father Jerzy's prophecy: "An idea which needs rifles to survive dies of its own accord."

I returned to a free Poland in November 1989, just as the rest of the Eastern Bloc was unraveling. At Saint Stanislaw Kostka Church, where Father Jerzy's grave is marked with a massive stone cross, I stood with the parishioners, lit a candle, and cried with them—not so much because he was gone and in a better place but because of that for which he gave his life.

Lessons from Jerzy Popiełuszko

"Be a witness to and defender of justice, goodness, truth, freedom, and love": Father Jerzy Popiełuszko preached a message that people of any faith can admire: it is not enough to condemn evil and lies; you must do your best to defend and advance truth, freedom, and justice. Father Jerzy was a living embodiment of this commitment.

"Live for what is true and good and lasting": Felix Adler's words capture Father Jerzy's approach to life. The brave young priest spoke truth to power, knowing the dire risks that doing so entailed. He paid for his candor with his life, but today he is remembered as one of the best examples of courageous resistance to tyranny.

35

Roberto Clemente

"I Learned the Right Way to Live"

In both Puerto Rico and Pittsburgh, more than four decades after his untimely death at the age of thirty-eight, the name of Roberto Clemente brings a smile to almost every face.

A member of the Pittsburgh Pirates for eighteen seasons (1955–1972), Clemente was one of the greatest right fielders in baseball history. He could run, hit, and throw better than almost anybody who ever played the game. Black and Puerto Rican by birth, he transcended race, nationality, and culture to become Major League Baseball's first Latino superstar.

Growing up in western Pennsylvania in the 1960s, I heard his name practically every day. The mentions were always admiring. Clemente had so much talent and character that Pulitzer Prize–winning author David Maraniss could write a four-hundred-page biography of him, *Clemente: The Passion and Grace of Baseball's Last Hero.*

A Loving Home

The youngest of seven siblings, Roberto Enrique Clemente Walker (in Spanish, the last name is the maternal family name) was born in 1934 in Carolina, Puerto Rico. As a young boy, he worked in the sugar cane fields with his father. "I learned the right way to live from my parents," he said years later. He always spoke well of his family: "I never heard any hate in my house. I never heard my father say a mean word to my mother, or my mother to my father, either. During the war, when food was hard to get, my parents fed their children first and they ate what was left. They always thought of us."

The Clementes were poor in material wealth, but the children enjoyed the riches of a loving home.

Roberto showed an early love of baseball, easily the island's favorite sport. The Brooklyn Dodgers offered the twenty-year-old a contract in 1954, but they left him unprotected the next year and the Pittsburgh Pirates wisely picked him up. The Pirates' general manager was the legendary Branch Rickey, who, while running the Dodgers several years earlier, had made Jackie Robinson Major League Baseball's first black player.

Rickey believed in giving every good person a chance. A devout Christian, he believed that prejudice was deep-seated and needed to be confronted. He wrote: "The American public not only in the south, but all over the place has a secret feeling that the Negro is really inferior by nature. The long years of unequal opportunity and menial service caused this sort of unconscious belief. I think the stark fact of it ought to be brought to the public's attention in every way we know how."

Maybe Rickey also knew that discrimination rarely pays in the marketplace. The owner or manager who passes up the chance to hire a winner will lose to competitors who do it instead. Both Jackie Robinson and Roberto Clemente made their teams proud and their owners financially well-off because they were great players.

"The Proudest Man on Earth"

Clemente donned the Pirate uniform at an inauspicious moment in the team's history.

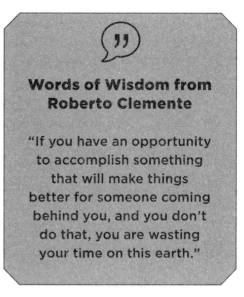

Words of Wisdom from Roberto Clemente

"If you have an opportunity to accomplish something that will make things better for someone coming behind you, and you don't do that, you are wasting your time on this earth."

Calvin Coolidge had been president the last time the Pirates won the World Series. That was in 1925. By the 1950s the team was a joke.

As a black Hispanic who knew little English when he came to the United States, Clemente faced daunting personal obstacles as well. Today Latino players account for nearly 30 percent of all major leaguers, but when Clemente debuted he was one of only a couple of dozen Hispanics in the game. He encountered anti-Latino and anti-black prejudice, especially at spring training in Florida. As Maraniss reports, "He spoke out strongly against Jim Crow segregation every chance he got." Up in Pittsburgh, sportswriters would describe him using terms like "chocolate-colored islander" and "dusky flyer." Fellow Puerto Rican and Hall of Famer Orlando Cepeda, who reached the majors in 1958, said, "We had two strikes [against us]: being black, and being Latin."

Clemente openly sympathized with the nascent civil rights movement, but he never let prejudice compromise his professionalism or his charitable attitude toward other good people, least of all the disadvantaged. "I don't believe in color," he said. "I believe in people." He spent considerable free time volunteering as a baseball coach and mentor to young boys in the barrios back in Puerto Rico. During the winter of 1958–59, he even joined the United States Marine Corps Reserve, spending his six-month active duty in the Carolinas and Washington, D.C.

Another challenge arose during his rookie year, when a car accident caused by a drunk driver left him with lower-back pain that plagued him for the rest of his life. Baseball players were expected to be stoic, never complaining about injuries. But when writers asked Clemente how he felt, the Pirate right fielder would respond honestly, giving rise to the exaggerated claim that he was a hypochondriac. His former manager Danny Murtaugh explained: "He was such a truthful man, it backfired on him sometimes. If you asked him if his shoulder hurt, he'd say, 'Yes, it does.' Then he'd go out and get three hits and throw out a guy at the plate. That's how he got the hypochondriac label."

Clemente played hard, all the time, whether he was hurt or not. It was a matter of pride. "When I put on my uniform, I feel I am the proudest man on earth," he said the year before he died. "The players should pay the people to come and see us play." On another occasion, he told an audience: "Why you think I play this game? I play to win. Competition is the thing. I want to play on a winning team. I don't want to play for sixth place. I like to play for all the marbles, where every game means something. I like to play for real, not for fun."

Thanks to Clemente and other great players like Bill Mazeroski, the Pirates' fortunes began to look up in the late '50s. In 1958 they scored their first winning season in a decade. Two years later they were the National League champions.

The Pirates entered the 1960 World Series as underdogs against the American League victors, the New York Yankees, who boasted big names like Mickey Mantle, Yogi Berra, and Roger Maris. In the ninth inning of game seven, the baseball world was stunned when Mazeroski slammed a home run and the Pirates won the game, 10–9. World champs for the first time since almost a decade before Clemente was born, the Pirates earned back the esteem that had evaded them for so long.

A Star on and off the Field

Throughout the 1960s, Robert Clemente's fame grew as his abilities awed fans year after year. He was an All-Star every season he played after 1960 but for one, 1968. He won the Gold Glove every season from 1961 on. He won the National League batting title four times— in 1961, 1964, 1965, and 1967—and received the Most Valuable Player Award in 1966, hitting .317 with 29 home runs and 119 RBIs. In 1967 he belted 23 home runs, batted in 110 runs, and logged a career-high .357 batting average.

The Pirates' next shot at a World Series came in 1971. After beating the San Francisco Giants for the National League pennant, they faced the Baltimore Orioles, the defending champions. In seven games once again, the Pirates won the series. Clemente, at thirty-seven years of age, hit a stunning .414 for the series and had a home run in the deciding game, claiming the World Series MVP.

But Clemente earned respect for more than just his play. He established himself as a person of character, pride, strength, and compassion. He also could be philosophical. Accepting an award in 1971, he offered these elegant remarks:

> If we have respect for our fathers and we have respect for our children, we will have a better life. I watched on TV when America sent men to the moon, and there were a lot of people whose names weren't given who helped make it possible. You don't have the names of those who run the computers and other things. But they worked together and this is what you have to have...Chinese, American, Jewish, black and white, people working side by side. This is what you have to do to make this a better life. When you can give opportunity to everybody, we won't have to wait to die to get to heaven. We are going to have heaven on earth.

During the same speech he offered another message about making the most of one's life, in words that became his motto: "If you have an opportunity to accomplish something that will make things better for someone coming behind you, and you don't do that, you are wasting your time on this earth."

Rushing to Help

On September 30, 1972—a month and a half after his thirty-eighth birthday—Clemente collected the three thousandth hit of his major league career. He became only the eleventh player to reach that milestone in major league history, and the first Hispanic player to do so. The hit came in his last at-bat of the 1972 regular season.

There would be no 1973 season for the superstar from Puerto Rico.

Just two days before Christmas 1972, the capital of Nicaragua was struck by a massive earthquake. In a country where Clemente had close friends and that he had visited just three weeks before, the casualty figures were heart wrenching: six thousand killed, twenty thousand injured, and more than a quarter million homeless. In Puerto Rico, Clemente watched the early reports on television with his family, just long enough to know he had to act.

Helping the needy came naturally to Clemente; he had done it personally, frequently, and often quietly for years. Within hours of the quake, he gathered medical and other relief supplies and organized flights to carry them to Managua.

But after the first three flights, Clemente learned that corrupt officials of the Nicaraguan government had diverted the relief supplies, keeping them from the victims. Angry, and determined to personally see that the material went where it was intended, he boarded the fourth flight himself, on New Year's Eve 1972.

The plane never made it. Mechanical trouble forced it into the ocean immediately after takeoff. Clemente's body was never found. He left behind his beloved wife, Vera, and three young boys.

In a special election on March 30, 1973, the Baseball Writers' Association of America voted to waive the stipulated five-year waiting period and posthumously elected Roberto Clemente into the Baseball Hall of Fame. Twenty-six years later, he was ranked number twenty on the *Sporting News*'s list of the hundred greatest baseball players of the twentieth century. He was the highest-ranking Latin American and Caribbean player on the list.

For all his accomplishments on the field, however, Clemente earned the respect and admiration of so many for his actions off the field, the way he carried himself, and the message of hope he conveyed. Each year Major League Baseball gives the Roberto Clemente Award to the player who "best exemplifies the game of baseball, sportsmanship, community involvement, and the individual's contribution to his team." It's a fitting tribute to a fine man.

Roberto Clemente: all these years later, the thought of him still brings a smile, and some tears as well, to the faces of many people, including me.

Lessons from Roberto Clemente

Don't "waste your time on this earth": Roberto Clemente was not only an incredibly good baseball player but also a fine model of a man. A person of character and compassion, he made the most of personal opportunities and worked tirelessly to help others. He implored people to do the same; failing to do so, he said, would amount to "wasting your time on this earth."

"Believe in people": Clemente fought prejudice all his life. But he also said: "I don't believe in color. I believe in people." One teammate, Al Oliver, recalled that his conversations with Clemente "always stemmed around people from all walks of life being able to get along well, or no excuse why that shouldn't be."

36

John Patric

Hobo, Screwball, and Hero

John Patric was a self-described "hobo" and "screwball" who lived out of a car for years at a time. He attended universities in seven states from California to Minnesota and was expelled from three (in Oregon, Michigan, and Texas). He ran for office at least fifteen times, as a Republican as often as a Democrat, and paid his campaign filing fees with loose change. To prove how gullible reporters could be, he often falsely claimed to be an FBI agent, the mayor, or deputy sheriff. He was, by all accounts, an odd duck.

So what makes this guy a hero?

Paeans to the "common man" abound in literature, magazines, and political speeches. I confess, however, to an attachment to the uncommon—an appreciation that goes back at least forty years, to the time I first read "My Creed" by a New Yorker named Dean Alfange, an immigrant from Turkey:

I do not choose to be a common man. It is my right to be uncommon, if I can. I seek opportunity, not security. I do not wish to be a kept citizen, humbled and dulled by having the state look after me.

I want to take the calculated risk; to dream and to build, to fail and to succeed. I refuse to barter incentive for a dole. I prefer the challenges of life to the guaranteed existence; the thrill of fulfillment to the stale calm of utopia.

I will not trade freedom for beneficence nor my dignity for a handout. I will never cower before any master nor bend to any threat. It is my heritage to stand erect, proud and unafraid; to think and act for myself, enjoy the benefit of my creations and to face the world boldly and say, "This I have done."

Sometimes the uncommon man is offensive, intrusive, or even violent. But on most occasions he's simply a little rebellious or peculiar—just *different*. How boring this world would be if everything and everybody were common and conventional!

John Patric was unequivocally uncommon and unconventional. He puts me in mind of "Think Different," a 1997 Apple ad campaign that paid tribute to the unusual among us.

Featuring footage of famous personalities from Albert Einstein to Bob Dylan to Thomas Edison, the ad celebrated diversity in thought and behavior:

Here's to the crazy ones. The misfits. The rebels. The troublemakers. The round pegs in the square holes. The ones who see things differently. They're not fond of rules and they have no respect for the status quo. You can quote them, disagree with them, glorify them, or vilify them. About the only thing you

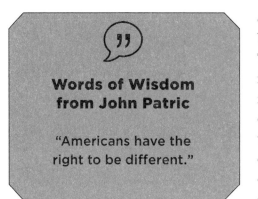

Words of Wisdom from John Patric

"Americans have the right to be different."

can't do is ignore them—because they *change* things. They push the human race forward. And while some may see them as the crazy ones, we see genius. Because the people who are crazy enough to think they can change the world are the ones who do.

Free Spirit

Patric was born in Snohomish, Washington, in 1902 and lived until his teen years in the family home on the floor above the town library. He was surrounded by books and read lots of them. His adventurism—some might call it rebellion—showed up well before he finished high school. He ran away from home and, as he explained it, "hoboed my way from Seattle to Mexico and back," hopping trains with railway men many years his senior. When he finally made it back to Snohomish, he finished high school as the valedictorian and president of the senior class (it was the only election he ever won).

Bitten by the travel bug, Patric began a peripatetic life. This free spirit never hung around long enough to earn a degree at any of the universities he attended. He earned some money selling rubber stamps and writing for publications like the *American Insurance Digest*. His first real "home" that he bought was a used 1927 Lincoln sedan, which he drove from coast to coast.

For a stretch of several months, one of his traveling companions was the libertarian political theorist Rose Wilder Lane, the daughter of novelist Laura Ingalls Wilder. According to Lane biographer William Holtz, Patric "had sought her out because he shared her political views."

With a breezy, quirky writing style and endless travel adventures to chronicle, Patric established himself as a freelance writer. He became a regular contributor to *National Geographic*, where he developed loyal readers. His best-known article, the March 1937 piece "Imperial Rome Reborn," described his travels in Italy near the peak of Benito Mussolini's power. Some of the most prominent architects of Franklin Roosevelt's New Deal were enthralled by Il Duce's central planning, but Patric's article—its photographs in particular—raised the chilling specter of an egocentric dictatorship.

A few years later, as Mussolini and his Axis allies waged war on the world, Patric stirred the ire of organized labor when, in *Reader's Digest*, he exposed union corruption and featherbedding in the nation's shipbuilding industry. Called to testify before Congress, he argued that the unions were crippling the nation's productivity in wartime.

Yankee Hobo

Patric's most widely read work was his 1943 book, *Why Japan Was Strong*, later retitled *Yankee Hobo in the Orient*. A repackaging of articles first published in *National Geographic*, the book was based on his two years of travel around Japan, China, and Korea from 1934 through 1936. True to his fiercely independent lifestyle and increasingly libertarian political views, Patric maintained that the book's most important argument was that every individual should try to diminish, "by whatever peaceful means his ingenuity may devise, the power of government—*any* government—to tell him what to do."

The *New York Times* reviewed *Hobo* favorably, stating that the author exhibited "qualities of good sense and poise and instinct for honest reporting sufficiently to give his excellent account of Japan's 'common man' the favorable reception it deserves." In less than two months, *Hobo* reached number seven on the bestseller list. *Reader's Digest* in the United States and *World Digest* in England produced abridged versions. All told, in both full and condensed versions, the book sold an astonishing twelve million copies worldwide.

Patric's style captivated readers. For many, it was their first encounter with daily life among a people who seemed inscrutable. One couldn't help but feel sympathetic to the ordinary citizen up against the mandarins of arbitrary rule. Of Koreans, he wrote:

> After centuries of servitude, taxes, and oppression, Koreans looked to me to be terribly beaten down.
>
> Why try to build a better farm? Why try to get ahead? If you succeeded, your farm might become the farm of a Japanese. So why not just produce the barest needs of your traditional life— food to eat and white clothes to be gentlemen in—and possess nothing your conquerors might covet?...
>
> In America as we have known it, there has always been something to strive for—always a goal ahead. Here there was nothing. Little matter how hard a Korean worked; if he acquired what passes in the Orient for a fine farm, and what is comparatively a degree of prosperity, a way would surely be found by the Government to relieve him of both. It usually would be by some new tax.

One of my favorite passages comes early in the book, when Patric explains the difficulties he had with American police as he made his way west to Seattle for passage to Japan:

> To save hotel bills, I took to sleeping curled up in the front seat of my car. The worst problem was where to park to avoid the police—for there seem to be laws about sleeping in cars. The more quiet the spot I found, the more likely it seemed that the police would pick me up, take me to the police station, finger-print me, talk to me as they talked to thugs, and finally let me go without any breakfast. If I resented the cruelty and arrogance of some policemen, and showed it, I was jailed. As I learned to be

meek, to act stupid, to say "sir," to pretend a respect and an awe I did not feel, I got along better.

Why is it that when otherwise decent men come to represent the majesty of law and government, they can become so discourteous, so arrogant, so cruel? It is no wonder to me that petty offenders, and even those who have committed no real offense whatever, sometimes become antisocial after a few experiences with "the law."

Could it be that if police had less power, and if there were fewer laws and regulations, people and police would both become more decent, so that still less law and fewer police would be needed, and honest men could spend on themselves some of the price they pay for government and for crime?

By 1945, *Hobo* was in its seventh edition. At that point Patric was his own publisher. He also owned a 160-acre backwoods ranch near Florence, Oregon, where he settled for about twelve years. *Settled* is too strong a word, though, as he still found plenty of time to "hobo" his way around the country, peddling thousands of copies of his book. He signed so many that you can buy an autographed copy online today for under fifty dollars. I possess a copy in which Patric wrote, "To Jack Slinn, and may this book be lent to many an honest borrower—8/9/52."

Gadfly

In 1957, Patric returned to his hometown of Snohomish, Washington, but didn't like what he saw. "When I came back I found the most rotten, corrupt political situation I've seen anywhere in the world," he wrote. "It was like a big stinking thunderjug with the lid clamped down."

To needle the local politicians and their ill-considered schemes for more government, he started a newsletter he dubbed the *Snohomish*

Free Press, later renamed the *Saturday Evening Free Press*, and wrote under the puckish pseudonym Hugo N. Frye.

Over the next quarter century, Patric ran for public office almost annually. Washington state authorities jailed him once for using his pseudonym rather than his real name. When the charges were dismissed, the *Spokesman-Review* of Spokane editorialized, "Hugo N. Frye may be a fictitious character. But in this case he symbolizes a spirit of individual freedom and independence that must always remain alive in a free America."

Local authorities didn't always agree. Incensed by Patric's rabble-rousing newsletter, they exploited his personal eccentricities to concoct charges of mental incompetence. They managed to have him remanded to a mental hospital for months until, acting as his own attorney and arguing that he had "always been a screwball," he won his release.

"What happened to me could happen to any of you," he told the jury. "Americans have the right to be different." He never transgressed against any man's life or property; the only "crime" of which he was ever guilty was being odd.

Later, after one of his many tongue-in-cheek political campaigns, Patric declared, "I was the only candidate who could prove he was sane; the others could only claim it."

"Reporters loved John Patric and the colorful copy he provided," recalled a fellow Washington resident. "Clayton Fox of the *Daily Olympian* enjoyed describing Patric with phrases like, 'the bearded bard of Snohomish,' 'gadfly of golliwoggs and gooser of governmental gophers'... 'the pricker of political stuffed shirts,' 'the scourge of junkmailers,' 'implacable foe of pollution and corruption,' 'aider and abetter of bees, trees, and ocean breezes.'"

David Dilgard, a librarian at Washington's Everett Public Library, knew John Patric. In an April 2, 2015, interview, he recalled:

John's lifestyle, including his diet, was highly idiosyncratic and he was a heavy smoker. The brief glimpses I got of his eating habits were startling. He apparently subsisted at times on canned mackerel and chocolate bars, washed down with large quantities of coffee. Although it may sound pretentious, his comparison of himself to the Cynic Diogenes was pretty convincing to me. Like Diogenes, his lifestyle was austere and he spent a lot of his time looking for honesty and virtue in his fellow man and loudly proclaiming that he had failed to find it.

John Patric passed away on August 31, 1985, at age eighty-three. His headstone in a Snohomish cemetery reads, "A Little Eccentric, But Justified."

Self-described screwballs can be heroes. John Patric was both.

Lessons from John Patric

Dare to be different: You don't have to be a hobo or a screwball like John Patric to want to emulate his daring, candor, and independence. His eccentricities should not overshadow his powerful reflections on protecting individual liberty from an overweening state, particularly his accounts of Imperial Japan and Mussolini's Italy.

Stand for something and say so: Patric needled politicians with hard-hitting sarcasm and by making himself a candidate for public office at least fifteen times. Throughout his writings he emphasized that a person should use "whatever peaceful means his ingenuity may devise" to diminish "the power of government—any government—to tell him what to do." Patric demonstrates the virtue of speaking out for your principles, even if some people think you're crazy.

37

Haing S. Ngor

"To Give of Your Soul"

Every year when the Academy Awards are presented, I seem to find something else to do that evening. The program is always too long and often celebrates movies I didn't like while ignoring ones I did. Wherever I am and whatever I'm doing, however, my thoughts turn to a friend who won an Oscar more than thirty years ago.

At the 1985 Oscars, *Amadeus* claimed best picture; F. Murray Abraham won best actor; Sally Field, best actress. Then came the announcement for best supporting actor. To the stage, bearing the widest grin of his life, came a man few Americans had heard of, a man who had acted in only one motion picture.

A physician in his native Cambodia, Dr. Haing S. Ngor witnessed unspeakable cruelty and endured torture and forced labor before escaping. He made it to a Thai refugee camp and found his way to America in 1980, less than five years before he claimed his Academy Award. His Oscar-winning performance in *The Killing Fields* gave him the platform to tell the world about the mass murder that occurred between 1975 and 1979 at the hands of Cambodia's Khmer Rouge communists.

When I met Ngor at a conference in Dallas a few months after his Oscar win, I was struck by the intensity of his passion. Perhaps no one loves liberty more than one who has been denied it at gunpoint. We became instant friends and stayed in frequent contact.

When he decided to visit Cambodia in August 1989 for the first time since his escape ten years earlier, he asked me to go with him. Dith Pran, the photographer Ngor portrayed in the movie, was among the small number in our entourage. So were Diane Sawyer and a crew from ABC's *Prime Time Live*. Experiencing Cambodia with Ngor and Pran so soon after the genocide left me with vivid impressions and lasting memories.

But Cambodia in 1989 was a universe away from the Cambodia of 1979. Although the country's suffering continued on a grand scale, I knew it was a playground compared to what Ngor and Pran had miraculously survived.

Cambodia's Killing Fields

In 1975 crazed but battle-hardened revolutionaries known as the Khmer Rouge had seized power in Cambodia. Their leader, Pol Pot, embraced the most radical versions of class warfare, egalitarianism, and state control. His model was the Chinese Cultural Revolution. Mao and Stalin were his heroes.

The "evils" the Khmer Rouge aspired to destroy included all vestiges of the former governments of Cambodia, city life, private enterprise, the family unit, religion, money, modern medicine and

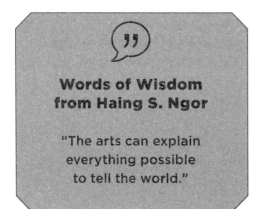

**Words of Wisdom
from Haing S. Ngor**

"The arts can explain
everything possible
to tell the world."

industry, private property, and anything that smacked of foreign influence. They savaged an essentially defenseless population already weary of war. Pol Pot's killing machine produced the "killing fields" for which the film was later named.

Signaling the goal to remake society completely, the regime declared 1975 to be "Year Zero," and the numbering of succeeding years would follow accordingly. To break with Cambodia's past, the Khmer Rouge changed the country's name to Kampuchea. Racial pogroms, political executions, and random homicides were instituted as public policy to discipline, frighten, and reorganize society. Any individual's life meant nothing in the grand scheme of the new order.

One day after taking power, the Khmer Rouge forcibly evacuated the populations of all urban areas, including the capital, Phnom Penh, a city swollen by refugees to at least two million inhabitants. Many thousands of men and women, including the sick, the elderly, and the handicapped, died on the way to their "political rehabilitation" in the countryside. Survivors slaved away in the rice fields, often separated from their families, routinely beaten and tortured for trifling offenses or for no reason at all, kept hungry by meager rations, and facing certain death for the slightest challenge to authority.

Thon Hin, a top official in the Cambodian foreign ministry at the time of our 1989 visit, told me of the propaganda blasted daily from speakers as citizens labored in the fields: "They said that everything belonged to the state, that we had no duty to anything but the state, that the state would always make the right decisions for the good of everyone. I remember so many times they would say, 'It is always better to kill by mistake than to not kill at all.'"

Churches and pagodas were demolished, and thousands of Buddhist monks and worshippers were murdered. Schools were closed down and modern medicine was forbidden in favor of quack remedies and sinister experimentation. By 1979, only forty-five doctors remained in the whole country; more than four thousand had perished or fled. Eating in private and scavenging for food were considered crimes against the state. So was wearing eyeglasses, which was seen as evidence that one had read too much.

With total control of communication, Pol Pot's gang of killers kept the Cambodian people unaware of the full extent of the state's atrocities. Most had little idea that the horror they were witnessing was a nationwide event. The rest of the world knew even less. Mass graves unearthed years later provided grisly evidence of the violence.

During our 1989 tour, Ngor and I visited Tuol Sleng. It was a former high school in Phnom Penh that the Khmer Rouge had converted into a torture center. Of twenty thousand men, women, and children taken there, only seven survived. Hideous devices and blood-soaked floors remained for visitors to see. The walls were lined with snapshots of the hapless victims—pictures taken by their captors.

Fifteen kilometers away we visited a place called Choeung Ek, where a memorial houses more than eight thousand human skulls found in an adjacent field. Cambodians say that nearby streams once ran so red with blood that cattle would not drink from the water.

An estimated 2 million Cambodians died from starvation, disease, and execution during Pol Pot's tyranny—in a nation of only 8 million inhabitants when he took power. Far more people died at the hands of the Khmer Rouge in less than four years than in the last decade of the Vietnam War, when 1.2 million perished on both the American and Vietnamese sides.

Torture, Forced Labor ... and Escape

Haing Ngor didn't just *see* these things; he endured them. He had to get rid of his eyeglasses and deny that he was a doctor. He pretended to be a cab driver, hoping he and his wife would not draw the regime's attention.

Nonetheless, he fell prey to the Khmer Rouge's brutality. He and his wife were among the countless expelled from Phnom Penh in Year Zero. Driven into the countryside to work as a slave laborer, he was forced to smash heavy stones from dawn until deep into the night and even to wear a yoke and pull a plow, like an ox, as guards whipped him. Khmer Rouge thugs sliced his finger off in one torturous episode. In another, they tied him to a post, burned his leg, and put a plastic bag around his head, nearly suffocating him. In still another, they jammed him and dozens of other prisoners into a hut filled with feces. After four days, the guards set fire to the hut—and then shot anyone who ran out. Ngor stayed in the burning hut and somehow survived.

The prison camps brought constant dread. "The terror was always there, deep in our hearts," Ngor wrote in his riveting 1987 autobiography, *Survival in the Killing Fields*. "In the late afternoon, wondering whether the soldiers would choose us as their victims. And then feeling guilty when the soldiers took someone else.... Then lying awake and wondering whether we would see the dawn. Waking up the next day and wondering whether it would be our last."

In the camp, Ngor's wife died in his arms from complications during childbirth. Ngor might have saved her; he was a skilled gynecologist and surgeon. But had he revealed he was a doctor, he and his family would have been executed on the spot.

In *Survival in the Killing Fields*, Ngor recounted his anguish: "The wind brought me her last words again and again: '*Take care of yourself, sweet*.' She had taken care of me when I was sick. She had saved my life. But when it was my turn to save her, I failed."

In 1979, as the Khmer Rouge contended with invading Vietnamese forces, Ngor seized the chance to escape. He, his ten-year-old niece, and other family members had to travel by foot through jungles, avoiding the land mines that littered the paths and eating rats to survive. Finally they made it to Thailand. Ngor spent more than a year volunteering at a medical clinic for his fellow Cambodian refugees.

"This Is Unbelievable"

Ngor left for America on August 30, 1980, a year and a half after the Vietnamese invasion ended the Khmer Rouge regime. He believed the world needed to know about the Khmer Rouge's atrocities, fully and graphically. When fate gave him the chance to act in a movie about the period, he grabbed it and performed brilliantly.

He had never acted before, but he was driven to do well in *The Killing Fields* so that the rest of us would remember what happened and to whom. He often said that he really didn't have to "act"; he had personally suffered through calamities much worse than those depicted in the film. But just imagine the pain and torment he had to revisit in making the movie. His director, Roland Joffé, was right when he said of Ngor: "He was very brave. Acting means you have to give of your soul, and he did that." Haing Ngor deserved the Academy Award that his riveting performance earned him.

When he accepted his Oscar on the night of March 25, 1985, Ngor began by saying, "This is unbelievable—but so is my entire life."

Educating for Liberty

After *The Killing Fields*, Ngor earned some money here and there from bit parts in film and on television. But he was too busy helping others and educating audiences about the catastrophe in his homeland to pursue a career in Hollywood. He volunteered for weeks at a time to provide free medical assistance to refugees along the Thai border.

I remained in frequent communication with him in the years after our 1989 visit to Cambodia. He always had time for his friends. If he wasn't home when I called, he never failed to ring me back.

One cold morning in February 1996, a reporter friend from the local newspaper called my office. He had just seen a wire report and wanted my comment. My friend Dr. Haing S. Ngor, then fifty-five, had been shot and killed the day before—not somewhere in Southeast

Asia, but in downtown Los Angeles. The perpetrators, it turned out, were ordinary gang thugs trying to rob him as he got out of his car near his modest apartment. They took a locket, which held the only picture he still had of his deceased wife.

It's impossible to make sense out of a senseless tragedy. I do know this, however: for Haing Ngor, rediscovering his freedom after experiencing hell on earth wasn't enough. He couldn't relax and resume living a quiet and anonymous life. He felt compelled to tell his story so others would know the awful things totalitarian government can do. He forced us to ponder and appreciate life more fundamentally than ever before.

We can be grateful to live in a country where we can celebrate our creative achievements in film, but we should be even more thankful for people like Haing Ngor, who did more to educate for liberty in a few short years than most of us will do in our lifetimes.

Lessons from Haing S. Ngor

Speak out for liberty: Perhaps no one loves liberty more than one who has been denied it at gunpoint. A victim of the Cambodian holocaust of the late 1970s, Dr. Haing S. Ngor worked tirelessly to inform the world of what happened so such atrocities might never occur again. Through his Oscar-winning performance in *The Killing Fields*, his autobiography, and his other work, he taught millions about the brutality of total government.

Don't rest on victories: Ngor could have been expected to retire to a quiet life in America after the horrors he endured in Cambodia. He had escaped; he was free. But he felt compelled to tell his story so others would know the awful things totalitarian government can do.

38

Vivien Kellems

"Please Indict Me!"

"**A**ll our liberties are due to men who, when their conscience has compelled them, have broken the laws of the land."

These words are often credited to John Clifford, an early-twentieth-century British politician and minister. The statement is inspiring, but did you catch the one glaring error? *It leaves out the women!*

Anyone who knew Vivien Kellems wouldn't make that mistake.

Kellems was a successful entrepreneur, an accomplished public speaker, a political candidate more interested in educating than in winning, and, most famously, a tireless opponent of the IRS and its tax code. She was an outspoken crusader to the end.

Innovator and Business Leader

Born in 1896 in Des Moines, Iowa, Kellems was the daughter of evangelistic ministers. Later in life she reflected on how her parents had influenced her fiery oratorical style: "I suppose in my case shouting about all that stinking, rotten business going on in Washington simply takes the place of shouting at the Devil."

Kellems attended the University of Oregon, where she displayed the spunk that would mark the next half century of her life. She became the first and only female on the college debate team, humbling many men in a competition widely thought at the time to be for males only. She graduated in 1918 and soon returned to the university to earn a master's in economics in 1921. Kellems began work toward a PhD at Columbia University but suspended her studies when business opportunities beckoned. Decades later, while in her seventies, she took up her PhD studies again, this time at the University of Edinburgh in Scotland. The focus of her dissertation was the issue that made her a household name in America: the income tax.

The Roaring Twenties were well under way when Kellems and her brother Edgar invented the Kellems cable grip, used for lifting and supporting electrical cables. With a thousand dollars she had saved and another thousand borrowed, she founded the Kellems Company in Stonington, Connecticut, in 1927 to manufacture and market the device. By the time World War II broke out, she was a wealthy woman with a loyal following among her hundreds of employees.

When the war demanded grips to lift 2,700-pound artillery shells, Kellems innovated and ended up selling two million of the resulting product to the armed services. Doing business with the military also introduced her to the seamy side of government—the often needless paperwork, the meddlesome bureaucracy, the complicated and dubious tax code, and even a dangerous naiveté about foreign regimes.

Most Americans were reluctant to criticize Washington in the early years of the war. More pressing matters occupied us as the Axis powers scored victory after victory. But when Kellems saw waste, bungling, and stupidity in government, she didn't hesitate to speak out and make headlines. She was incensed by the U.S. government's shipping thousands of tons of vital materials to Stalin's Soviet Union at a time when our own war effort demanded them. To a Chicago audience, she prophetically warned: "Mark my words. This temporary ally will soon pose a mortal threat to the United States and the entire free world."

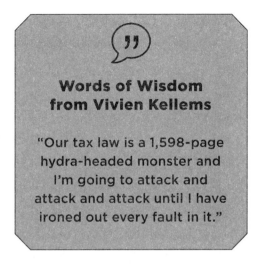

Words of Wisdom from Vivien Kellems

"Our tax law is a 1,598-page hydra-headed monster and I'm going to attack and attack and attack until I have ironed out every fault in it."

Franklin Roosevelt's minions were not amused by Kellems's very public disapproval. Her private correspondence was intercepted by the Office of Censorship (yes, we had one of those), then leaked to two newspaper columnists and a congressman friendly to the administration. Nothing in her letters was in any way incriminating, and no action was ever taken against her, but it was plain that the government wanted to embarrass and intimidate her into silence. The feds underestimated Kellems.

As the tax burden soared, so did Kellems's resentment of the confiscatory marginal rates (as high as 94 percent on personal and corporate income) and the bullying tactics of the "revenuers." In speeches around the country, she ripped into FDR for promising lower taxes during his first presidential campaign in 1932, only to deliver relentlessly higher rates.

Treasury Secretary and FDR crony Henry Morgenthau hinted at treason charges and proceeded toward legal penalties against Kellems. But then a scandal enveloped the Bureau of Internal Revenue (BIR, the predecessor to the IRS).

Thanks in part to Kellems and the women around the country she had stirred up, congressional investigations led to the indictment or resignations of hundreds of BIR employees who had violated the very tax laws they were supposed to enforce.

Attacking the "Tax Grabbers"

Kellems opposed intrusive government at any level. When the state of Connecticut passed a law in 1947 forbidding women to work after 10 p.m., she sprung into action. The Hollywood movie star Gloria Swanson, who supported Kellems's efforts, described how her friend and fellow activist characterized the law as "rank discrimination" and started the resistance. Kellems, Swanson said, "brought several hundred women in to work at her factory one night," but Connecticut authorities made no arrests. "Finally, she got a job in an all-night diner and threatened to work there every night until the legislature acted. Two days later, the law was repealed."

In 1948 Kellems challenged the federal government again. What had started out as a temporary and "voluntary" wartime measure—tax withholding—was now permanent and compulsory. Kellems would have none of it. She was not about to become an unpaid tax collector for the feds without a fight.

In February she began paying her employees in full, which meant that they had to pay the required taxes directly to the federal government. Within days, she was on NBC's new show *Meet the Press*—only the second woman to appear as a guest on the program. She said the withholding law was unconstitutional. The very rationale for creating it—to make the costs of big government less visible to workers—was, in her mind, a reason to get rid of it. People needed to know what their government was costing them. As she later put it in her 1952 book, *Toil, Taxes, and Trouble* (which is still available), employer withholding enabled the federal government to "hide" taxes from citizens and keep them from being "tax-conscious."

Going after President Truman in 1948, Kellems said: "If High Tax Harry wants me to get money for him, then he must appoint me an agent for the Internal Revenue Department. He must pay me a salary for my work, he must reimburse me for my expenses incurred in collecting that tax, and I want a badge!"

Violating the law was the only way to settle the issue. Kellems wrote to the treasury secretary to inform him of her decision. She added, "I respectfully request that you please indict me."

The indictment never came. Instead, the IRS sent agents to her bank and seized the $6,100 it said was due—an amount far greater than her company would have withheld.

Kellems fired back with a lawsuit against the government, and in 1951 a jury ordered the feds to return the money, with interest. She continued to press for a decision on constitutionality, and finally, in 1973, the United States Tax Court formally rejected her argument. Before that, however, she had relented to prevent her company from going bankrupt from IRS seizures. With great reluctance, she had begun withholding taxes from her employees.

But she never backed away from the views of the federal government that she expressed in her speeches and in *Toil, Taxes, and Trouble*. Kellems railed against the "tax grabbers and tax planners," calling the feds "yellow cowards" and "mangy little bureaucrats."

"A Spine of Pure Steel"

In the 1960s, with the withholding issue still to be resolved, Kellems took up another tax crusade—to remove the built-in penalty against single people. Income tax rates for an unmarried person were as much as 42 percent higher than those for married couples making the same income.

Gloria Swanson captured what made Kellems such an effective antitax lobbyist: "Vivien could quote passages from the Constitution by heart, recite the legislative history of obscure sections of the Internal Revenue Code, and do it all in a grandmotherly, finger-wagging manner that disarmed even the most experienced politicians."

Congress gave her a partial victory in 1969, when it cut the disparity to a maximum of 20 percent.

The *Bridgeport Post* paid tribute to Kellems in an editorial:

> When it comes to possessing a spine of pure steel, we wonder if there is any man or woman in Connecticut who can match Miss Kellems. One lone woman against the whole U.S. government! If there are persons—and we know there are—who think she is simply a pugnacious person making a personal fight over the withholding tax, they are doing her a great injustice. Her interest is one of deep conviction and firm principle based on study of the history of the Constitution of the United States. She understands the circumstances which gave birth to this country, the firm realization of the founders that the power to tax is the power to destroy, and the steps which they took to prevent this power from being misused.

Kellems ran four times for public office in Connecticut, once for governor and three times for U.S. Senate. Though she never won, she did something all too many candidates seldom do: she *educated* people. After a Kellems campaign, nobody could say she stood for what she thought people would fall for.

Kellems lived until 1975, when she was seventy-eight. She never changed her mind about the income tax. The personal income tax forms that she filed for the last ten years of her life were all blank. Apparently not even the IRS wanted to tangle again with this scrappy patriot.

Whether you agree or disagree with Vivien Kellems on the issues, you have to give her credit. She had principles—*sound* ones, in my estimation—and the courage to stand for them no matter the legal, economic, or political consequences.

Lessons from Vivien Kellems

Don't roll over when unjust laws are passed: The rule of law is a prerequisite of a free society. But that does not mean every law is just or constitutional. Vivien Kellems challenged the government whenever she believed that a law violated individual liberty or exceeded the limits of federal or state authority.

Bring attention to your cause: "Of course I'm a publicity hound," Kellems once said. "Aren't all crusaders? How can you accomplish anything unless people know what you're trying to do?" Her fiery oratorical style, command of the issues, and ability to get to the nub of complex subjects made her a natural publicist for her causes.

39

Homeschoolers

It's for the Children!

The hero in this story is not any one person but rather the moms and dads of some 2.3 million American children. Often at great sacrifice to themselves, they are rescuing children in a profoundly personal way.

They are the homeschoolers, parents who give up time and income to supervise directly the education of their children. They teach, they arrange learning experiences in cooperation with other parents, and they inspire a love of learning.

The Most Important Ingredient

Of all the ingredients in the recipe for education, which one has the greatest potential to improve student performance?

No doubt the teachers unions would put higher salaries for their members at the top of the list, to which almost every school reformer would reply, "Been there, done that!" Teacher compensation has gone up in recent decades, while indicators of student performance have stagnated or fallen.

Other standard answers include smaller class size, a longer school year, more money for computers, or simply more money for *fill-in-the-blank*. The consensus of hundreds of studies over the past several years is that these factors exhibit either no positive correlation with better student performance or only a weak connection.

On this important question, the verdict is in and it is definitive: *The one ingredient that makes the most difference in how well and how much children learn is parental involvement.* Homeschooling is the *ultimate* in parental involvement.

When parents take a personal interest in their children's education, several things happen. The child gets a strong message that education is important to success in life; it isn't something that parents dump in someone else's lap. Caring, involved parents usually instill a love of learning in their children—a love that translates into a sense of pride and achievement as their students accumulate knowledge and put it to good use. As one might expect, time spent with books goes up and time wasted on screens or in the streets goes down.

But there's so much more to the homeschooling experience. My colleague Marianna Brashear, curriculum development manager at the Foundation for Economic Education (FEE), explains:

> Much time is spent not just in books but also in seeing the world and participating in field trips with hands-on learning. There is so much knowledge that is gained through real-world exposure to a vast array of subjects far more lasting than reading out of a

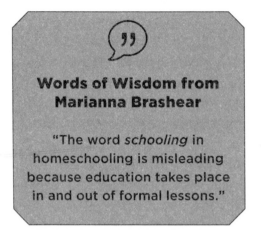

Words of Wisdom from Marianna Brashear

"The word *schooling* in homeschooling is misleading because education takes place in and out of formal lessons."

textbook. The word *schooling* in homeschooling is misleading because education takes place in and out of formal lessons. The biggest waste of time in schools comes not just from indoctrination but also from "teaching to the test," where kids memorize, regurgitate, and forget.

The Homeschooling Boom

American parents were once almost universally regarded as the people most responsible for children's education. Until the late nineteenth century, the home, the church, and a small nearby school were the primary centers of learning for the great majority of Americans.

American parents have largely abdicated this responsibility, entrusting supposed "experts." The context for this abdication is a compulsory system established to replace parental values with those preferred by the states and now, to an increasing degree, by the federal government. (Remember J. Gresham Machen, our hero from chapter 19? He wrote, "This notion that the children belong to the State, that their education must be provided for by the State in a way that makes for the State's welfare . . . , is inimical at every step to liberty.")

Twenty years ago, a Temple University report revealed that nearly one in three parents was seriously disengaged from his or her child's education. The Temple researchers found that about one-sixth of all students believed their parents didn't care whether they earned good grades, and nearly one-third said their parents had no idea how they were doing in school. I can think of no reason to believe things have improved in the two decades since.

Teaching children at home isn't for everyone. No one advocates that every parent try it. There are plenty of good schools—private, public, and charter—that are doing a better job than some parents could do for their own children. And I certainly praise those parents who may not homeschool but who see to it that their children get the most out of education, both in school and at home. Homeschooling almost always goes the extra mile, however, and it is working extraordinarily well for the growing number of parents and children who choose it.

This outcome is all the more remarkable when one considers that homeschooling parents must juggle teaching with all the other demands and chores of modern life. Also, they get little or nothing back from what they pay in taxes for a public system they don't patronize. By not using the public system, they are saving taxpayers billions of dollars annually—more than $27 billion, according to the National Home Education Research Institute—even as they pay taxes for it anyway.

In the early 1980s, fewer than 20,000 children were homeschooled. From 2003 through 2012, the number of American children ages five through seventeen who were being homeschooled by their parents climbed 61.8 percent, to nearly 1.8 million, according to the U.S. Department of Education. That's probably a conservative estimate, but it equals 3.4 percent of the nation's students in this age group.

Parents who homeschool do so for a variety of reasons. Some want a strong moral or religious emphasis in their children's education. Others are fleeing unsafe public schools or schools where discipline and academics have taken a backseat to fuzzy, feel-good, or politically correct dogma. Many homeschool parents complain about the pervasiveness in public schools of trendy instructional methods that border on pedagogical malpractice. Others value the flexibility to travel with their children for hands-on educational purposes, the ability to customize curricula to each child's needs and interests, and the potential to strengthen relationships within the family.

"When my wife and I first decided to homeschool our three children," says Bradley Thompson, a political science professor who heads the Clemson Institute for the Study of Capitalism at Clemson

University, "we did it for one reason: we wanted to give them a classical education—the kind that John Adams and Thomas Jefferson might have received when they were young boys." He continues:

> Within a couple of years, we added a second reason: we didn't want our children exposed to the kind of socialization that goes on in both government and some private schools. Over time, however, we added a third reason: homeschooling became a way of life for our family, a way of life that was irreplaceable and beautiful. By the time our third child goes to college, we will have been homeschooling for eighteen years. Those years have been, without question, the most important of my life.

Proving the Critics Wrong

Homeschool parents are fiercely protective of their constitutional right to educate their children. In early 1994 the House of Representatives voted to mandate that all teachers—including parents in the home—acquire state certification in the subjects they teach. A massive campaign of letters, phone calls, and faxes from homeschool parents produced one of the most stunning turnabouts in legislative history: by a vote of 424–1, the House reversed itself, and then it approved an amendment that affirmed the rights and independence of homeschool parents.

The certification issue deserves a comment. We have a national crisis in public education, where virtually every teacher is duly certified. There is no national crisis in home education.

Critics have long harbored a jaundiced view of parents who educate children at home. They argue that children need the guidance of professionals and the social interaction that comes from being with a class of others. Homeschooled children, these critics say, will be socially and academically stunted by the confines of the home. But the facts suggest otherwise.

Reports from state after state show homeschoolers scoring significantly better than the norm on college entrance examinations. Prestigious universities, including Harvard and Yale, accept homeschooled children eagerly and often. And once homeschoolers get to college, they tend to perform better than students from public or private schools: *U.S. News and World Report* cited various studies showing "that on average homeschooled students have higher grade point averages in their freshman years and have higher graduation rates than their peers."

But what about socialization? That's probably the question homeschooling parents hear more than any other. The evidence contradicts claims that homeschooled students will be socially stunted. In fact, as homeschooling expert Diane Flynn Keith put it in an interview with Homeschool.com: "Socialization is actually meant to prepare children for the real world, which means learning to interact and deal with people of all ages, races, and backgrounds. In this case, homeschooling actually does a *better* job of this because homeschoolers spend more actual time out in society." A 2013 article in the *Peabody Journal of Education* supports this claim. After reviewing the research on homeschooling and socialization, the author, Professor Richard G. Medlin, concludes: "Homeschooled children are taking part in the daily routines of their communities. They are certainly not isolated; in fact, they associate with—and feel close to—all sorts of people."

Homeschooling parents emphasize this engagement. Writing in *The Freeman* in May 2001, homeschool parent Chris Cardiff observed that because parents aren't experts in every possible subject, "families band together in local homeschooling support groups." Cardiff continued: "From within these voluntary associations springs a spontaneous educational order. An overabundance of services, knowledge, activities, collaboration, and social opportunities flourishes within these homeschooling communities."

My former FEE colleague B. K. Marcus, also a homeschool parent, agrees. "Homeschooling produces communities and participates in a division of labor," he says. "Homeschooling is social and cooperative, contrary to the stereotype of the overprotected child under the stern watch of narrow-minded parents. Traditionally schooled kids show far fewer social skills outside their segregated age groups."

A quick Internet search reveals thousands of cooperative ventures for and among homeschoolers. In Yahoo Groups alone, as of July 2016, about 8,400 results pop up when you search for the keyword "homeschool." Close to 1,500 show up in Google Groups. Facebook is another option for locating a plethora of local, regional, and national homeschool groups, support groups, events, co-ops, and communities.

As homeschoolers reach high school age, they can participate in early-college and dual-enrollment programs. Marianna Brashear reports that these programs "are quite eager to admit homeschoolers for their ability to take responsibility and to self-motivate, for their maturity, and for their determination to learn and succeed." Her own daughter, at fourteen, began a program at a nearby technical institute that gave her high school and college credit simultaneously.

The few longitudinal studies that have been conducted all show that homeschoolers fare well as adults. In measures of employment, community involvement, and even happiness, homeschool graduates do better than the rest of the population.

Educational Heroes

In every other walk of life, Americans traditionally regard as heroes the men and women who meet challenges head-on, who find solutions when the conventional responses don't work, and who persevere to bring a dream to fruition. At a time when troubles plague education and educational heroes are too few in number, recognizing the homeschool champions in our midst may be both long overdue and highly instructive.

Common to all homeschool parents is the belief that the education of their children is too important to hand over to someone else. Hallelujah for that!

Lessons from Homeschoolers

Don't be so quick to entrust important decisions to "experts"—and certainly not to the government: We have a national crisis in public education, not in home education. The next time you hear someone calling for more federal funding for education, or more spending on technology in classrooms, or some other government reform, remind the person that *parental involvement* makes the most difference in how well and how much children learn.

Question the conventional wisdom: Parents might never start homeschooling if they accept at face value the skeptics' common criticisms, such as that parents aren't qualified to teach their children in most subjects or that homeschooled children will be socially stunted. Dig deeper and you'll see that the evidence contradicts these claims. In fact, homeschoolers perform better academically and develop stronger social skills than their peers in public or private schools.

40

——•——

Larry Cooper

Never Too Late for Character

On a fateful day he'll never forget, eighteen-year-old Lawrence ("Larry") Cooper, an unmarried black man and high school dropout, found himself on the wrong side of the law. He attempted an armed robbery of a store in downtown Savannah, Georgia. It was April 1987. The cash involved? A mere eighty dollars, enough to finance his cocaine habit for less than a day. Larry was caught and sent to a maximum-security prison.

One month after Larry's arrest, his son was born. The boy wouldn't see his father outside a cell until November 2015, when his dad was finally released. "I wasn't there even to sign the birth certificate," Larry told me in February 2016.

These lamentable chapters of the Larry Cooper story are distressingly familiar in America.

Today, incarcerated black American males number about 750,000. That's more than the entire prison populations of India, Argentina, Canada, Lebanon, Japan, Germany, Finland, Israel, and England combined. An August 2013 report from the Sentencing Project on Racial Disparities in the United States Criminal Justice System revealed that "one of every three black American males born today can expect to go to prison in his lifetime."

The leading cause of incarceration of black males is nonviolent drug offenses. This is no accident. President Richard Nixon's domestic-policy adviser and Watergate coconspirator John Ehrlichman revealed in a 1994 interview:

> We knew we couldn't make it illegal to be either against the [Vietnam] war or black, but by getting the public to associate the hippies with marijuana and blacks with heroin, and then criminalizing both heavily, we could disrupt those communities. We could arrest their leaders, raid their homes, break up their meetings, and vilify them night after night on the evening news. Did we know we were lying about the drugs? Of course we did.

For black men, the next leading causes of incarceration are false accusations, then crimes against persons, followed by crimes against property. Economist Thomas Sowell argues convincingly, as do many others, that the genuinely criminal behaviors—the violations of person and property—have much less to do with racism and poverty than with the debilitating, family-busting policies of the welfare state. (It doesn't help that poor, inner-city families are often trapped in lousy government schools.) Sowell observes:

> Murder rates among black males were going down—repeat, *down*—during the much-lamented 1950s, while [they] went up after the much-celebrated 1960s, reaching levels more than

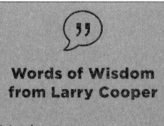

**Words of Wisdom
from Larry Cooper**

"It took me so many years to realize how important your character is…. I'm not going to ever let it slip again."

double what they had been before. Most black children were raised in two-parent families prior to the 1960s. But today the great majority of black children are raised in one-parent families.

Such trends are not unique to blacks, nor even to the United States. The welfare state has led to remarkably similar trends among the white underclass in England over the same period…. You cannot take any people, of any color, and exempt them from the requirements of civilization—including work, behavioral standards, personal responsibility, and all the other basic things that the clever intelligentsia disdain—without ruinous consequences to them and to society at large.

Larry Cooper was one of the statistics, exhibit A in this national tragedy. But today he's well on his way to a life of honor and redemption. Perhaps the jury on him is still out, but I'm betting he is a hero in the making. Symbolic of his determination to live a repaired life, he advised me firmly when he reviewed this chapter: "Lawrence Cooper is dead. I'm Larry Cooper now." So that's the last time in the chapter you will see "Lawrence."

"A Different Man"

Growing up in Savannah in the 1970s and '80s, Larry faced the challenges posed by a broken family.

"My dad had thirty-three kids with six or seven women," he informed me over breakfast when we met in February 2016. "Mom and Dad separated early, so Dad just wasn't around. I saw him maybe twice a year."

As a teenager, Larry started skipping school, stealing, smoking marijuana, and then doing cocaine. "I dropped out of school when I was sixteen and it broke my mama's heart," he said. His mother implored him to find employment, so he took a landscaping job. It lasted only a week before he was in the streets again.

Hanging out with the wrong people, trapped in a vicious circle of using drugs and stealing to afford more—and with only a broken-hearted mother at home to offer any hope for a better life—Larry was headed for destruction. His poor choices caught up with him two years later with a ten-year sentence for armed robbery. Things would get much worse before they got better.

Bad behavior, including aggravated assault, earned Larry additional prison time—a grand total of twenty-eight years. He went in at age eighteen and emerged at forty-seven. It will be another decade before he can say he has been a free man for as long as he wasn't.

"Over the years while behind bars," Larry told me, "I thought more and more about what my mama had told me. She said this would happen if I didn't straighten up. She prayed hard for me, all the time. She visited me as much as she could. I still remember how bad I felt when she once came to see me but was turned away because I was 'in the hole' for bad things I had done. But she never gave up on me."

I asked Larry what the low point of his time in prison was. I expected it might have been a run-in with a guard or another inmate, an ugly incident of short duration. His answer: "Seven years in solitary confinement."

"*Seven years?!*" I exclaimed.

"Yes, and every day it was the same: one hour out in the yard, fifteen minutes in the shower, and then twenty-two hours and forty-five minutes in solitary. At first I was in despair. But then I started reading and then writing to folks, exercising in my cell and thinking hard about what had happened to me and what was going on in my life. It took those long hours by myself to make me come to my senses and start feeling bad about the people I stole from, all the friends and family I had hurt. Things mama told me finally started to have an effect on me."

Larry's mother arranged his baptism when he was a child, but he never made time to read more than a few words of the Bible—or anything else, for that matter. A prison chaplain introduced him to a Bible study course conducted by mail. Larry enrolled and completed it.

"That's when my life really began to change," he told me. "Ever since that course, I've been a different man. I've settled down. I use my brain now. I'm no longer the man I used to be."

Freedom

Larry's personal and spiritual recovery were well under way before I had ever heard of him. His reading had brought him into contact with ideas of political and economic liberty. He wrote my former place of employment in Michigan, the Mackinac Center for Public Policy, asking for more information. My old colleagues there forwarded his letter on to me at the Foundation for Economic Education (FEE), and that began a correspondence that now fills two shoeboxes on a shelf in my home office.

Never before had I contemplated forming a friendship with a man in prison. I wouldn't have known how to begin. If Larry hadn't taken the initiative to contact me, a relationship would never have developed. I now count it as a great blessing in my life.

Larry was much more diligent in writing than I was, I confess with some remorse. "I had more time on my hands than you did," he jokes.

But I'm pleased to have helped deepen his understanding of liberty by sending him many books and articles.

"Were there any particular things I sent you that made a big impact?" I asked.

Without skipping a beat, he replied, "Yes. One was your book *A Republic—If We Can Keep It*, and the other was *What It Means to Be a Libertarian* by Charles Murray." The reader will excuse me, I hope, if I report this with a smile and considerable pride.

Larry and I corresponded but never spoke by phone until after his release. I was looking forward to the day when I could finally drive down to Savannah to spend time with him. Until we met, I didn't even know what he looked like, but we embraced as if we were brothers.

We dined at the Bonefish Grill on Abercorn Street, then went to see the film *Race*, about Olympic hero Jesse Owens (see chapter 24). The next morning we had breakfast, where I recorded the interview on which this chapter is based. After the interview we visited the public library on Bull Street so I could show Larry how to create his first e-mail account.

I learned much from Larry during our time together. For example, he opposes the drug war from a vantage point I have never experienced—from inside prison walls, where, he said, "drugs are everywhere." I asked him where they come from.

"All sorts of ways and places," he said. "Guys out on work detail get 'em. People throw 'em over the prison gate. Guards and officers bring 'em in."

Larry's views on current issues are interesting, but his personal transformation is, to me at least, positively captivating. The sad part of it is that Larry's mother, one of the few anchors in his life, died just three months before he earned his freedom.

"At first I couldn't believe it," he recalled. "She was living for the day I would get out, which was the day after Thanksgiving, 2015. It really hit me at Christmas. At my first Christmas dinner as a free man in twenty-eight years, family and old friends got together. Everybody was there but mama. It took me so many years to realize how important your character is. Thanks to mama and my faith, I'm not going to ever let it slip again."

For a few months after his release, the Salvation Army in Savannah provided Larry with a place to live and a church to attend on Sundays. He started putting his new life together working two jobs, one with a prestigious catering service and the other with a local staffing firm that placed him in short-term stints at manual labor. He doesn't want welfare.

"I try to earn every penny I get," he told me proudly. He's both optimistic and excited about his future. He would love to start a new family.

"I want to prove to myself that I can be a good independent man and make amends for what I did. I take one day at a time, but my spirits are real good."

After all Larry has been through and with freedom so new to him, I suppose there's a chance of a relapse. Surely he will encounter occasional bumps in the road. I hope I've encouraged him and can continue to do so.

Hero in the Making

There are many lessons here: Strong families and good parenting can make all the difference in the world. Building character for navigating life's pitfalls is a priceless undertaking. Don't underestimate the value of a mother who never gives up on a wayward son. Through an inner transformation, in this case facilitated by a spiritual renewal, even the seemingly incorrigible can turn his or her life around. Never miss an opportunity to encourage someone who is clearly trying to do the right thing.

I intend to stay in touch with Larry Cooper. I'll watch his progress and assist with it if and when I can. He has already taught me a valuable truth: that heroes aren't always the ones who make the headlines or the history books. They may just be on the other side of a wall.

Lessons from Larry Cooper

Remember that it's never too late to build character: Larry Cooper, who has spent more time in prison than as a free man, says that it took him "so many years to realize how important your character is." But once he realized it, he learned from his mistakes and began building himself into a person of character. Anyone—even the seemingly incorrigible man—can turn his life around.

Encourage someone who is trying to do the right thing: Before Larry Cooper reached out to me, I never would have considered forming a friendship with someone in prison. But I am immensely grateful that he did. I count our relationship as a great blessing in my life, and I am gratified that I played some small part in encouraging him along his path of recovery.

Epilogue

⸻

Though only three of the chapters in this book focus on heroes who are still living, my primary purpose here will be lost if readers conclude that heroism is a bygone ideal. It isn't.

Men and women of courage, principle, and character are all around us. Look and you'll find them. When you do, recognize and encourage them. Set your own standards high so that you, too, may join their ranks.

Remember that we're talking about real people here, which means imperfection is rife. Heroism is never a straight line upward. Even the best will disappoint on occasion. But what looks like a setback or a mistake will often prove in hindsight to have been a critical, character-building moment. If a hero falls but then picks himself up, learns from his failures, and becomes an even better person because of them, he has proven he was, and still is, a hero.

All of us are tested every day, just like everyone I write about in this book. We may not pass every test, but that doesn't have to mean we stop learning or cease improving.

After composing the last chapter of this book, on my friend Larry Cooper, I tried to reach him so he could read my draft and point out any errors. I e-mailed, wrote, texted, and phoned him. Almost a month passed with no response from Larry. I wondered whether something really bad had happened, perhaps something so serious that I should remove the chapter. Then finally a text message popped up on my phone: "Call me when you can!"

Larry had hit one of those bumps in the road I wrote about. He lives in a tough neighborhood and got into a fight. He spent most of

March 2016 in jail until he was cleared. When I spoke with him again, he was out, back at work, his spirits renewed. My real disappointment is with myself, because without knowing the circumstances, I had flirted with the temptation to give up on him. That's no way to encourage anybody, let alone a hero.

If this book inspires more people to heroism, or if it prompts you to help others achieve it, it will—in my mind at least—have been well worth both my time and yours.

Acknowledgments

The author extends a special thanks to John Hartwell for his portraits leading into each chapter, and Sara Seal and the team at Crowdskout for their cover artwork. Thanks to B. K. Marcus, former editor of the Foundation for Economic Education's magazine, *The Freeman*, for his editorial suggestions throughout the book. Thanks also to FEE's chief operating officer, Richard Lorenc, and ISI's vice president for publications, Jed Donahue, for stewarding this collaboration between these two great organizations dedicated to liberty.

About the Author

L awrence W. ("Larry") Reed is president of the Foundation of Economic Education (FEE). Prior to joining FEE in 2008, he served for twenty years as president of the Mackinac Center for Public Policy. He also taught economics full-time from 1977 to 1984 at Northwood University in Michigan.

Reed is the author or coauthor of seven other books, including *Excuse Me, Professor: Challenging the Myths of Progressivism* and *A Republic—If We Can Keep It*. A frequent guest on radio and television, he has written thousands of articles for newspapers, magazines, and journals in the United States and abroad. He delivers at least seventy-five speeches each year, and his public speaking has taken him to dozens of countries, from Bulgaria to China to Bolivia. His lectures "Seven Principles of Sound Policy" and "Great Myths of the Great Depression" have been translated into more than a dozen languages and distributed worldwide.

Reed holds a bachelor's degree in economics from Grove City College, which has awarded him its Distinguished Alumni award, and a master's in history from Slippery Rock State University. He has also received honorary doctorates from Central Michigan University and Northwood University. A native of Pennsylvania and a thirty-year resident of Michigan, he now lives in Georgia.